The Best American
Newspaper Narratives,
Volume Six

THE BEST AMERICAN NEWSPAPER NARRATIVES, VOLUME SIX

Gayle Reaves, editor

Number 6 in the Mayborn Best American Newspaper Narrative Series

University of North Texas Press

Mayborn Graduate Institute of Journalism

Denton, Texas

Permissions:
University of North Texas Press
1155 Union Circle #311336
Denton, TX 76203-5017

The paper used in this book meets the minimum requirements of the
American National Standard for Permanence of Paper for Printed Library
Materials, z39.48.1984. Binding materials have been chosen for durability.

Library of Congress Cataloging-in-Publication
Data is available from the Library of Congress

The Best American Newspaper Narratives, Volume Six is Number
6 in the Mayborn Best American Newspaper Narrative Series

The print and electronic editions of this book were made
possible by the support of the Vick Family Foundation.

TABLE OF CONTENTS

ACKNOWLEDGMENTS

There's a reason the Mayborn Literary Nonfiction Conference has been called a "summer camp for writers." It's a place where journalists and writers from around the country gather to take a deep dive on the art and craft of what they love to do best: storytelling. This isn't the typical conference where you bounce around to concurrent sessions. Writers come here to learn how to be better writers. Reporters come here to improve their skills and become better reporters. That's why, since 2004, the conference has attracted both experienced and aspiring writers who are committed to journalism.

In 2013 we launched a new writing initiative for narratives previously published in the nation's dailies. This Best American Newspaper Narratives contest, co-sponsored by *The Dallas Morning News*, is designed to encourage narrative nonfiction storytelling at newspapers across the United States. BANN represents this conference's commitment to recognizing the great work of those writers. As a young journalist at the Miami Herald, I learned how to report and write from the best. The late Gene Miller, a two-time Pulitzer Prize winner, served as a writing coach. I recall as clearly as yesterday how he worked with me on a profile I was writing about a woman who ran a foster home in northwest Dade

County. We went word by word, sentence by sentence. Gene peppered me with questions, challenging me to provide depth, details and character regarding the people and the home where these children lived. Like any young journalist, I felt demoralized and frustrated by the process. When we were done, I realized how much more reporting I had to do. I realized how much better a writer I could be. That's why BANN is so important to this conference— and to journalism. It showcases journalism that inspires all of us to make one more phone call, do one more interview, sift through one more stack of documents to tell great stories.

Yes, it's hard nowadays. We live at a time when the 24/7, 365-day news cycle, driven by bursts of Twitter posts, is blurring the lines between real news and fake news. It is even more important, then, that this and other writing contests are strengthening the importance and role of journalism and particularly long-form storytelling. These stories capture all aspects of life — the rich, the poor, broken government and institutional systems, and heart-wrenching personal journeys of discovery.

Over the years, BANN has attracted entries from staff writers at such publications as *The New York Times*, the *Los Angeles Times*, *The Boston Globe*, the *Milwaukee Sentinel*, *The Washington Post*, the *Oregonian*, the *Tampa Bay Times*, and *The Dallas Morning News*. Additionally, freelancers for major publications such as *GQ* and *Outside* magazine are submitting their works, which only makes the job that much harder for our outstanding judges.

Contest judges were Karen Blumenthal, an award-winning financial journalist and book author with more than 25 years of experience, including more than two decades spent with *The Wall Street Journal*; Kelley Benham French, a many-times-honored former narrative journalist for the *Tampa Bay Times* who now serves as a journalism professor at Indiana University; Adam Playford, who serves as director of data/digital enterprise for the *Tampa Bay Times* and was honored by *Editor & Publisher* in its 2012 "25 Under 35" listing that recognized "the next generation of publishing leaders;" Steve Wilmsen, narrative editor at *The Boston*

Globe, and Gayle Reaves, an award-winning journalist and former faculty member at the University of North Texas' Mayborn School of Journalism. While a member of *The Dallas Morning News* newsroom, Reaves was honored with a Pulitzer Prize and George Polk Award for her work.

A special thanks to George Getschow, whose vision for the Mayborn Conference and these writing contests has raised the profile of the Mayborn School of Journalism, and, in so doing, has allowed the school to become the mecca for literary nonfiction. Thanks to Gayle Reaves, currently managing editor of *The Texas Monitor,* who has done an outstanding job writing the introduction and serving as a judge. Thanks to UNT alumnus Eric Nishimoto, who designed the cover. Karen DeVinney, assistant director/managing editor of UNT Press, deserves much gratitude for editing the collection with competency and patience. This publication could not happen without the huge support of Ron Chrisman, the director of UNT Press, who continues to demonstrate his commitment to "literary nonfiction."

-- Neil Foote, co-director, Mayborn Literary Nonfiction Conference, and principal lecturer, Mayborn School of Journalism

Recipe for the Future

Immerse, Innovate, Repeat

By Gayle Reaves

If you only like short stories, don't read this book, which presents the 2018 winners of the Best American Newspaper Narratives contest, sponsored by the Mayborn Literary Nonfiction Conference. Or maybe you should give it a try. Start with "His Heart, Her Hand" or "The House on the Corner" or "Dirty John." You may be surprised at how you're drawn in, even to the series that ran over several days. The stories don't represent Journalism Past, however. With any luck, they represent the future.

If you skip this anthology, you'll also miss our first-place winner, an amazing series by Kale Williams for the *Oregonian* about a polar bear cub's struggle to survive, with dogged, inventive help from humans. It's a key narrative of our time, being repeated in different ways for different species around the globe. The series was accompanied by a documentary film, a children's book, and other extras. It drew thousands of fans to follow the cub's journey and, as a byproduct, to absorb information about the effects of climate change.

You'd miss the story that caused a Florida city to re-think its treatment of young repeat-offender car thieves and helped inspire a national think tank's study of that crime wave. Another Florida story, a gritty and hard-to-believe tale, drew 35,000 readers on a single website and moved a prosecutor to offer a plea deal to a man on trial for shooting a drug dealer who'd taken over his property and threatened his wife. And then there's the somewhat terrifying story from a reporter who watched and listened and rode along as a former pro football player with a young daughter dealt with the self-destructive urges he believes were caused by a degenerative brain disorder brought on by his injuries on the field.

In short, you'd be missing the kind of excellent narrative writing, deep reporting, and smart presentations that are pulling many thousands of readers back to newspapers (online, if not in print). The articles collected here focus attention on problems like global warming, the treatment of refugees, domestic violence, and gun violence, and they do it without the trite conclusions or melodrama that too much daily news coverage —particularly broadcast coverage and online infotainment— relies on. The stories come from both coasts and the heartland, from the Pacific Northwest to Florida.

Some of them will renew your faith in ideas like tolerance and humanity. Others will leave you wondering about governmental dysfunctions so persistent that, without evil intent, they can ruin or end lives. These are stories that inspire change, including one that helped push the government to begin saving babies with a rare disease.

The underlying lessons for me, in this year's batch of 11 winners, are twofold: immersion and innovation. Immersion takes different forms. The reporting in several of the stories ran for several months to more than a year. When the major players aren't available for extensive interviews, it can mean immersing oneself in records work — following a daisy chain from document to document, requesting them, fighting for them, reading, sifting, unlocking their secrets.

Take "Dirty John," by Christopher Goffard of the *Los Angeles Times*, the tale of how a con man romanced a woman, attacked her daughter, and got killed himself. The series became one of the most popular podcasts of 2017, inspired a TV "true crime" series, and won third place in this year's contest. As an editor pointed out in the cover letter to Goffard's entry, the *Times* has clearly made a "commitment to innovative storytelling."

Goffard went back many times to talk to the people involved, as well as doing extensive records research to show how John Meehan used intimidation, gaslighting, and other techniques to bring a woman under his psychological control.

Many of these stories immerse the readers in their characters' lives by carrying the narrative back and forth in time. In "The Loneliest Polar Bear," Williams takes readers into the Ohio trailer where zookeepers watch and worry over Nora, the only surviving polar bear cub born in the country in 2015. But he also shows them a day 27 years earlier when a hunter in Alaska pulled another cub, who would become Nora's father, from a den after shooting the mother bear. The *Oregonian* series tracks the relentless efforts of zookeepers and veterinarians to keep Nora healthy after her mother abandons her— the intricacies of diet, the "Nora Moms," the move to another zoo and another to find bear companionship for her.

A very different story, "The House on the Corner," by Lane DeGregory of the *Tampa Bay Times*, is another winner that illustrates those same strengths. The story, chosen by contest judges as a "notable narrative," started with a crime brief that caught DeGregory's eye, about a drug dealer getting shot 17 times. When DeGregory started digging into the story, she found the task anything but easy. Anthony Roy admitted to the shooting and wanted to explain why he did it. But he was awaiting a murder trial, so she got only one interview. Many others involved refused to talk at all, and police dragged their feet. It took six months of fighting to get copies of call records, and another six months to get an interview with the police chief. By the end, the reporter had many hours of audio depositions to listen to, as well as taped police interrogations and interviews.

Even though most of her immersion in the subject came via paper and recordings rather than live interaction with her subject, DeGregory amassed a powerful testimony about what happened. The "voice" carried by those materials was so strong that DeGregory at first tried something very non-journalistic: She wrote the story as a play. When that approach ran into opposition from editors, she turned it into something else almost as unusual for newspapers: After a fairly traditional opening section, most of the story is told as dialogue, or direct quotes, with each short section headed by an explanatory paragraph and, in places, with tiny sentences in between the quotes— akin to stage directions, just enough to help the reader understand what is going on. The result was maddening, in a good way. You want to reach into the story and grab people and shake them, change the outcomes. It's hard to turn away from.

That's also true for "There's Nowhere to Run," by Kent Babb for *The Washington Post*, named a "notable narrative" in our contest. The profile follows a former pro football player suffering from what he believes is a degenerative brain disorder caused by his on-field injuries but which, for now, can only be clearly diagnosed after death. Babb mostly leaves to others the arguments about the underlying issue of the disorder — chronic traumatic encephalopathy — that the NFL and its players are wrestling with. Instead it focuses on what life is like now for Larry Johnson, a former star with the Kansas City Chiefs. Johnson is trying to be a good father to his young daughter while dealing with demons that include memory loss, paranoia, and self-destructive impulses, driving recklessly with his daughter and getting angry with the reporter. After years of taking hits on the field, he tells Babb, aggression "became a switch I couldn't turn off." Babb accompanies Johnson through his day, recording father-daughter dialogue and taking readers back through Johnson's life, to build the mosaic of a fractured human being. The story is so full of tension and tenderness that I had to put it down and come back to it a few times to finish reading.

That same combination of tenderness and tension, plus dogged records research and immersion in a subject, inform one of what I consider the most important of this year's winners, in terms of clear humanitarian results. Following a doctor's tip, *Chicago Tribune* reporter Patricia Callahan learned that the launch of mandated testing of babies for a deadly neurological condition called Krabbe disease had repeatedly been delayed by bureaucracy. The condition can only be treated if caught within days of birth; testing delays had produced a decade of needless, agonizing deaths.

Callahan did the digging and reporting that identified each misstep along the way. Then, in "Doomed by Delay," which won second place in our contest, she told that story through the eyes of parents whose children had weakened, suffered and died or were facing death because of the blunders. One little boy, Kenan, and his mother, Natasha, were at the heart of the story. As her editor wrote in the cover letter for her entry, the reporter "made the sluggish bureaucracy the foil to Kenan's rapid deterioration." Using records from many sources, and quotes from Natasha's blog and Facebook posts, Callahan turned medical terminology into the actual suffering of a little boy. She turned a faceless bureaucracy into the specific people who, time and again, failed to get a life-saving job done. Repeatedly, state officials diverted the funds intended to pay for the critical tests. Callahan's story ran in October 2017. By December, Illinois had begun screening of newborns for Krabbe, giving families and doctors the chance for the stem-cell transplants that could save the babies' lives.

"Doomed by Delay" put readers there beside Natasha in her fight, not because the journalist herself had been there through all of Kenan's illness, but because seven months of reporting allowed her to write in such a way as to make that place for readers. Jenna Russell, writing for *The Boston Globe*, pulled off a similar effect by starting her work months before the refugee family she would profile arrived in this country.

Russell's immersion in the experiences of this Syrian family began with getting to know the Jewish community near Boston that had put together the pieces of a resettlement project. Once the family arrived, Russell, with a translator and photographer Suzanne Kreiter, then gained the trust of the refugees by being present as they cooked and learned and built a new life in America. The result was "The Last Refugee," a runner-up in our contest, an eloquent series filled with beautiful imagery. The family would begin unpacking, Russell wrote, "hanging up the remnants of their past in empty closets." Volunteers didn't just provide supplies and information; they installed child-safety latches on cabinets, posted instructions in Arabic, and included baby dolls for the family's two little girls. Russell's portrait of the refugee family and the volunteers who helped them is indelible. Readers responded by offering sewing machines, books, services— and welcome.

Readers also responded to Lisa Gartner and Zachary T. Sampson's story, "Wrong Way," in the *Tampa Bay Times*, named a "notable narrative." They thanked the reporters for giving them a look at troubled teenagers that went beyond crime statistics to reveal the teens' humanity. The article, about an epidemic of auto thefts by teenagers in a suburban county, got its genesis from a tragic incident in which three young women drowned when they accidentally drove the car they'd stolen into a pond.

Gartner filed it away; months later, when she joined her paper's enterprise team, she and Sampson started looking for the deeper story. Their version of "immersion and innovation" included creating their own database of the crimes, sitting in juvenile court, doing police ride-alongs, reading endless police reports, and monitoring the Facebook accounts of the teens involved. The reporters went back repeatedly to talk to Isaiah, brother to one of the teenagers who had drowned. Finally one day, the tough exterior broke, and he told them he believed in heaven and hoped he could be with his sister there.

As a result of the story, Gartner wrote in her cover letter, local police also began to see the young repeat-offender car thieves as people. Officers started talking to the teens to figure out their motivations and ways to head off the trauma that so often pushes young people toward the juvenile justice system and blighted futures.

The intersection of juvenile and adult justice systems and that of guilt and forgiveness are examined in Jennifer Emily's work for *The Dallas Morning News* that was named a notable narrative in the contest. In "Hope for the Rest of Us," she tells the story of Buz Caldwell, a Texas man who, over years of sorrow, eventually found himself able to forgive his daughter Krissi and her then-boyfriend for killing Caldwell's wife and wounding him. Emily dug deep, interviewed a wide range of people, read medical records and Krissi's own letters. And, over and over, she talked to Caldwell himself, getting new insights and details from the story he had been living through for so long. Her series destroyed stereotypes, replacing them, scene after scene, with rich details of actual, wounded, imperfect, unpredictable human beings.

In "Twelve Seconds of Gunfire," one of the runners-up in our contest, John Woodrow Cox of *The Washington Post* had a different challenge than dealing with emotions and conversations recalled from years earlier. Instead, he interviewed a group of first-grade students about things they remembered all too well from only a few months earlier: the killer who came to their school playground one day and started shooting, fatally wounding one of their classmates, wounding two other students and a teacher less seriously, and hurting other children in ways that will only unfold with time. Cox got to know parents, school officials, and medical personnel, and researched other school shootings to put the Townville, S.C., tragedy into perspective. Most importantly, he listened to the students themselves, who told stories that no seven-year-old should ever have to tell:

> When the shooting started, Ava dropped her cupcake and ran. Jacob— "Jakey," the only boy she'd ever kissed — was behind her but didn't make it.

Long after the shooting, Siena kept asking her parents about the 14-year-old attacker, who'd killed his own father that day before driving to the school: What if he gets out? What if he gets out? Each day, she tried to talk her parents out of making her go to school.

Siena and her friends started carrying stuffed animals, another way of feeling protected.

Ava began having episodes of rage, hitting herself and pulling out her eyelashes. And she'd started screaming what the shooter had yelled on the playground: "I hate my life."

Two of the most engaging stories in our list this year use versions of the technique of reconstructed conversations. Like the first-place story, both are from the *Oregonian*. "His Heart, Her Hands," by Tom Hallman Jr., was named one of three runners-up, and Casey Parks' "About a Boy" was a notable narrative. Clearly, editors at the *Oregonian* have realized the power of narrative writing, immersive reporting, and innovation, and their readers are richer for it.

Parks' series tells about Jay and the transgender teen's painful, hopeful, complicated journey of understanding himself and then changing his life and his body. Thoughtfully reported and written, it opens on the morning of his first day in a new high school, where fellow students would meet and get to know him, from the first, as a boy.

"Jay woke in darkness, the summer and a girlhood behind him," Parks writes. The teenager's siblings are still asleep, so only his little dog "marked Jay's passing from one life to the next."

Most readers will never experience anything like Jay's profound reshaping of his identity. But those who read Parks' narrative have a real hope of understanding Jay, because they are right there with him over several years, from his discovery of videos and other information online that explained what he was feeling to the point when he can tell his story to the girl he has a crush on. The strongest parts of the story are about the teenager's thoughts and strategies to deal with his situation, his conversations with family and close friends, his mom's own journey to acceptance.

"His Heart, Her Hands" is the most sparely written of all this year's winners and one of the most creative. It tells about another journey, taken by Steve Goodman, a pianist and composer with early-onset Alzheimer's, and Naomi LaViolette, a fellow musician. Melissa, Goodman's daughter, had accepted her best friend Naomi's offer to work with Goodman to help him save the music he had created but that was slipping from his grasp. Hallman's poignant article alternates between more traditional third-person reportage and first-person sections in which Goodman tells his own story. Those sections are choppy, full of very short sentences, eloquently depicting a man struggling with memory, language, and the things and people he loves. Over two years, LaViolette helps draw from Goodman 16 of his favorite songs, and the family arranges to have a recording made of her playing them. But she doesn't stop there: With the family's help, she arranges for the music to be performed in concert.

"Naomi crawled up into my brain and found the parts and pieces, all of them broken, and brought them back to me," Goodwin says in the story's final section. He knows what is ahead for him with his disease, he says, but his heart is happy. "I was just a man who learned to play the piano as a little boy. And I loved it."

Goodman's story, Jay's story, the refugee family in Massachusetts, the father who forgives his wife's killers, the young car thieves in Florida, Dirty John's victims, the polar bear cub and her human helpers, the young children who survived a gunman's bullets, the families fighting to save children from disease and bureaucracy, the athlete dealing with rage, the man who shoots a drug dealer to protect his wife — these are journalism's future delivered, and damn good reads. We commend them to you.

THE BEST AMERICAN NEWSPAPER NARRATIVES, VOLUME SIX

The Loneliest Polar Bear

The Oregonian

October 15-22, 2017

By Kale Williams

Abandoned

As the sea ice shrinks, polar bears have found a home in zoos and a friend in humans. One cub born in captivity faced harsh odds as zookeepers weighed their role. This is Nora's story.

In the den, the walls were white like ice. Light came from a single red bulb. The air smelled of cool concrete, of straw piled thick, and of a heavy, captive musk. Somewhere, tucked under her 600-pound mother, was Nora. She was the size of a squirrel, deaf and blind. Translucent fur barely covered her pink skin. Soft paws paddled against the straw, and her nose led her in one direction: toward her mother. The bear cub woke only to nurse, which she did greedily and often, with a soft whir that sounded like a tiny outboard motor. She suckled even in her sleep, her curled, comically large tongue lapping at the air. On the morning of her sixth day, her mother, Aurora, rose and stretched and ambled out of the den. Nora felt the chill return. As the minutes crept by, she searched for something familiar, casting her head side to side, unmoored from her mother's gravity and heat. Her screech sounded like a baby dragon.

When she got no answer, Nora began to wail.

In a trailer just outside the denning compound, zoo veterinarian Priya Bapodra squinted at a grainy, red video — a live feed from inside the polar bear den. Nora was a shifting shadow of pixels, barely discernible.

Zookeeper Devon Sabo took notes. For five days, Priya, Devon and a curator kept watch in rotating shifts. They craned their necks and pressed headsets to their ears.

Nora was the first newborn polar bear to live more than a few days at the Columbus Zoo and Aquarium since it opened in 1927. Her birth in a concrete den in central Ohio represented all the ways humans and polar bears were inextricably tangled — from the day nearly three decades before when an orphaned cub was pulled from an icy den in the Alaskan wilderness, to the political battle that appointed her species the sad-eyed symbol of climate change. She represented the damage humans had done to the Earth, and she offered the thinnest hope of setting things right.

To her species and to the zoo, she was priceless.

And so, at 8:55 a.m., as Aurora took one step away from Nora and then another, the women willed themselves to stay calm.

Aurora had left Nora alone for brief periods. But in the wild, a mother polar bear doesn't leave the den, even to eat. Devon made a note in the log.

"Aurora gets up and goes into pool room."

An alert went out over a text message thread to the rest of the animal care team.

Ten minutes passed.

Maternal instincts are innate in animals, but the young mom appeared conflicted.

Priya kept an eye on the clock. Twenty minutes now.

***

Alone in her den in November 2015, Nora was the only surviving polar bear cub born in the United States that year. A twin brother had lived less than two days and died with an empty stomach. Zookeepers believe he never tasted his mother's milk.

Polar bears epitomize independence, savagery and power, but their newborn cubs are fragile and rare.

Adult bears mature late, have few litters and expend a great amount of time and energy raising their young. Every cub — wild or captive — shoulders a share of the burden of a species in peril.

No one knows how many wild polar bears exist because counting them is nearly impossible in the remotest regions of the planet. But only a few of the 19 subpopulations of polar bears are growing. At least three have been in steep decline in recent years.

In the Southern Beaufort Sea, along the northern coast of Alaska and Canada, researchers saw a 40 percent drop in polar bears in less than a decade. In Canada's western Hudson Bay, the bear population has dwindled at least 22 percent since the early 1980s. And in southern Hudson Bay, bears are thinner and dying younger.

The best guess puts the total count somewhere around 26,000 — about the population of Tualatin.

To survive, polar bears need sea ice, and sea ice is melting fast. NASA researchers using satellite imagery have seen the summer ice across the Arctic shrink 13 percent per decade on average since the 1980s.

Nora's wild counterparts hunt seals from atop that ice. As the ice breaks earlier in the season, bears are forced to swim farther to find food and must fast on land for longer periods, disrupting their ability to breed. If trends continue, some experts say, two-thirds of polar bears could be extinct by 2050.

One of the few places on Earth where polar bear numbers are growing is in zoos. And at the Columbus Zoo, thousands of miles from those shrinking frozen seas, Nora was alone and in trouble.

***

Aurora had been gone for 30 minutes. She'd never left Nora for this long.

She wandered the rooms of the compound, seemingly deaf to the sounds of her daughter.

Inside the trailer, the tension was thick. Nora's cries reminded the keepers of their own children, only louder and more urgent. As long as her vocals were strong, they were willing to wait.

The women watching had decades of experience hand-raising jungle cats, livestock and primates. The prospect was starting to hit them: Would they have to raise a polar bear?

At the one-hour mark, something had to be done. Devon went into the compound, carrying more straw to coax the wandering mom back to the den. She walked along the narrow path called "keeper's alley," beckoning.

"Aurora."

The bear wouldn't respond.

"Aurora."

She sniffled and shuffled about.

"Aurora."

Devon put the straw next to the room where Nora lay crying. Though she wasn't ready to say it aloud, Devon couldn't help but think that Aurora had given up on motherhood.

***

Twenty-seven years before Nora was born and 3,600 miles away, Eskimo hunter Gene Rex Agnaboogok grabbed his rifle, got on his snowmobile and headed onto the ice.

The morning had been disappointing and painfully cold.

Gene searched for three hours for a seal or fox or anything he could haul back to his village to eat. Then, just before 11 a.m., he found prints so large they could come from only one animal. In his village of Wales, Alaska, an adult polar bear could feed several families for weeks.

Gene followed the tracks onto the Bering Strait.

Close to shore, 4-foot waves of ice sat frozen in time — a rough, unmoving sea. Wind whipped the barren expanse, picking up snow and piling it in drifts.

Gene's snowmobile bumped along over the ice until the desolate sea stretched flat for hundreds of yards. There, where the ice had been blown smooth, Gene lost the bear's tracks. He throttled back the engine.

Now nearly a mile from shore, Gene hiked up the slope of an iceberg. It looked like a good place to take a coffee break and figure out his next move.

He pulled a Marlboro Light from his shirt pocket and poured coffee from a Thermos. His perch gave him a 360-degree view, but when he looked through binoculars, all he saw was emptiness and blowing snow. Hot coffee didn't stand a chance in below-zero conditions, but he took one more sip. Gene flicked his spent cigarette and started walking back down the iceberg.

Halfway down, coffee in hand, he heard the ice crack. His weight felt suspended in air for a split second, and then he was falling.

He crashed waist-deep into one of the many cavities beneath the surface. As Gene struggled to gain his footing, he realized the ground below him was moving.

Gene had broken through the roof of a den, and he was standing on a polar bear.

Adrenaline flooded his nervous system and his legs scrambled against the ocean of fur. It felt like he was running on a waterbed.

Gene managed to plant the butt of his rifle in the snow. He spun, struggling to free himself.

He thrashed, heart hammering. As the bear moved underneath him, he leapt from the hole.

But behind him, the bear lunged. A claw pierced Gene's right leg just above the knee.

Her nose hit the back of his leg and her lower jaw struck his heel. Had she turned her head sideways and latched onto his leg, the story might have ended there.

Instead, her head landed like a log, propelling him farther from the cave and onto the slope of the ice.

The bear circled behind the den, toward the top of the iceberg. Gene turned and saw her rearing on her haunches, tall and angry.

At a dead sprint, polar bears can cover nearly 30 feet per second. She was 15 feet away.

He aimed his rifle and squeezed the trigger. All 150 grains of gunpowder in his Remington .270 ignited and flung the lead slug in the direction of the bear. The bullet struck where her neck met her torso.

She crumpled, sliding down the iceberg back toward the den, using the last of her energy to draw her body as close as she could to the opening in the ice.

Breathless and exhausted, Gene thought he saw the bear move. He approached her carefully, then fired a second shot, just below the skull, to make sure she was dead.

As he stood over the bear, Gene saw movement inside the den and jumped back. He looked into the dark. Two small, white fluffs of fur peered back.

Baby polar bears, motherless on the ice.

It was at that moment that Gene noticed his pants were warm and wet. Assuming he had spilled coffee, he reached under his ski pants. His hand came up red, covered in blood leaking from the hole in his leg.

He was 20 miles from home, nearly a mile out on the sea ice and injured. The cubs would have to wait.

***

The next day, Gene's father and nephew followed the snowmobile tracks back to the iceberg to salvage the hide and meat from the dead bear.

Gene's dad stripped the fur from the animal, while his nephew approached the collapsed den. He saw the cubs, quiet and still.

Each was the size of a small raccoon, and they'd already grown sharp teeth. Gene's nephew took off a glove and dangled it in front of the first bear as a distraction. When it lunged, he grabbed it by the scruff of its neck and put it in a cardboard box strapped to the back of the snowmobile.

He repeated the process with the second bear, lamenting the puncture marks the cubs were putting in his new gloves. With no room left in the box, he tucked the second bear into a backpack, its head poking out of an opening in the zipper.

Neither of those cubs would ever see the wild again. One was given the name Nanuq, and 27 years later, he would have a daughter, born in a zoo, named Nora.

Most polar bear cubs born in captivity live less than a month. Only about a third survive to adulthood. For hand-raised cubs, the odds are worse.

They can't regulate their temperature. They succumb to disease and infection. They suffer from malnutrition and bone issues because their mother's milk is impossible to replicate.

Zoos rely on a comprehensive birth plan, drafted long before the mother goes into labor. Aurora's 23-page plan was kept in a binder in the denning compound. The keepers each had a copy on their phones.

The plan accounted for all conceivable scenarios, including pulling a cub from its mother.

"It will not be possible to return the cubs to the female when their condition improves or they have been stabilized, as she will not accept them," the plan read.

At the two-hour mark, Devon went into the denning compound again. This time she brought fish.

"Aurora," Devon called out.

"Aurora."

On the text thread, Devon relayed what was happening. Soon, other keepers showed up to watch. Questions swirled in their heads. Could something have driven Aurora from the den? What else could they do to coax her back? How long should they wait?

Three hours had gone by, and now the keepers gave Aurora a deadline: one more hour. If Nora appeared to weaken, they would swoop in sooner.

None of them wanted to raise Nora themselves. Her odds would plummet the instant they plucked her from the den. But they didn't want to stand by and watch her die, either. Left alone, her odds were zero.

They grabbed a plastic bin and lined it with heated water bottles and blankets. Without her mother's warmth, Nora had to be getting cold.

At 12:43 p.m., almost four hours after Aurora left the den, Nora's cries weakened ever so slightly and she looked sluggish.

It was time.

Devon went to the far side of the denning compound with a plate of smelt, one of Aurora's favorite snacks. She grabbed a fish with a pair of tongs and called Aurora. She was distracting the bear so Aurora wouldn't notice as the door slid shut behind her. Moving slowly, a curator quietly secured the door with a padlock. As it clicked into place, any remaining bond between Aurora and her daughter was severed.

Priya unlocked a second door and entered the den, crouching to avoid the low ceiling. It was just a couple of steps to Nora. Priya knelt, pushed aside some straw and scooped her up.

Nora fought, wriggling against the intrusion, the strange smells, the alien touch.

She was just a pound and a half, and dangerously cold. Intervening was a radical move, and it came after decades of human meddling in her world. There was wildness in Nora, who bleated and squirmed. But the untamed expanse of ice that her father had once known was shifting, melting, fading away. There was no perfect home for her, not anymore.

Nora and the fate of her species were in human hands now.

The Moms

Without her mother, Nora's chances of survival were slim. It would be up to a group of women to keep her alive and healthy.

The veterinarian stared at the thermometer and at the white cub, who was screeching.

The digital screen said simply "low." Just as the vet had feared. Nora, who had now been without her mother's warmth for more than four hours, was so cold her body temperature wouldn't register.

She was about a pound and a half, disoriented and angry. Priya Bapodra knew if she didn't stabilize and warm the little bear, she would lose her.

Odds were, Nora would die no matter what anyone did. Few zoos had attempted to hand-raise a polar bear. Most had failed.

Priya chose a 22-gauge needle, the second smallest she had, and searched Nora's thigh for the femoral vein to draw blood. It was a vein she knew she could hit the first time, even on something so small and squirmy.

"Hang on, girl," Priya said, as the needle pierced Nora's skin. The vet always talked to the animals. This time, the one she was trying to reassure was herself.

***

The very idea was audacious and terrifying: to raise by hand one of the world's fiercest and rarest apex predators, with little precedent or guidance. Of the roughly 70 polar bears living in accredited zoos and wildlife refuges in North America, only four newborns had been successfully hand-raised.

The keepers at the Columbus Zoo would not only have to save Nora's life but also preserve the things that made her wild. And even though every face she saw would be human, they would have to somehow teach her to be a bear.

Nora had a role to play. She could grow up and contribute to the biodiversity of the species. She could help scientists understand her distant cousins who still walked the shrinking Arctic ice where her father was born. She could endear herself to millions of visitors who might think of her when they filled their gas tanks or tuned in to the latest political debate.

But first, the women who became known collectively as the Nora Moms would have to guide her through these tenuous days. They had to get her warm, then get her fed.

They had a 23-page plan, with step-by-step instructions in the subsection "Removal of Cub." They had a manual: "Hand-Rearing Wild and Domestic Mammals." They had an incubator the size of a double-wide refrigerator. Priya set the small-animal compartment to 88 degrees and lined it with clean baby blankets from Target.

They were as ready as they could possibly be, and they were not ready at all.

***

Dana Hatcher, who ran the nutrition center at the zoo, got a call in the early afternoon that seemed like a simple request.

"Can you come over to the animal hospital so we can talk about polar bear formula?"

She headed to a meeting in a large conference room — joining a group of Nora Moms, curators and administrators — and explained the recipe she had on hand.

"So, if you pull the cub ..."

Someone interrupted her.

"Dana, we've already pulled the cub."

They needed the formula within an hour.

Dana experienced a brief moment of tunnel vision, mentally transporting herself to the nutrition center, cataloging every ingredient and its place in the cabinet.

She was a scientist in the kitchen. Even at home, she cooked using Excel spreadsheets and metric weights. She had cooked for lemurs, flamingos and her 7-year-old. But never a polar bear cub. This would be like one of those harried time challenges on a Food Network cooking show. But if she failed, Nora would die.

Dana knew that polar bears were among the most difficult animals to feed. In the wild, they live almost entirely off of ringed seals, fatty animals that add richness to polar bear milk. In making formula, the zoo had no handy substitute for seal fat, and Dana knew that roughly a quarter of hand-raised cubs had developed bone problems due to an inadequate diet.

Fortunately for Dana, a veterinarian from the San Francisco Zoo had managed to study wild polar bear milk just a few years earlier. To get the milk, scientists in Norway fired darts at mother polar bears from helicopters, then hand-milked them on the ice. The nutritional profile of that milk gave Dana an advantage over the failures of the past couple of decades. She knew, roughly, what nutrients Nora would need.

The zoo kitchen, housed in a beige warehouse out of public view, looked like the storeroom of a large grocery store. The 500-square-foot walk-in refrigerator was stocked with fruits and vegetables. The freezer, nearly three times larger, was loaded with fish and meat.

Dana started with a can of powdered kitten milk replacer — baby formula for cats — and sifted it so it wouldn't clump. The formula was low in fat, leaving Dana room to add calories however she saw fit.

She knew the sugars in the cat formula would be hard on Nora's stomach, because polar bears can't digest cow milk or goat milk. Through experimentation, she figured out that heating the water helped break down the lactose. Dana also knew that polar bears needed lots of taurine to help absorb vitamins, so she crushed taurine tablets with a mortar and pestle and added it to the mixture.

Then came the biggest piece of the puzzle: Nora needed fat, and lots of it, to grow. But what kind?

Human milk and cow milk contain around 3.5 percent fat. Polar bear milk is 10 times as rich, with a fat content upward of 30 percent. The closest thing in the supermarket is whipping cream.

The birth plan recommended herring oil, but that was only available from Canada, and Dana didn't have any. She considered her options and went with safflower oil. It had a mild flavor and was easy to work with.

Dana poured it all into a Vitamix and hit the button for low. The oil and the creamy formula spun together but stratified like old yogurt. Dana tried turning the machine to high. The mixture frothed but ended up too thick to drink.

After a few tries, Dana still couldn't get the consistency right. The big Vitamix was too powerful. If only she had the Magic Bullet she used to make salsa at home. It was the perfect size, and it had a pulse function.

She sent a staff member on a quick trip to Target.

The smaller mixer proved to be the key. Dana heated the water and added the pre-sifted powder. Once those ingredients were blended smooth, she poured in the oil. She hit pulse on the Magic Bullet once, twice. Three times.

It was ready.

Cindy Cupps was charged with Nora's first feeding. She was a zoo veteran whose presence calmed the younger keepers. Cindy was serene when others were stressed, tranquil when they were frenzied. As she headed to the zoo's intensive care unit, she locked eyes with another keeper.

Shannon Morarity was known as the crier in the group, and sure enough, her eyes were welling.

Cindy looked at Shannon and clenched her fists.

"We can do this," Cindy said.

Shannon looked back at her and took a breath.

"OK."

As Cindy arrived at the intensive care unit and opened the door to the incubator, she marveled at Nora's head, just a little bigger than a golf ball. Cindy scooped her up. Thin, white fur covered Nora's back and legs. Her squeals fluctuated between a high-pitched whine and a miniature roar. Her tongue lapped about freely in search of something to suckle. After not feeding for roughly five hours, Nora was hungry.

Cindy couldn't help but think about the threat facing Nora and her species.

This is unreal, she thought.

Cindy draped a towel across her thigh. She slid her hand under Nora's soft belly and held her upright, so she wouldn't inhale any of the formula.

Cindy tipped the bottle toward the cub and Nora latched on. She fed so tenaciously that a small milk moustache formed around her mouth. Cindy encouraged her in a soft voice, using a nickname that would stick.

"Good girl, Bean."

***

The next day, the zoo's public relations staff posted 78 seconds of video from one of those first feedings. Viewers saw Nora, eyes still fused shut, gnaw on Cindy's gloved thumb. They watched Cindy stroke her with a finger. Nora became an international phenomenon.

It was a risk to introduce her to the world so soon. The odds favored Nora dying, and if she did, her budding global fan club would expect answers. Critics would say the zoo had exploited Nora and doomed her from the start.

Babies are currency for zoos. And few animals are as rare or appealing — or as valuable — as a newborn polar bear. In the mid-'90s, the Denver Zoo saw attendance double after two polar bear cubs were pulled from their mother. Family memberships went up by a third as zookeepers hand-raised Klondike and Snow. The zoo raked in hundreds of thousands of dollars on merchandise, from oven mitts to Christmas ornaments, emblazoned with the likenesses of the cubs.

If she lived, Nora would be good for the zoo's bottom line, and the marketing machine in Columbus was ready to make the most of her.

Nora also represented something more pure. Zoos offer most of us our only chance to witness firsthand the diversity and splendor of life on Earth. Few people will work to protect something they have never seen and don't understand. Without zoos, children would never hear the low rumble of a tiger, or feed a giraffe, or look an orangutan in the eye and see something undeniably familiar staring back. Nora could lead a generation of children to consider their role in preserving the planet.

People clicked on the video of Nora feeding and watched it again and again. They said they wished they could be like Cindy, holding something so rare, feeling the strong tug of her mouth on the bottle, hearing the satisfying swallows that meant Nora now had a chance.

***

Of all the Nora Moms, Priya worried most. Nora had spent just six days with her mother in the polar bear birthing compound before keepers rescued the abandoned cub. Had Nora gotten enough antibodies from her mom to ward off pneumonia? Was she too cold? Was she too warm? Every action came with a round of second-guessing.

Nora left her cozy incubator only for meals and medical checks. While she was out, Priya counseled the other Moms to finish their tasks and put Nora back.

"What are you doing?" she teased them. "It's been like 20 minutes! Get her back in there."

From the start, the Moms found it hard to let go. They kept Nora wrapped tight to their chests, where she could smell them and feel their heat. Cindy talked to her softly and stroked her head. Shannon scratched the cub's round belly as Nora tried to bury her head in the crook of her arm.

On day seven, Shannon noticed that the pink pads on Nora's feet began to turn black, followed by her nose the next day and her ears the day after that. Soon, the wispy, translucent hair on her ears and feet thickened and she turned whiter and softer. She grew a little more than an ounce every day.

The keepers gradually dialed down the incubator, allowing Nora to regulate her own body temperature. They kept the ICU dark like a den, and they didn't talk much around Nora, so she could sleep and grow undisturbed.

Shannon would stare at Nora in the dark, through the window of the incubator, and watch her roll or snore or sleep.

She would ask herself: What does this baby need?

Nora slept belly-up, tongue-out, paws twitching as she dreamed.

Each of the Moms had a job at the zoo outside of caring for Nora, and those responsibilities didn't end with the arrival of the baby bear. Shifts for Shannon sometimes lasted 28 hours. Through the holidays, she barely saw her family. Priya ate Thanksgiving dinner on the floor of the ICU, near Nora's incubator. Their families understood. They could tell how much Nora meant to them.

Around week three, Nora grew more feisty. Her eyes were still closed, but she began moving around the incubator on her own. Her head was too big and her tummy too round for her to stand.

The Moms allowed her more freedom, sitting with her on rubber mats on the floor so she could learn to walk.

At the 30-day mark, Nora's odds of survival, once so remote, improved to 50-50. A coin flip. The Moms breathed a little easier.

Four days later, Nora opened her eyes for the first time. No one can say what she made of the scene before her, but there were no bears in it, and no snow or ice.

She saw Priya, the analytical one, anticipating every contingency. She saw Shannon, the tender-hearted one, who was often crying. She saw Cindy, the veteran, telling the others it was going to be all right.

***

While the Moms were busy raising Nora, Dana had been in the nutrition center doing research on how to import herring oil. The fish oil had a better fatty acid profile than the safflower oil they'd been using. Once she'd found a supplier in Canada, Dana began to slowly add the new fat to Nora's formula.

In late December, Priya noticed that Nora was passing oil in her stool. Just as Dana began introducing the herring oil, Nora's growth slowed.

Priya was concerned, but there was so little data on hand-raised cubs that she wasn't sure what to make of it. Nora was 54 days old now, and Priya ordered a full exam. The results were not encouraging.

Nora's vitamin D and calcium levels were low. Critical building blocks for growth and bone development were passing right through her system.

Priya also took X-rays.

In the darkened radiology room just outside the ICU, Priya looked at the images of Nora's bones, and her face dropped. Shannon, standing just outside the doorway, saw the look in the veterinarian's eyes. She knew something was wrong.

The X-rays showed curves where bones should have been straight. She had a fracture in her left radius, one of the bones between the wrist and the elbow.

Metabolic bone disease.

Despite everything Dana had done, Nora had not gotten the nutrients she needed.

Priya stepped out of the X-ray room and headed to the ICU. Shannon was already there, lying on the floor next to Nora, who was still groggy from anesthesia. Nora was crabby and hungry. She growled at her keepers.

When Priya walked in, Shannon read everything on her face. This time, both women cried.

Letting go

As Nora grew, her keepers did all they could to keep her healthy. But with plenty of human fans, she still needed the company of another bear.

The line stretched through Polar Frontier, past walls plastered with facts about climate change, past a time-lapse projection showing shrinking sea ice, past posters urging people to conserve fossil fuels, and ended at the floor-to-ceiling glass that looked out onto the enclosure, where throngs of adults with fancy cameras and children with expectant smiles waited for Nora.

She strutted into the yard, 70 pounds of pigeon-toed fluff, and immediately got her head stuck in an orange traffic cone, tromping around like a confused construction worker. She played with a yellow ball. She buried her nose in a pile of ice chips. She belly-flopped into the pool, scattering fish.

"Do it again!" someone shouted. "Jump again!"

Nora's debut at the Columbus Zoo was covered by nearly all the local media. Shannon Morarity, who had been with Nora for all but a few of her first 159 days, teared up on Channel 10.

"We're proud of her," she said.

Over the next five months, the zoo counted 261,126 people who came through the line to see her. Some ran through the gates. Some visited so often that the keepers recognized their faces.

A bear who didn't appear to know she was a bear, Nora thrived on human attention. She spent much of her time in front of the window that separated her from her fans.

She seemed to love people, and they loved her back.

***

In the 13th century, King Edward III kept a polar bear, a gift from the King of Norway, at the Tower of London. The bear was led, muzzled and shackled, to the River Thames, where it was allowed to swim and fish on a chain. In the 18th century, polar bears and other exotic animals traveled Europe in menageries for public amusement. One owner said he was doing "more to familiarize the minds of the masses of our people with the denizens of the forest than all the books of natural history ever printed."

That's still the essential argument for zoos.

The arrangement never seems quite fair to the bears, which, left alone, roam the tundra for hundreds of miles. Some zoos, such as the one in Columbus, offer expansive, multi-million-dollar habitats, while others muster little more than a lukewarm pool and an iceberg mural.

Getting the climate right is tough. Polar bears easily overheat, and in Beijing, captive bears endure summer temperatures of more than 100 degrees. But as zoo habitats expand and wild habitats disappear, zoos become more central to the survival of the species.

Nora's keepers had scoured the research on how to care for her, and the cub seemed happy, if the happiness of another species is a thing that can be judged.

She would never have to roam the vanishing sea ice in search of food, or be forced to rummage through garbage or raid goose nests or eat berries, like her northern cousins. The keepers known as the Nora Moms would exhaust themselves to attend to her needs.

But could they offer her enough open space? Were traffic cones and oversized toys enough to engage her mind? Could they build her a family? Mature polar bears in the wild spend months alone as they search for food, but when their needs are met, they seem to want to be around other bears. Nora had never known another polar bear.

***

The people who watched Nora bob in her blue pool were unaware that her keepers harbored a nagging concern.

Despite everything — the extensive research, the careful monitoring, the round-the-clock care, the 28-hour shifts, the missed holidays — the Nora Moms had fallen short.

When Nora was only a month old, four months before she met her public, her keepers had learned that the cub wasn't absorbing enough vitamin D and calcium. Her bones were crooked and cracked. If the problem wasn't fixed, Nora faced a bleak future.

Zoo veterinarian Priya Bapodra had dried her tears and pored over the research to figure out how to balance Nora's diet. Priya suspected the problem began when the team switched Nora's formula from safflower to herring oil. The research said herring oil would be better, but that wasn't the case for Nora.

Nora's keepers switched her back to safflower oil and gave her extra calcium. She also started getting vitamin D injections. Nora wasn't in obvious pain, but polar bears don't always show when they're hurting, so they gave her light painkillers. When the Moms took her out of the incubator, they tried not to handle her too much so her bones could heal.

Babies recover quickly, and it took only a few weeks for some of the issues to right themselves. Priya and the rest of the Moms were overjoyed at how quickly she seemed to improve. They gave her one more vitamin D shot on Jan. 21. X-rays taken later showed the fracture in her forearm had healed. Nora appeared to be a healthy baby bear.

Inside the ICU, the Moms gradually lowered the temperature from 88 to 70 to 55 degrees. They brought electric blankets, beanies and thick sweatshirts to stay warm. They rested on an air mattress in the corner, so they could be close to her all the time.

They dressed in thick Carhartt outfits, to protect themselves from her curved claws and new teeth. Nora would appear content one second, and then an unfamiliar noise would set her off. Under different circumstances, her mother might have set her straight with a firm paw.

Nora still pulled herself along like a seal, back legs splayed behind her. She'd push herself up and then topple and roll, no particular structure to her, just fur and feet and dark, curious eyes.

While the Moms worked on email or entered data in the corner of the darkened ICU, Nora scooted over to them and wrapped her paws around their ankles.

They were always strategizing, always worrying, but there were moments they stopped and just stared at her, lovestruck. Shannon sometimes held Nora while the cub napped, and at least once, she nodded off herself, snuggling a warm armful of polar bear.

On day 78, Nora learned to walk. On day 82, she lapped from a green bowl, and the Moms cheered. On day 88, they gave her a tub of water to explore, and she parked her rump in it.

The head veterinarian told Priya what she already knew: "You're going to have to let her go."

So Priya declared Nora medically clear, and they moved her from the animal hospital to Polar Frontier. She had more space there, in the 1.3-acre enclosure. The exhibit was new by zoo standards after a $20 million face-lift, and it could host multiple bears in separate areas. The 167,000-gallon pool had a geothermal heating and cooling system. Columbus featured three adult bears and Nora, more than any other zoo in the country, and its habitat reflected the zoo's commitment to the species.

***

Visitors saw few walls, in keeping with modern zoo design. It appeared that Nora could wander north, leave the zoo, hang a left when she got into Canada and join her Alaskan kin. She explored her new surroundings tentatively, looking back to Shannon and the rest of the Moms every time she encountered something new.

As Shannon watched her in the yard, she felt her shoulders relax and thought, OK. She's good. Getting Nora to this point had been exhausting but worth it. Now the bear had room to play with all five of her Moms at once, and they romped with her in the yard like a bunch of kids.

After about two weeks, Shannon and another keeper pulled on wetsuits and waded into the 7-foot-deep pool to show Nora it was safe. Nora stalked the edge of the water before tentatively dipping in a paw. A few minutes later, she waded in. She was a natural swimmer. Seeing her take off in the water, paddling with her outsize paws, assured them that there were things about being a bear that, somehow, Nora already knew.

In the log the Moms kept of Nora's milestones, the "swimming" entry is accompanied by four exclamation marks.

When she reached five months, they had to pull back. Her claws and teeth had gotten longer and sharper. Staying in the enclosure with a growing bear was dangerous.

She was too big to be with the keepers but too small to be with the other bears, who could easily injure or kill her.

The Moms interacted with her through glass or netting. They still talked to her and told her they loved her. But inside the enclosure, she was alone.

When Nora roamed the yard, Shannon stood at a door where the cub could see her. For a while, Nora looked to Shannon every time a new noise or strange smell wafted across the enclosure.

And then, one day, she stopped looking. It was the moment all moms work toward, and all moms dread. Shannon would never get to cuddle her nose-to-nose again.

But Nora had a whole world full of people lined up to see her from the other side of the glass.

***

Two thousand miles away, at the Oregon Zoo, a very different polar bear also found herself alone.

Tasul was 31, one of the world's oldest known polar bears. She had lived an extraordinary life in captivity, and she represented the best of what humans and bears could accomplish together.

She had just lost her twin brother, Conrad. The two bears had been close. Tasul and Conrad sometimes slept curled up together. When Tasul wanted to play, she bonked her brother with her head or batted a ball at him with her giant paw.

After Conrad died, the elderly bear wandered the enclosure, sniffing and searching for her brother.

Like most polar bears, Tasul was smart. Bears have to be great problem solvers to survive in the Arctic, home to some of the harshest conditions on the planet. But their intelligence, combined with their size and power, means they can't be tricked into doing anything.

Portland zookeeper Nicole Nicassio-Hiskey built a relationship with Tasul over 15 years. It started simply. Nicole fed the bear smelt and trout from her hands, talking to her softly from behind the bars. Tasul learned to follow Nicole, who never forced her to take any action she didn't want to take. Everything they did was on the bear's terms.

Nicole's biggest challenge was getting Tasul comfortable when keepers reached through the bars to touch her. It spooked Tasul at first. Polar bears don't like to be touched. But Tasul learned to enjoy it. Cooperation earned her papayas, bananas — peel and all — and squirts of fruit juice. She even got sherbet when her keepers were feeling generous.

The first time Nicole held Tasul's paw, she was humbled.

It was the size of her head. She felt a deep sense of honor that one of the world's fiercest predators would allow her so close. It reminded her of the first time she held her own child.

Nicole remembers the date of their biggest breakthrough, because it came on her birthday, Dec. 4, in 2011. It had been a rough stretch for Nicole. She had just lost her father, and her emotions were raw.

Tasul had trained for this moment for years. A local company built a unique cage that attached to one of the dens. That morning, Nicole stood in front of the cage near Tasul's head, where she could hand-feed her and monitor the bear's demeanor. Another keeper knelt in the back, where a second door provided access to Tasul's hind paws.

As Nicole occupied Tasul with carrots, the other keeper shaved the top of Tasul's paw and searched her black skin for a vein. The fact that Tasul could be handled so easily was extraordinary.

And then, the other keeper popped up.

"Oh my god," she said. "We got blood! We got blood!"

It marked the first time a polar bear had given blood without being tranquilized. It was a high point for Nicole in a difficult year, and it would make Tasul famous in the zoo world.

Karyn Rode noticed. The wildlife biologist had spent years studying polar bears on the ice of the Chukchi Sea, where Nora's dad had been orphaned. Karyn read about Tasul's blood draw in The Oregonian and saw an opportunity to bolster her research. She'd been tracking wild bears using radio collars. But the collars told Karyn only where the bears went. She wanted to know what they did when they got there.

Tasul gave her that chance. Karyn fitted her with a collar and sensor, like an oversized Fitbit.

She and other scientists took video of Tasul while the bear wore the collar. The readings gave researchers a benchmark to compare with collared bears in the Arctic. Now they could tell when the wild bears were resting, running or swimming, and when they were being forced to roam long distances in search of ice.

Tasul was the first polar bear to walk on a treadmill in a metabolic chamber and to swim in a one-of-a-kind flume. Researchers used the data to compare how much energy she expended on land versus water.

Nicole and the other keepers changed Tasul's diet from fish to meat so Karyn and her team could study any changes in Tasul's blood and fur. That information helped researchers understand how climate change affected wild bears, who scavenged for food on land.

Tasul had been born in a zoo, had learned to trust humans, and had spent her life with other bears. She was arthritic and a little slow, but calm and wise. She was just the kind of bear Nora could look up to.

***

Nora would never be reunited with her mother, Aurora. As much as she needed the companionship of other bears, and as much as the zoo adored her, it didn't make sense for her to stay.

In the spring, keepers at the Columbus Zoo saw Nora's father, Nanuq, mating with Aurora and the zoo's other female bear. If they were pregnant, they'd be giving birth in November or December. The zoo had to make room, and Nora was occupying the space they needed.

The Association of Zoos and Aquariums, the organization that recommends placement for bears, looked at every zoo in the country capable of housing a cub. None was quite right until the group's leaders looked to Portland. Nora seemed the perfect company for a lonely, old bear at the Oregon Zoo.

That summer, Nicole traveled with a team of keepers from Portland to Columbus to meet Nora and her Moms. The team was there on Nora's last day in front of the public, when 6,750 people came to see her. But now, many of her fans felt as if they knew her. They'd watched her grow.

As Nicole walked through the exhibit, a group of volunteers gathered around her, eyes fixed on the Oregon Zoo logo on her shirt. They peppered her with accusatory questions, some jokingly, some not so much.

"So, you're the one taking our Nora?"

***

That they knew she'd be leaving didn't make saying goodbye any easier.

It was early September, and Shannon stood on the runway in front of a FedEx cargo plane.

Nora sniffed the unfamiliar smells of an airport from inside her shipping crate next to the hangar. She'd been weighed and checked in.

Shannon and another keeper took turns saying goodbye, with equal feelings of accomplishment and sadness. They'd done the nearly impossible. This 10-month-old bear, who faced long odds of survival, was starting a new life.

"We love you," Shannon told Nora through the metal bars. "You have so much to look forward to, and we're so excited for you."

The other keeper stood by, taking video with her phone. They were proud of the job they'd done. The whole zoo had come together to cover their shifts while Nora pulled them away. If so many people could devote themselves to just one long-shot baby bear, maybe the planet could pull together to save the others.

A curator and veterinarian hopped on the plane to accompany the young bear for her flight. Shannon watched the door close.

As the plane lifted into the sky, Nora let out a low, rumbly growl.

***

The Oregon Zoo, tucked into the densely wooded West Hills of Portland, is a vastly different institution than the Columbus Zoo. At 64 acres, it's one-tenth the size of the Columbus Zoo. Its polar bear exhibit is nearly a full acre smaller.

For much of its 112 years, the Oregon Zoo's history with polar bears had been abysmal. The zoo's first polar bear stayed in a 20-foot-wide pen in the early 1900s and ate only milk and cod liver oil. Conditions were so awful that Portland's mayor sought unsuccessfully to shut down the zoo.

The zoo built a 0.4-acre polar bear exhibit in 1956. But it didn't get much better for the bears. One died after swallowing a rubber ball that blocked its intestines. Two died of food poisoning. One mauled a zoo worker and had to be shot.

Shortly after a 1985 remodel of the exhibit, Conrad and Tasul arrived. With the longevity of the twin bears, the zoo began to put its sad legacy to rest. Young Nora represented a hopeful new chapter.

There are no visible bars in the Portland polar bear exhibit, but tall, concrete walls surround the three yards. The public looks into the enclosures through thick windows. The ground in each of the polar bear yards is a mix of concrete and grass, usually littered with toys and tubs of ice.

It was in those yards that Nora and Tasul would meet.

After a 30-day medical quarantine, the keepers had orchestrated a series of introductions known in the zoo world as "howdies." First, the zoo staff positioned the bears so they could see each other. Then Nora and Tasul were put in adjacent rooms, separated by only a metal screen.

Nora hadn't been so close to another bear since she was a helpless, blind cub. By October 2016, she was nearly 200 pounds and almost a year old.

Nora didn't seem interested in interacting with Tasul through the screen, but the keepers knew that socialization was key to her development, and they were eager for Nora to have a companion. It was time to put them together.

***

Nicole watched from the roof of the bear building, radio in hand. Catwalks rimmed the enclosures, and Nicole had a bird's-eye view. She was charged with reporting, every 20 seconds or so, exactly what the bears were doing.

At least 10 other keepers and veterinarians were stationed around the exhibit at every door, in case they needed to close one in a hurry. The entire exhibit had been set up to limit dead ends, so Nora couldn't be backed into a corner. Keepers had frozen oranges and grapefruit they could toss to distract the bears. They had powerful hoses and fire extinguishers to separate the bears in a worst-case scenario. They cleared a channel so their constant updates wouldn't clog the zoo's radio frequencies.

They also had instructions: Don't intervene unless you see blood.

Polar bears usually growl or hunch their shoulders before their tempers flare, and Nicole knew the kinds of things that might trigger a reaction in the older bear.

The keepers gave Nora access to the main part of the exhibit, while Tasul was confined to the den.

After a few minutes, the door slid open, and Tasul walked out.

"Tasul is stopped, facing north," Nicole's voice crackled over the radio. "They're about 10 feet apart."

As soon as the elder bear saw Nora, she broke into a run straight at the cub. Nora, confronted with an unfamiliar animal more than twice her size sprinting right at her, spooked.

She turned and ran.

Nicole's radio fell silent. This wasn't going as any of them had hoped.

Breaking point

Nora finally had a chance to meet another bear, but it wasn't going as planned and her keepers began to worry about her health — mentally and physically.

Nora darted over a log and through a fake-rock tunnel.

The old bear, Tasul, lumbered behind. Nora jumped in the pool and zookeepers held their breath. It was the only part of the Oregon Zoo polar bear enclosure where she could be cornered. For a moment, it looked as if Tasul might go in after her.

"T-bear!" the keepers called, fire hoses at the ready. The older bear backed off.

Animal introductions could be tricky, but zookeeper Nicole Nicassio-Hiskey remained calm. She had known Tasul for more than 15 years, and she could tell when the bear was frightened, irritable or aggressive. Tasul showed none of those signs as she followed Nora. She was just curious.

The older bear had gotten used to company. She'd been with her twin brother, Conrad, for years before he died two months earlier.

Over the next few days, the older bear tried to make herself approachable. She looked away when Nora got close. She lowered herself to the ground to appear smaller. She tried to entice Nora to play, but Nora wasn't interested.

Everyone involved with Nora's upbringing — the Nora Moms in Columbus, her caretakers in Oregon and experts brought in to consult — stressed the importance of socialization. Nora needed to learn to be a bear, and the only way to do that was to spend time with one.

The exhibit was closed to the public for the introductions, but the zoo released a video of Nora tentatively walking the yard, obviously alarmed by Tasul's presence. In the news release accompanying the video, the zoo described their first meeting as "extremely positive," but going in "slow motion."

In truth, Nora was starting to buckle under the stress.

***

Back in the dens, Nora grew inconsolable. She barked like an angry seal, loud enough to be heard outside the building. Not even her favorite toys and treats could pierce the fog.

Soon after the keepers from Columbus dropped off Nora in Oregon, she'd begun exhibiting stereotypical behaviors, repetitive actions that have no obvious purpose. She pawed at the concrete, digging imaginary holes. She paced in circles, bumping into toys but ignoring them.

She fixated on her keepers, and any time they left the room, she threw a tantrum.

Captive animals can develop emotional and psychological problems. Elephants sway, gorillas hold their knees and rock, birds pluck themselves bald. Perhaps the most famous animal to exhibit these symptoms was Gus, a polar bear at the Central Park Zoo in New York.

In the mid-'90s, Gus started swimming laps in the pool. Over and over again, sometimes for 12-hour stretches, he swam the same figure-eight pattern. Zoo visitors found it whimsical and ticket sales jumped, but his keepers grew concerned. Gus was called "neurotic" and the "bipolar bear." The zoo paid $25,000 to a consultant who concluded Gus was bored.

The zoo gave Gus complicated puzzles, toys and a playroom. His repetitive behavior lessened but never went away.

Nora wasn't bored — just lonely and scared. Her symptoms got worse as the meetings with Tasul continued. After a session with Tasul, Nora panicked and paced for hours. Even when the bears were apart, her keepers sensed Nora was apprehensive, as if she thought the older bear might be lurking.

She wasn't getting better.

Mitch Finnegan, an Oregon Zoo veterinarian, prescribed Alprazolam, commonly known as Xanax. She took a pill once in the morning and another in the evening, hidden in ground horse meat, for a total of 4 milligrams a day. She paced less, but she remained anxious. Her dosage was upped to 6 milligrams per day.

Two weeks after that, Nora still paced. The zoo called in an animal behavior specialist who recommended a different approach. Nora was put on Fluoxetine, a generic version of the antidepressant Prozac.

***

At the heart of Nora's story is a complicated question: Are zoos helping animals or hurting them? People for the Ethical Treatment of Animals has taken a hard stance against zoos. Some parents won't take their young children to see animals they say are being exploited for our entertainment.

But few animals live as nature intended anymore. Not the rhinos, who are butchered for their horns; or the elephants, who are out of space; not the orangutans, who have lost their homes to palm oil plantations. Not the manatee, the mountain gorilla, the poison dart frog or even our own pets. We dose our dogs with Prozac, like Nora, as they chew their tails and bark all day.

More than 195 million people around the world visit zoos every year. By that measure, the demand for them is self-evident.

Animals at reputable zoos are vaccinated, dewormed and fed on schedule. Bears get their teeth brushed. Elephants stand for ultrasounds. Giraffes get their hooves trimmed. Zoo animals live much longer than their wild counterparts, and when they get sick, they don't fall prey to a faster predator or get picked apart by scavengers.

Animal rights groups argue that zoos focus on endangered species that are considered charismatic, such as the polar bear, because they draw crowds. But a zoo full of frogs could never generate enough ticket sales to pay for the research into why frogs are disappearing in the wild. To save frogs, zoos need animals like Nora.

More than anything, though, critics of zoos say containing animals for any reason is cruel and makes them crazy and bored.

That criticism puts zoos on the defensive with the media. Keepers and PR staff refer to "enclosures," "habitats" or "exhibits," but not cages. Access behind the scenes, when granted, usually comes with a caveat banning photography to prevent the public from seeing bars.

PR staff at zoos rarely release information when animals are faring poorly. None of Nora's ailments, physical or emotional, were revealed to her adoring fans when they were discovered. Not in Columbus and not in Portland. Metabolic bone disease and Prozac never made it into press releases about her milestones or into videos of her cute antics. It's anyone's guess how many other zoo animals suffer through similar problems.

Zoos sell a narrative of research, conservation and the highest standards of animal welfare. In most cases, the narrative is true. But it doesn't fully answer the charge made by animal rights groups that some creatures just don't do well outside their natural environment.

Animals like Nora present an impossible predicament. In the wild, she would have died soon after her mom left her alone. Without human intervention back in Ohio, she likely wouldn't have survived the day. But confinement was crippling her body and her mind.

The love of her keepers, and her fans, was not quite enough.

***

Tasul had been slowing down for months. She was old and arthritic. In the wild, she probably wouldn't have lasted this long. Wild bears usually don't live past 20. Captive bears rarely make it to 30.

When keepers noticed blood in her mucus, they ordered an ultrasound. It showed abnormal growths in her abdomen. A biopsy confirmed early-stage kidney failure. Veterinarians also suspected an ovarian tumor.

She needed surgery.

Mitch fired a dart filled with sedatives into the old bear's thick hide and she went down in minutes. Together, the keepers rolled her onto a cargo net and lifted her into a zoo van for the short ride from the polar bear enclosure to the medical center.

In the operating room, Mitch stood to the side as the surgeon made a nearly 10-inch incision lengthwise along Tasul's belly. When they opened her up, it was worse than they had suspected.

Cancer lined the inner wall of her body cavity from her pelvis to her kidneys. Her lymph nodes were inflamed. She had likely been in a great deal of pain.

Mitch believed she couldn't be helped. He picked up the phone.

Nicole was home with a bad case of the flu when she got the call.

The decision was heartbreaking but clear. Mitch helped administer a cocktail of pentobarbital to further sedate her and potassium chloride to stop her heart. Tasul died within minutes.

Afterward, Nicole arrived at the zoo. Tasul lay on the operating table while her keepers cried and traded stories during a makeshift wake.

They could touch her as much as they wanted now.

***

Just a few weeks after she had met Tasul, Nora found herself alone again. For the first time in Oregon, the keepers put her on public display, allowing her to build a whole new fan base. She seemed to thrive when she had an audience.

Before Tasul died, the gift shop had devoted its most prominent real estate to polar bear T-shirts, polar bear snow globes, polar bear ceramic statuettes, polar bear water bottles.

Nora's name was embossed in gold letters on black ribbon tied loosely around the neck of every one of the smaller stuffed bears.

A fluffy, jumbo polar bear sat atop the display case with a much smaller stuffed animal tucked under its big left paw. It was meant to depict Nora's new harmonious life with Tasul. But the staging on the display shelf was the closest the two bears would get.

Winter brought snow to Portland, and for the first time, visitors saw Nora in an environment that looked similar to her natural habitat. She romped through the yard as fat flakes fell around her. She pressed close to the glass as zoo staff engaged her in a game of peekaboo. In one of the coldest and snowiest winters the Pacific Northwest had ever seen, Nora's warm breath steamed the glass.

After the visitors left, she interacted with the security guards, following them along the exhibit and splashing in the pool to get their attention. She put her nose to the glass, trying to smell their coffee. When custodians washed the windows with giant, furry cleaning mitts, Nora's paws mirrored them from the other side.

Nora was ornery before the crowds arrived. She stomped and chuffed. To Nicole, it seemed like Nora was complaining that no one had come to see her.

As soon as the first people showed up, the growls stopped and Nora belly-flopped into the pool straight toward the windows.

It was great for social media videos and for the crowds.

But that isn't how polar bears are supposed to act.

***

It's impossible to know all the lessons Nora would have learned from her mother if she'd stayed with her, but experts know that key skills are impulse and temper control.

Of the eight species of bear, only polar bears are dedicated hunters. They rarely scavenge or forage. They hunt seals on sea ice, a skill that requires cunning and patience, traits usually taught by mom.

Nora had not learned those lessons. She paced less, either because of the medication or because she was settling in now that Tasul was gone. But she was still prone to tantrums. She barked and batted her food bowls across the floor. When frustrated or anxious, she turned her back on her keepers, shunning them.

The fits were hard for the keepers to watch, but all animals, even humans, need to learn to deal with adversity. Her handlers talked constantly about how to help her.

Soon after Tasul died, Jen Degroot and the other keepers started a relaxation exercise for polar bears they called "Zen sessions."

On a rainy day in December, Jen prepared for one of the sessions, loading a pie tin with lake smelt. Nora was only a year old, but she could read people and their energy. Jen took a series of deep breaths to center herself.

A few steps from the zoo kitchen, down a corridor lined with barred doors, Jen called out to Nora, who came lumbering up to an opening. Jen knelt on a piece of cardboard to insulate her knees from the cold concrete and began to offer fish through a gap in the bars.

No words were spoken, but Nora lay down immediately, head resting on her fluffy paws. Jen began feeding Nora the smelt at 5-second intervals. To a casual observer, it wouldn't look very Zen, but Jen took careful mental notes.

Between fish, the cub let out a low growl and shook her head. Her vocalizations were important. If she could wait for the next fish without stressing, it meant she was learning patience.

Nora was still in a critical stage of development. What she learned during her first two years would dictate how she interacted with other bears, which would be important for breeding. And it would affect her quality of life, which, to her keepers, was most important.

The keepers practiced the Zen sessions with Nora every day. She improved through winter and early spring, but Nora was still missing something that her keepers couldn't provide: the companionship of another bear.

The zoo had been planning for years to tear down its polar bear facility and build a new one. Demolition had been postponed twice for Nora's sake.

With Tasul gone, the zoo would not be bringing in another bear. They'd be shipping Nora out.

She needed a new home. Again.

***

One April morning, Nicole watched Nora walk up a ramp toward her den. The young bear seemed playful, as usual, but her gait was off.

That's really weird, Nicole thought to herself. That's new.

Nora was favoring her front left leg. It looked like the elbow bowed out just a little. Nicole called the zoo vet, who came by later that day.

By the time Mitch arrived, Nora couldn't put pressure on her left front leg, and her elbow jutted out as she walked.

She'd developed a habit of jumping into the pool and slamming against the window with her front paws. Mitch hoped she was just sore from playing, but he suspected it was more.

Mitch knew about her history with metabolic bone disease, so he asked the vets in Columbus for Nora's old X-rays.

In May, Nora was still limping. Mitch sedated her and took another set of X-rays.

One of the bones in her forearm was stunted, and because the pieces didn't fit right, her elbow was being forced out. He sent the X-rays to orthopedic surgeons around the country.

"All joints are trashed," a vet from another zoo wrote in the assessment. "She is or will be an arthritic mess, especially because she is such a big animal."

The surface where Nora's bones met was "so F-ed up," the vet wrote.

Joints require a high degree of precision, especially in an animal like Nora, who now weighed 330 pounds. If the bones don't match perfectly, like a piston in a cylinder, the joints wear out.

That was happening to Nora. During those few weeks back in Columbus when she didn't get sufficient vitamins and calcium, Nora's bones had softened and her left elbow had become deformed. Her keepers in Ohio thought they had corrected the problem, but they hadn't.

Any surgery would be complicated and might make things worse. Operating on Nora was ruled out.

Meanwhile, her anxiety and aggression intensified. It was hard to tell if she had outgrown the dose of antidepressants or if she was in pain, but Mitch upped her dose of Prozac either way.

He added two daily doses of anti-inflammatory pain medications to the schedule of drugs Nora was taking. Experts recommended she spend as much time as possible in the water to ease the load on her joints. Nora already loved the water.

Other than that, there was little they could do.

Survival

As Nora's journey takes her to a new zoo, the home of her counterparts in the wild is melting away

Nora's nose quivered as the smells of the Oregon Zoo blew through her yard. • Polar bears can detect a seal from 20 miles, so she must have inhaled the scent of the penguins over in Pacific Shores, the hot fried dough of the elephant ear cart, the orangutans dangling from their fingers in the Red Ape Reserve and even the coyotes roaming the West Hills of Portland. None of it would seem strange to her. The aromas of many continents had mingled in her imagination all her life.

On land, she moved awkwardly, her back feet pigeon-toed and front legs slightly bowed, but in the water, she was majestic.

She clambered out of the pool and shook a cylindrical aura of droplets from her thick fur. She blinked in the sunlight fracturing off the turquoise water. She loved to snag the head of a bristle brush and position herself with her rump in the pool. With a swift arc of her neck, she would fling the toy over herself and then execute a back dive after it.

Every time she did, the shrieks of her fans echoed through the viewing area and off the climate change infographics.

"Don't you want to snuggle her?"

"She must be so lonely."

Over in the zoo's gift shop, Nora's name had disappeared from the polar bear merchandise as her time in Portland neared an end. All that remained were a few polar bear baby bibs, a smattering of refrigerator magnets and the last of the shiny ceramic figurines relegated to a remote corner of the store.

Her final day on public display was a mild Sunday in September, a respite from a scorching summer. That morning, keepers tossed down cardboard boxes wrapped like going-away presents. After she shredded the colorful paper, the enclosure looked like a polluted, abused beach.

"Nora is going to a new home in Utah to be with another bear," a volunteer explained to the crowd, though he left out the extent of her emotional troubles.

The Association of Zoos and Aquariums had found a companion to join Nora in her new home. A bear named Hope would be traveling from Toledo, Ohio. Hope's mom was Nora's grandmother, so Hope was Nora's aunt.

Both bears would be sent to Utah's Hogle Zoo in Salt Lake City, which had recently lost its beloved bear, Rizzo, to kidney failure. Hogle had an experienced staff and a newer polar bear exhibit called Rocky Shores.

The cubs had vastly different upbringings, but that was good. Hope had been raised by her polar bear mother and knew more about being a bear than Nora did. Nora and Hope were both about to turn 2, the age when wild bears leave their mothers and set out on their own.

For much of her last day, Nora padded gingerly around the yard, her limp imperceptible to those who didn't know to look for it.

She pressed her face against the bars that led to her swim flume, where a researcher had measured her oxygen use on the zoo's underwater treadmill. In the afternoon, she napped in a mound of manufactured snow.

"She may not understand the importance of this day like we do," the volunteer said to the crowd.

In the back of the viewing area, spinning placards showed visitors "10 things you can do to help save polar bears," such as driving less or turning off lights.

A toddler fiddled with the first sign indifferently as his father sat on a bench posting a video of Nora online. A few feet away, a globe showed the Arctic sea ice in stark relief.

"That's where it was in 2005, and that's where it was in 2016," another father said to his son.

"It's all shrinking," the boy replied.

***

In the Arctic, the problems Nora's wild counterparts face can be reduced to one thing: the search for food.

Polar bears have been observed eating walrus and small whales, but up to 90 percent of their diet is ringed seal. Seal blubber is the only food dense enough in calories and plentiful enough in Arctic waters to support an animal that can grow to 1,200 pounds.

Polar bears rely on cunning, patience and brute strength to hunt their main prey. A bear can smell a seal through 2 feet of ice. It locates the air holes the seal uses to breathe, and it waits. The wait can last for days. When the seal surfaces, the bear plunges its long neck into the water, hauls out the seal and crushes its skull.

Even a small seal contains 100,000 calories, enough to sustain a bear for a week. When the ice melts in the summer, most bears head to land to forage or fast. Polar bears have been seen eating birds, grass and trash on the outskirts of villages and towns. But nothing they eat on land comes close to satisfying their caloric needs.

Without ice, polar bears can't hunt. They lose weight and give birth to fewer, weaker cubs. Sickly cubs are less likely to survive, so as ice disappears, so does the polar bear.

Off the coast of Alaska, the shadow of a helicopter swept across the snow. A hundred feet up, in the passenger seat, Karyn Rode wore a headset and goggles and scanned the craggy landscape for tracks.

Every spring since 2008, Karyn had traveled to her remote research base 100 miles north of the Arctic Circle on the Chukchi Sea. The open terrain was Nora's ancestral homeland. Her father, Nanuq, was orphaned about 200 miles from here. Polar bears can roam farther than that in a week.

The frozen sea looked like a whitewashed version of the moon. It always amazed Karyn that anything could live out here.

"Is that a track?" Karyn's voice crackled over the headset as she guided the pilot. "I think that's a track."

The paw prints crossed and faded out in blown snow.

A wildlife biologist with the U.S. Geological Survey based in Portland, Karyn had studied polar bears long before she started working with Tasul at the Oregon Zoo. Her research was cited in 2008, when polar bears were identified as threatened under the Endangered Species Act — the first imperiled animal ever listed due to climate change.

The helicopter bobbed and lurched. Early in the afternoon, Karyn spotted a bear lumbering across flat, open ice.

"You see it right in front of us there?" the pilot asked over the headset.

"I do," Karyn said.

The helicopter swooped low, and the bear broke into a lope heading north. Another biologist stood in her seat, aimed a tranquilizer gun at the bear's shoulder and fired a dart.

Within minutes, the pilot landed near the sleeping bear and Karyn went to work.

First, Karyn took samples: blood, hair, stool and a biopsy of fat. The bear groaned and twitched. She ran a tape measure along the bear's length and around its midsection. She and another biologist set up a heavy-duty tripod with a net and a chain hoist. They rolled the bear onto the net and lifted it to get its weight: 542 pounds.

To track the bear if it were ever caught again, they tattooed its inner lip. This one was Bear 21736.

It was a female, so Karyn fitted it with a radio collar. Male necks were too big.

"Good looking bear," Karyn wrote in her log.

She stuffed the test tubes into a box lined with hand warmers so they wouldn't freeze. Later, Karyn would analyze the samples based on what she learned from Tasul at the Oregon Zoo. The results would tell Karyn what the wild bears had eaten.

About an hour later, the bear began to rouse and lifted its head in time to see Karyn's helicopter take off.

The information she gathered illustrated how bears were adapting to their changing habitat. The ice in the Chukchi Sea was retreating faster than elsewhere on the continent: nearly 20 percent per decade. And it was breaking up earlier than she'd ever seen it.

Because the sea was shallow, the bears still found seals. But the wide, flat areas Karyn needed to sedate the bears were few and far between. Many parts of the Chukchi were slush and open water.

In a good year, Karyn tagged more than 30 bears. This year, she caught three.

Ten days before her trip was to end, the ice ran out. For the first time, Karyn and her team had to pack up early and leave.

***

The Hogle Zoo sits at the foot of the Wasatch Mountains, which tower over the eastern edge of Salt Lake City. Nora arrived at her new home in mid-September on a 100-degree day.

Zookeeper Kaleigh Jablonski had worked with the zoo's previous polar bear, Rizzo, for almost three years. But the Rocky Shores exhibit, an $18 million project built in 2012, had been vacant since Rizzo died in April.

Kaleigh had imagined the exhibit would stay empty for a while, because polar bears aren't in abundant supply. When she heard two cubs were coming, she was overjoyed.

She'd loved animals since she saw a marine mammal show at age 6. She'd worked with giraffes, cape buffalo and seals before moving to the zoo in Salt Lake City, where she spent most of her time with bears.

Kaleigh knew Nora and Hope had fans who would be watching to see that everything went smoothly. Meeting after meeting had been held to plan for their arrival.

Nora's long-term prognosis remained unknown. Her keepers were confident that once she got comfortable with her companion, she wouldn't need anxiety medication anymore.

As for her bones, they wouldn't know much until she finished growing in a couple of years. In the worst case, her adult weight would stress her joints and cause so much pain that she would have to be put down. More likely, she would deal with some discomfort and a slight limp for the rest of her life.

When Nora arrived, Kaleigh felt the pressure of it all.

Then she saw her. Nora walked out of her travel crate and into the small yard where she would spend time in quarantine alone. Flood lights illuminated the gravel as Nora cut straight to the pool.

"Hey, baby girl! You're here!" Kaleigh squealed. She couldn't help it. Even the fiercest animals at the zoo got the baby talk.

***

About 200 miles south of where Karyn Rode conducted her research, in an Eskimo village on the westernmost point of mainland Alaska, the story of Gene Rex Agnaboogok and the polar bear is legend.

Just 155 people live in Wales along a quarter-mile strip with one road, one public internet connection and one truck buried to its windows in snow.

On a clear day, villagers can see Russia across the Bering Strait.

Gene still lives here, in the house where nearly 30 years ago he played with two orphaned cubs, including Nora's father.

His straight, black hair is streaked gray, and a white goatee circles his mouth. The scar on his leg that the polar bear gave him has nearly faded. He still hunts by snowmobile, but he is 60 now and careful when climbing icebergs.

"You don't heal easy like when you're younger."

At Gene's house, the wind has weathered the green siding gray. Inside, the faint smell of old fish mixes with the aroma of cigarette ash. Most of the floor, chipped down to the plywood, is taken up by his mattress, piled with sheets and blankets. The house is warmed by an electric heater and a stove, which Gene fed with wood as he boiled dried cranberries into juice.

His job cleaning out honey pots doesn't afford him as much time to hunt as he had in 1988. Besides, hunting is harder now. The seasons are unpredictable.

The walrus and whales come a month earlier than they did when Gene hunted as a teenager. Ice that used to support the weight of a hunter and a snowmobile now flexes and sinks weeks earlier. He used to hack through more than 4 feet of ice to hit water. Now, maybe 2 feet.

The last time Gene killed a walrus, the iceberg he butchered it on drifted 20 miles, rocking in the waves the whole time. He had a boat, but

Gene was afraid and a long way from home. The same thing happens to polar bears. Ice drifts farther and faster with the warming climate. Scientists found that bears in the Chukchi need to catch three more seals per year to make up for the extra energy they use.

The people of Wales rely more these days on the two stores in town. But food is not easy to bring to the remote Alaskan coast. And it's not cheap — especially when 40 percent of the villagers are unemployed and the median income is less than $30,000 a year. Most planes that land here are loaded with food like mayonnaise, ramen and powdered drink mix. A gallon of water is close to $9. A sack of sugar is almost $20. Gas, which runs the boats, four-wheelers and snowmobiles, can cost $8 a gallon.

Down the road from Gene's house, the tribal elders say that boys still learn to tell when a fox is rabid, to track a moose, to kill an animal without letting it suffer and to use every part. It's been that way in Wales for hundreds of years.

Gilbert Oxereok learned by listening to stories his grandmother told, then by earning his way onto a hunting boat. Now he teaches his nephews.

"The first thing you're taught is respect," he said. "You hunt with respect. When you kill something, you use it. It's not a game. It's a way of life."

He's 60, just like Gene, and still hunts at least twice a year. In the spring, he hunts to replenish what has been used up over the winter. In the fall, he hunts so he and his family can eat through the cold months. Gilbert, Gene and the others have noticed that things are changing fast.

"I'm not an expert" on climate change, Gilbert said. "I just have to live with it."

Gilbert sees bare ground where he used to see snowbanks. He sees insects he hasn't encountered before. A recent issue of *National Geographic* informed him that shipping is expanding as the waters become easier to navigate, polluting the sea. But Gilbert already knew that. He pulls seals from the water coated in oil and covered in sores because parasites thrive in warmer temperatures. He can't eat seals like that.

"We just slit the belly and let them sink."

***

Hunters killing fewer polar bears will not save them. Neither will Karyn Rode's yearly trips to study them. Every bear in every zoo could give blood and walk on a treadmill, and polar bears would still face a grim future.

The only thing that can save polar bears is for the sea to stay frozen. And that can happen only if humans stop spewing heat-trapping gases into the sky.

That's according to a report by the U.S. Fish and Wildlife Service called the "Polar Bear Conservation Management Plan," written by more than two dozen scientists. The 100-page document, released in late 2016, is frank.

"Short of action that effectively addresses the primary cause of diminishing sea ice, it is unlikely that polar bears will be recovered."

For most bears to remain in their habitat, the Arctic can warm no more than 2 degrees Celsius by the end of the century. In the Paris climate accord, 195 countries agreed to take steps to limit global warming to below that level.

In June, President Donald Trump announced plans to withdraw the United States from the agreement.

The native people and the polar bears hunt on the same ice under the same sky in the same cold air. Gene's people, the Inupiaq, say that polar bears are smarter than most people, and they understand their native language. If a polar bear attacks, the legend goes, just talk to it in Inupiaq — "Adaa-piglutin!" — and it will listen and go away.

They see that the bear Gene made an orphan, and the daughter of that bear born in a zoo, and the women who raised her, and the researchers who studied her, and the people who come to see her are all connected, just as commuters in Atlanta and factories in Detroit are connected to fishermen off the Alaskan coast. Just as ice melting in one place causes flooding in another.

After Gene shot Nora's grandmother, he walked close to her and shot her again. He did that because his parents taught him that respect means never letting another creature suffer.

If you do, they warned him, you will eventually suffer the very same fate.

Two keepers from Oregon had accompanied Nora to Salt Lake City. Now they stood to the side.

They knew that at Hogle, Nora would have, in theory, everything she needed for a good life. She'd have bucketloads of smelt. She'd have more open space. She'd have an expert medical team keeping an eye on her bones. She'd have a polar bear her own age — a relative, even — to keep her company.

And there would always be her fans, more and more of them flocking to see this beautiful, charismatic girl, limp and all.

Would that be good enough?

Her keepers in Columbus could make her warm, hold her tight and wade into the water to show her it was safe. Her handlers in Portland could teach her patience. And now her keepers in Salt Lake City would manage her pain and help her adapt yet again.

But they couldn't conjure the Arctic from concrete, or turn the ocean into ice or set Nora free. No matter what anyone did, Nora's life would never unfold as nature intended. But neither would the life of the bear that Karyn Rode's research team darted in the snow.

They knew Nora's odds were long, and they had weighed those odds against the consequences of doing nothing. Their promise to Nora, and to Bear 21736, was not that they always get it right, but that they try.

They try because polar bears will die out unless people care enough to change. Making people care is what Nora does as well as any animal on Earth.

On that first day in Salt Lake City, when Nora left her crate, she walked past her Oregon keepers and went straight toward Kaleigh. The keeper crouched on the other side of the metal fence as Nora approached until the two stood nose-to-nose, faces inches apart, for what felt like forever.

Then Kaleigh started to cry.

Doomed by Delay

Chicago Tribune

October 5, 2017

By Patricia Callahan

How Illinois bureaucracy robbed parents of a chance to save their children from a deadly disease

Nine months pregnant, Natasha Spencer watched anxiously from her eighth-floor window as the abandoned cars and buses piled up on South Shore Drive.

One of the worst blizzards in Chicago history gripped the city in the winter of 2011, and Spencer was past her due date. Her obstetrician had offered to induce labor before the storm hit, but Spencer declined. As she watched the snowdrifts devour the vehicles on the road below, Spencer wondered if she should have listened.

Spencer was nearing 40, so she was keenly aware that her pregnancy was high-risk by medical standards. Throughout her pregnancy, she hadn't been able to shake a foreboding that was so intense and so out of character she didn't even tell her husband about it.

She had opted for all the tests, even the amniocentesis, and all came out clear. At Spencer's 21-week ultrasound, the doctor went through her son's anatomy part by part and offered reassurance, his comforting words etching themselves into her memory: "That's a beautiful brain."

Spencer's son also had impeccable timing. Kenan Spencer Witczak— 8 pounds, 11 ounces with a full head of hair— was born on Feb. 5, three days after the snowstorm ended, enough time for the streets to become passable, enough time for doctors to get back to work.

Spencer introduced Kenan, her second child, to her Facebook friends with a photo of him swaddled and sleeping. "We are in love!" she wrote.

Before Kenan headed home from the hospital, there was one final test, a routine one for Illinois newborns. A nurse pricked his heel and used special filter paper to collect blood that a state lab would screen for dozens of rare diseases.

The Illinois Department of Public Health followed up with a sheet of paper bearing an unmistakable message:

"All results are normal."

Those four words doomed Spencer's child.

***

A few drops of blood. That's all it takes to determine whether a baby who appears healthy at birth requires swift medical attention to avoid early death or severe disability.

Though every state screens newborns, legislators in Springfield in 2007 passed a law that envisioned Illinois as a leader. The state lab in Chicago was to be among the first in the nation to test all infants for a group of diseases in which lysosomes -- sacs of enzymes that serve as recycling centers for human cells -- malfunction and wreak havoc on a child's body. Early treatment can extend life and prevent extreme suffering.

Among the worst of these lysosomal disorders is Krabbe disease. Babies with Krabbe (pronounced crab-AY) are born with beautiful brains that later deteriorate. Their lysosomes don't have enough of an enzyme that helps sustain the protective coating around nerve fibers. Without that protection, nerves throughout the body can't transmit their signals properly.

The babies' bodies go limp; their jaws go slack. They lose their sight, their hearing and their sense of taste. As the swallow reflex wanes, they choke on their own saliva. The mere act of holding them upright can restrict an airway. Children with the most aggressive form of Krabbe disease typically die before age 2.

New parents are used to chronicling the firsts of childhood: the first time a baby smiles, sits up, crawls. But for parents of infants with Krabbe, this tradition is turned inside out.

Instead, they are mindful of the lasts: the last time a baby smiles, laughs, turns his head to make eye contact.

The Illinois law set a goal of having statewide testing in place by November 2010, three months before Kenan was born.

Dr. Barbara Burton, who for decades has treated patients with Krabbe at Lurie Children's Hospital in Chicago, pushed for this screening after a study in *The New England Journal of Medicine* reported that a transplant of stem cells from umbilical cord blood could slow or halt the nerve damage in newborns with Krabbe.

That study found that stem cells harvested from umbilical cord blood donated after birth could be lifesaving for babies born with Krabbe, but only if the transplant occurred before the nerve damage started. When the same doctors performed transplants on children already experiencing the devastating symptoms of Krabbe, the stem cells didn't reverse the damage or prolong life.

The treatment wasn't a cure. A follow-up study of 18 babies transplanted in the first seven weeks of life showed that three died of transplant complications, one died of a surgical complication unrelated to Krabbe and one died of Krabbe at age 15. As the newborns grew up, all but a few used walkers or wheelchairs and needed speech therapy.

But many families who had watched babies suffer and die from Krabbe saw these transplants as miraculous. Not only did most of the children survive a fatal disease, they could see, hear and express themselves. Though most developed cognitive skills at a slightly slower rate than typical children, they were able to attend school and learn.

All of the newborns in the initial study were identified because they had an older sibling with Krabbe. Without screening, the only way to save a child with Krabbe is to lose one first.

New York became the first state to test all newborns for Krabbe in 2006, spurred by NFL Hall of Fame quarterback Jim Kelly, whose son, Hunter, died of Krabbe.

That same year, Burton prodded the Illinois Department of Public Health to begin testing but was turned down by a lab official who said he didn't have enough equipment or staff, records show.

Burton didn't give up. She's someone who has to break the news to parents that the baby they thought was healthy was actually dying. And by the time these families showed up in her office, it was too late to do anything about that.

Too many of her patients entered hospice when they should have been taking their first steps.

She and families of children with lysosomal disorders took their cause to Springfield. With passage of the 2007 law, the Lurie doctor thought she'd finally be able to offer these babies and their families a chance at a better life.

Instead, Burton got a lesson in how a sclerotic Illinois bureaucracy can be deadly.

***

On Kenan's first Father's Day, Spencer snapped a photo of her son and 2-year-old daughter, Tamsen, curled up on the lap of their father, Dann Witczak. Brother, sister and father -- all sleeping peacefully.

A short video that summer shows Kenan cooing and grabbing at a board book about zoo animals as Tamsen plops down and kisses one of his chubby legs. Another video captures Kenan's contagious laugh -- more a squeal of delight, really -- as Witczak lifts up his son repeatedly and kisses his cheek.

"Kenan's laugh ... around 5 months!" Spencer wrote on Facebook. "What a joy it is to hear!"

Within weeks, Kenan became a fussy baby. Everyone suspected lingering pain from an ear infection was the culprit.

Spencer looked for meaning in the moments when Kenan was at ease. She told her Facebook friends that her son always wanted to be outside -- even in stifling temperatures -- strapped to his mom's chest in the BabyBjorn carrier. Kenan liked facing outward, and Spencer wondered if this in itself was a personality trait, a sign that Kenan was an adventurer who would leave home at 18 and never come back.

"As we roamed the neighborhood, my mind would wander to the creative thinker I obviously had on my hands as he liked to be in constant motion," she wrote. "It was easy to fantasize about his potential."

With Kenan tucked into that carrier on her chest, Spencer had the perfect vantage point to spot the head tilt when it started.

***

The state's newborn screening program was supposed to be immune from the budget pressures weighing on state officials as the Great Recession took hold.

Screening newborns in Illinois is funded by a testing fee charged to hospitals for each baby born. The legislature directed Public Health to raise that fee to cover the new testing for Krabbe disease and other lysosomal disorders.

But the state took so long to change the rules to allow a $19 increase for each baby— an extra $3 million a year— that the money didn't start accumulating until January 2010.

"It takes forever to get administrative rules through," recalls David Jinks, who was chief of the newborn screening lab at the time. "It's a crazy system. You shouldn't have to do that."

To make matters worse, the legislature in October 2008 passed a law that allowed the state to raid the newborn screening fund, taking $500,000 from it to pay for unrelated expenses. Lawmakers called this a "sweep," as though the money taken from this account were dust bunnies on the statehouse floor.

Public Health officials periodically gave progress reports to panels of medical advisers, including the Genetic and Metabolic Diseases Advisory Committee and its subcommittees. They warned the committee that the newborn screening fund was running low and that this sweep could delay their testing plans for the lysosomal disorders.

Indeed, the lab never even tried to hit the November 2010 goal the law had set for statewide testing. Instead, Public Health committed only to pilot testing by that date.

Top state officials at that time, Jinks recalls, told managers throughout the department: "Do more with less."

Jinks and Michael Petros, the newborn screening lab's operations chief, studied the testing costs for lysosomal disorders closely. No other state was screening its newborns for so many lysosomal disorders.

New York's Krabbe screening relied on tandem mass spectrometers— machines that the Illinois newborn screening lab already owned.

But Jinks and Petros figured out that Illinois still would need $2.1 million in additional equipment, plus costly lab renovations, to perform all the new tests using mass spectrometers, according to an analysis Petros included in his doctoral dissertation.

When a private company proposed a cheaper alternative to mass spectrometers that looked promising, it was hard to pass up— even though the technology was new and unproven.

Jinks says a scientist he trusted recommended this new technology, so in 2009, he made a fateful decision.

He told the genetic diseases committee that this method was "less expensive," "requires fewer staff to run" and "has a shorter turnaround time," state records show.

Jinks and Petros calculated in their cost analysis that the ongoing price of the alternative tests would be $2.43 cheaper per baby.

Looking back, Petros likens trying out the new test method to taking a car for a test drive.

"Being a government employee, you have a limited amount of money and staffing resources," he recalls. "Is there a way to do this equally well but at a cheaper cost?"

But there was a major problem. The vendor pitching this new method had developed testing materials for three of the other lysosomal disorders but not for Krabbe.

Public Health contracted with the company anyway, after receiving assurances from the firm that the Krabbe testing supplies were being developed, state records show.

The state lab began a pilot test, screening babies from two Chicago hospitals for some of the lysosomal disorders.

But the lab never tested any babies for Krabbe because the vendor failed to provide the necessary materials. The equipment couldn't accommodate the large number of blood samples the lab needed to process each day, and some results for one of the lysosomal diseases were not reliable, records show.

Lab officials complained to an advisory panel that the testing process that sounded so promising wound up being "very labor and time intensive."

***

In just two weeks in September 2011, Kenan lost the ability to use his hands.

At first, he clenched his thumbs and flexed his wrists in odd ways, favoring one hand over the other. Then Kenan balled up both hands into tight fists and wouldn't let them go.

The fussiness, the head tilt -- there were plenty of reasons why healthy babies might display those behaviors. But there was no rationalizing this sudden loss of hand control.

Kenan's pediatrician was alarmed too. The doctor grabbed the first available slot Lurie Children's Hospital had for an emergency MRI, a week away.

But before that could happen, Kenan's screaming grew so extreme that it frightened Spencer. That night Dann Witczak watched Tamsen while Spencer took Kenan to the nearest emergency room, Comer Children's Hospital at the University of Chicago.

Around midnight, a medical resident told Spencer that a scan of Kenan's brain showed abnormalities that nobody could immediately explain. More tests were needed.

The glare of the fluorescent lights felt sharp as panic welled up inside Spencer.

"I now understand what fear is," she recalls thinking.

That's an astonishing statement coming from Spencer, who as a graduate student was mugged by a man who pressed a gun to her back and demanded money. But that horrifying encounter involved *her* life.

This was her baby's life, and there was nothing she could do to help him.

At one point, Spencer told Kenan's nurses that she was so overwhelmed she was unable to take even a sip of water and asked that they give her an IV.

A flurry of tests on Kenan followed. All were inconclusive.

Dr. Darrel Waggoner, a University of Chicago geneticist who is the crosstown counterpart to Burton, told Spencer he suspected her son might have a form of leukodystrophy, the umbrella term for Krabbe and other diseases in which the protective coating around nerve fibers gets destroyed.

She remembers insisting Waggoner and his neurologist colleague had to be wrong. Kenan had a beautiful brain; a doctor had told her so. She remembers trying to defend Kenan's ability to engage with his environment by showing videos from her phone: See, Kenan could play with the zoo animals board book. He could laugh at his dad.

This had to be temporary.

"My pleas seemed to go in one ear and out the other," she wrote on Facebook. "Little did my frantic mind know that they could see what I couldn't: the road we were about to walk down."

Waggoner ordered tests that would tell them definitively whether Kenan had leukodystrophy and, if so, which kind.

They would have to wait two weeks for the results.

***

Jinks retired from his job as newborn screening lab chief at the end of 2010, just before the pilot testing derailed. Public Health didn't fill his position.

Instead, the department gave Jinks' newborn screening duties to George Dizikes, a scientist who already was overseeing quality control and regulatory issues at all three Public Health labs. Newborn screening is handled by the Chicago lab, but there are also labs in Springfield and Carbondale. Together these labs test for contaminants in drinking water, lead in children's blood, pathogens in food, sexually transmitted diseases and other sources of outbreaks.

Dizikes became the next in a parade of managers who were supposed to get Krabbe screening up and running.

In May 2011 he told a state advisory panel that lab technicians had to repeat too many of the testing runs in the pilot program because of the poor performance of the materials the contractor provided. He halted the pilot later that week.

"You have to be a good scientist and say, 'This is not going to work,' " recalls Petros, the newborn screening lab's operations chief.

Changing course, Dizikes asked the lab scientists to learn how to conduct the tests for all of the lysosomal disorders -- including Krabbe -- using mass spectrometry machines, the method in New York state.

He told an advisory panel that the state lab had enough equipment to start new pilot testing that fall.

Burton, the Lurie doctor, sat on those advisory panels. Once so hopeful about what the new law could accomplish, she was now frustrated and skeptical. How could Dizikes switch out the two technologies so quickly?

"I don't like it, but I guess I'll have to eat it," Burton vented in an email to the father who helped shape the 2007 law. "Honestly, the whole thing gives me a headache."

Four years after the Krabbe screening law had passed, Public Health was back where it had started.

Later that month, the Illinois legislature passed a new law mandating screening for two more lysosomal disorders. It gave the lab an extra two years to launch statewide testing for the original lysosomal diseases in the 2007 law, including Krabbe.

***

Waggoner, the University of Chicago geneticist, was on his way to a conference in Montreal when Kenan's results arrived. He called Spencer to break the news: Kenan had the most aggressive form of Krabbe disease.

Her son soon would be trapped in a body unable to communicate anything but the sensation of extreme pain. The question wasn't whether he would go blind and deaf but when. Before long, he would be paralyzed and eventually would lose his ability to breathe.

Kenan had a year, maybe two, to live.

At a subsequent appointment, the genetic specialist gently explained there were decisions to make: Did Spencer and Witczak want Kenan to get a gastronomy tube, an easy surgical procedure that allows food to be delivered directly to his stomach?

Without the feeding tube, Kenan would die sooner. Just 9 months old, he already was having trouble nursing. The sucking reflex is one of the first skills lost to Krabbe.

Spencer couldn't bear the thought of Kenan starving to death. The answer, which seemed so obvious at the time, was "yes."

Years later, after witnessing the suffering that would follow, Spencer would question whether that was fair to Kenan. "I often think of the inherent nature of the illness," she wrote on Facebook. "It does not ask the child to live past the point of non-nourishment. But with a g-tube, we do. With that well-intentioned decision, and the next, and the next, he gets to live through the unraveling of his brainstem.

"Who is the cruel one in this dynamic?"

***

As Spencer suspected, it was too late for a transplant.

She had flown with Kenan to Children's Hospital of Pittsburgh of UPMC to see Dr. Maria Escolar, the Krabbe expert who was the lead author of *The New England Journal of Medicine* study on transplants. Spencer learned from Escolar how to stay ahead of Kenan's symptoms with therapies and medications.

On the last day of tests for Kenan, Spencer met a Dayton, Ore., family with two young boys who had Krabbe.

Oregon doesn't screen newborns for the disease. One-year-old Michael Wilson had been tested as a newborn only because his older brother, Marshall, started suffering the symptoms of Krabbe.

By the time he was diagnosed, it was too late for Marshall to be helped by a transplant.

When Spencer saw him, Marshall was 2 1/2 years old, lying motionless in a reclined wheelchair. His mouth was slack, his facial expression absent. Over and over, his mother, Tammy, suctioned the secretions from Marshall's throat so that he didn't choke to death or wind up with pneumonia.

Spencer couldn't imagine herself doing that. It terrified her. Yet, this was what was in Kenan's future.

And there was Michael, who was just 4 months older than Kenan, holding himself upright in his mother's arms, hugging her. He'd undergone a stem cell transplant earlier that year.

Two brothers with the same disease— two boys with dramatically different futures— were there in front of Spencer.

Spencer and the Wilsons struck up a lasting friendship in a way that only parents who share that kind of devastating diagnosis can.

Spencer and Kenan returned home with a new vision of the future. Rather than making their annual trek to Ohio for Christmas with the families of Spencer and her husband, they remained in Chicago that year.

Kenan spent his first Christmas in pain. He was going through withdrawal from one medicine, and the two other drugs meant to replace it hadn't yet reached full strength. The muscle spasms and nerve pain were intense.

The family made room for what would become a new tradition. Horizon Hospice sent a Santa to their home, as it does for all children in its care nearing the end of their lives.

The Santa hoisted Kenan and Tamsen onto his lap, as though nothing in this ritual were out of place.

***

That winter, another Illinois baby was starting to have symptoms of Krabbe.

Robin Maubach, who lived in Washington, Ill., wondered if something was wrong with her son, Dylan. The first sign was a head tilt, a condition that physical therapy couldn't solve. Then there was Dylan's fussiness, which the pediatrician treated as reflux.

Dylan initially met his early milestones, but his mother, a first-grade teacher mindful of child development, soon began to worry. Dylan's older brother sat up at 6 months; Dylan reached that age and never did. When he was 9 months old, Dylan stopped feeding himself.

At first doctors diagnosed Dylan with cerebral palsy. A visit to Children's Hospital of Illinois in Peoria led to the Krabbe diagnosis when he was 14 months old.

Like Spencer, Maubach took her son to the Krabbe expert in Pittsburgh to see if he could have a transplant.

But it was too late for Dylan too.

***

Burton was right to be skeptical that the changeover from one technology to another would happen quickly. What was supposed to take months dragged into years.

Another source of frustration for Burton was that the committee of scientists advising Public Health kept debating whether Krabbe screening was worth doing at all.

Newborn screening for Krabbe is controversial in the medical community, and some doctors complain that parents of sick children are pushing prematurely for screening. After reviewing the available research, a federal advisory panel in 2010 chose not to add Krabbe to the core group of diseases that the federal government recommends for newborn screening programs.

During Illinois meetings of the advisory committee on genetic diseases, Dr. Lainie Friedman Ross, a University of Chicago bioethicist and pediatrician, repeatedly warned Public Health officials that screening every newborn for Krabbe was akin to conscripting babies into an experiment without their parents' consent.

New York's experience screening newborns, Ross says, heightened her concerns.

Newborn screening for Krabbe involves two rounds of tests, both using blood from an infant's heel. The first test, which checks for an enzyme deficiency, can yield false positives, so blood samples flagged in the first round undergo a second and more intensive test that looks for certain genetic defects.

One mutation -- the kind Kenan has -- clearly indicates the most severe form of Krabbe, which appears in infancy and is fatal without a transplant. But the testing in New York also identified other genetic variations for which there is less certainty.

A form of Krabbe that appears later in life also can be fatal, but symptoms vary. In the early years of testing in New York, dozens of families were told that their babies had a moderate to high risk of developing Krabbe but doctors didn't know when the disease might arrive, if ever.

To Ross, giving frightening but uncertain information to parents who never asked for their babies to be tested is a form of psychological harm.

"People are told their child has this potentially horrific condition, and they're waiting for the other shoe to drop," Ross says. "And it might drop in the next six months, or it might not drop for 30 or 40 years."

Also troubling to Ross were the experiences of New York babies who received transplants. Of the first four children treated, two died of complications and a third wound up with severe developmental and physical disabilities.

Ross told Public Health officials that the Krabbe screening they planned to do was actually research requiring a formal protocol, where parents are informed of the risks and choose to have their baby tested. Such research, she said, must be overseen by an independent board that protects the rights of research subjects.

After Dr. LaMar Hasbrouck became director of Public Health in 2012, he declined to take that advice. In an August letter, he stated that the law had assigned the department a narrow role: "to pilot, calibrate and scale-up testing." This role didn't involve research and didn't require the approval of an institutional review board, he wrote.

Burton says she doesn't discount the anxiety parents must feel knowing that Krabbe may be in a child's future. But knowledge of that risk, in her view, gives those families a chance to intervene with a transplant when it's needed.

Escolar, the Krabbe expert in Pittsburgh, says her transplant patients with later-onset Krabbe have done "remarkably better" than those treated as newborns, in part because their form of the disease is less aggressive. "The later you develop symptoms, the better outcome you have from the transplant," Escolar says.

In recent years, a new blood test for elevated levels of a lipid called psychosine has provided more clarity to families who once faced uncertainty. Public Health includes this test in the Illinois screening protocol.

A high level of psychosine is an early marker of active disease, signaling the need for an immediate transplant, Burton says.

Doctors also have improved the transplant process and figured out that children who undergo the procedure in the first month of life fare better.

To Burton, the decision whether to have a transplant should rest with parents, not doctors or bureaucrats. By failing to implement the 2007 law, she says, Illinois is robbing parents of that choice.

"Even the ones who die of transplant complications, their families haven't said, 'I wish we didn't.' They know they gave their child a chance," Burton says. "And there are examples of kids who've done beautifully."

On paper, Gina Rugari had one of the worst outcomes of any child in the original *New England Journal of Medicine* study: The Cincinnati girl died of Krabbe, 15 years after her transplant.

Gina used a power wheelchair to get around and an assistive technology device to communicate. But to her mom, Anne, those disabilities never defined Gina, a smart social butterfly who wanted to travel the world. Like many teenagers, Gina had strong opinions— from the designs painted on her fingernails to the sites in Paris and Hawaii she wanted to visit. Gina was a Girl Scout, a movie buff, a good friend.

Anne Rugari lost her son Nick to Krabbe just after his first birthday, which is why Gina became one of the first children with Krabbe to receive a transplant. If Gina's mom could go back in time, would she make the same choice?

"God, yes, I'd do it again and again and again to have those experiences, for her to have life, for her to have love," Anne Rugari says. "I was given 15 1/2 wonderful years with Gina. That's 14 1/2 more than I had with Nick, and I wouldn't change any of it."

***

Spencer is an artist who spots beauty in places where others see trash. Through Spencer's lens, a discarded bag animated by a Lake Michigan breeze became the image of a bird. A deflated balloon splattered with paint transformed into a clownfish. A River North gallery featured both photographs.

Krabbe disease left Spencer with an eye for scenes of what might have been.

In July 2012 Spencer was driving to pick up Tamsen at summer school in the West Loop. Kenan was asleep in his car seat.

They stopped at a red light, and Spencer caught sight of a young man waiting on the corner.

He was in his 20s, she figured, attractive and well-dressed. He had dusty blond hair, just like Kenan.

The young man smiled as a car pulled up. A woman inside got out, and they embraced.

"My mind immediately races into the future— a future for Kenan that will never be," Spencer wrote later that day on a blog she had started about Kenan. "Before me is a mirage of potential and possibility shifting in the sunlight trying to take shape.

"There will be no culmination of collected moments to answer my questions: What will HE look like? Who will HE be?"

Spencer's eyes lingered on the couple until the light turned green, snapping her back into the life she had now.

She glanced into the rearview mirror at Kenan. He was awake then.

"No one," she wrote, "wants a parent to project on him what he isn't and can never be, least of all Kenan."

***

Public Health came close to screening all Illinois newborns for Krabbe in 2014.

Early that year, the Chicago lab tested at least 15,000 randomly chosen newborn blood samples for Krabbe and the other lysosomal disorders.

New York's state lab agreed to perform the second-round tests that would flush out false positives and confirm real cases. Those tests showed that none of the babies initially flagged had Krabbe disease.

Dizikes, the Illinois labs' regulatory director, included Burton and other medical advisers on the email he sent to hospitals announcing the start of a broader pilot testing program that August.

"I think it is finally going to happen this time!" Burton wrote to her Lurie colleagues.

When it came time for Public Health to sign a contract with the New York lab for the confirmatory tests, however, everything fell apart over a single clause, records show.

The boilerplate in Illinois state contracts includes an indemnification clause that provides legal protections for the state. Attorneys for the New York lab pushed for their own language.

Public Health lawyers, unwilling to put the state at risk, rejected New York's clause.

Burton, once again, was exasperated. Public Health had known for seven years that this crucial testing was needed to avoid unnecessarily alarming families and putting their babies through unneeded, invasive tests. And yet, the state had no backup plan?

An advisory subcommittee Burton chaired held an emergency conference call with Public Health officials that September. The officials explained that Mayo Clinic was willing to do the same tests at its lab, but the state hadn't started the lengthy bidding process to secure a contract.

That November, Public Health went forward with pilot testing for the other lysosomal disorders, which didn't need second-round tests, but put Krabbe on hold. The state lab's mass spectrometry machines were actually screening blood spots for the Krabbe enzyme while they performed the other tests, but the lab made adjustments so the Krabbe data weren't recorded.

Once again, the lab's Dizikes told Burton and her colleagues this would be only a short delay: less than four months.

After waiting so long for Krabbe testing, a few months didn't seem like a big deal to Burton.

"If I had known then what would happen later, I would have objected," she says. "Over and over again, they made us think it was going to happen."

But it didn't.

***

As Kenan's brain deteriorated, he reached birthday after unexpected birthday.

When Kenan turned 2, Spencer and Witczak held Tamsen's hands as big sister jumped on her parents' bed dancing to Green Day's "Holiday." Spencer iced Kenan's cake with red buttercream frosting — red because it was the easiest for his dwindling vision to see and buttercream because the smell is unmistakable.

On his third birthday, the one Spencer didn't think she'd see, she wrote to her Facebook friends: "Although there will be much celebrating, none is required because 'Kenan is three' is a self-contained celebration. My heart beats in fireworks for you today, Kenan."

Kenan made it to his fourth birthday, then his fifth.

Those early years with Krabbe were filled with a different sort of firsts for Kenan. First seizures. First need for supplemental oxygen. First time he turned blue.

Being upright restricts Kenan's airway, so he needs to be either lying down or reclined in his wheelchair when he is struggling to breathe.

As the disease damaged Kenan's nervous system, his spine curved unnaturally. His shoulders hunched up to his ears, and his chest became concave. Eventually, his hips dislocated.

Before Kenan got sick, Spencer ran an art installation business with her husband. Dann Witczak took over the lion's share of the family business duties while Spencer devoted her time to Kenan— a full-time job.

She spent day after day trying to undo the constriction of Kenan's muscles with heating pads, massage and range-of-motion exercises.

His eyes grew distant as he lost most of his sight. His senses of hearing and taste were fading. And yet, it was obvious when he was in pain, his face contorting when the disease forced his muscles from head to toe to contract in spasms.

Spencer grew awed by Kenan's ability to adapt to physical adversity. A typical preschooler takes at least 20 breaths per minute. Kenan was able to keep the oxygen concentration in his blood at a near perfect 98 percent while taking only four to six breaths per minute.

"What Kenan is performing on a physiological level makes him a BREATHING GENIUS, a SUPERSTAR, a GOLD MEDAL OLYMPIAN," Spencer wrote on her blog. "If you need something AMAZING to happen today, it is him."

The normal respiratory ailments of childhood are perilous for children with Krabbe. Any one of them can be deadly. Many times Spencer reached out to Facebook friends asking that they hold Kenan in their thoughts and prayers. She described one particularly bad bout of seizures and wheezing as an "awake coma: eyes open but physically and mentally unresponsive."

Yet, Kenan pulled through when many of his peers with Krabbe did not.

Though she once couldn't imagine herself using the suction machine, Spencer began threading the catheter into Kenan's throat so often to clear his secretions that the machine's jarring sounds became the background noise of their lives.

Spencer pulled over in traffic so frequently to suction Kenan that their trips to pick up Tamsen from school didn't feel safe anymore. She needed help, and got some when Kenan qualified for nursing assistance at home.

At first, nurses came for several hours each weekday. As Kenan got older, the hours increased.

Spencer, who has slept beside her son since his diagnosis, became chronically sleep-deprived. She feared she would nod off and miss the fact that Kenan was suffocating. Spencer wakes up regularly, not only to suction him but also to thump on his chest with a percussor cup, a rubber device that helps breaks up congestion.

"Each night as Kenan sleeps, his chest lifts in the gesture of an inhale but stops short: no air enters his lungs, no oxygen passes to his blood," Spencer wrote on Facebook. "... His mouth opens wider. He is trying harder. His chest. Stuck. Again. All the air right here in this very room without a means. Please Enter.

"I beat on his chest, force air into his mouth, lift him up in my arms. Jumpstart the mechanism. 'Thank you, Kenan. Thank you for breathing.' "

***

Dylan Maubach, the Washington, Ill., boy with Krabbe, died in his sleep in November 2014.

"We always hoped his death would be peaceful," says his mom, Robin Maubach. "It went just how we hoped and prayed it would. Something tells me that's what Dylan wanted for us."

***

The following spring, Logan Nichols was born at Stroger Hospital on Chicago's West Side.

He was sick, but as his mother took him from doctor to doctor, no one could agree on why.

This sort of medical odyssey is common with a rare disease when there is no screening. Krabbe is estimated to occur in 1 in 100,000 people, and New York found that the form that appears in infancy is even more rare. Many pediatricians will never encounter a case.

As a group, though, lysosomal diseases are more prevalent. In the first 15 months of screening newborns for five lysosomal disorders, 1 out 5,000 Illinois babies was diagnosed with one.

It would take nearly two years of uncertainty and multiple hospitalizations before Logan's mom, Shermane Jenkins, would learn that her son had Krabbe.

***

Spencer woke up one night in June 2015 to find foam pouring out of Kenan's mouth. She suctioned him, but he made more.

He had been on supplemental oxygen for allergies that whole month. When she went to sleep, a pulse oximeter showed Kenan's blood oxygen levels were safely above 90 percent.

But now the oximeter showed his levels were in the 50s, dangerously low. He was taking short, sharp breaths. It was 3 a.m., and Spencer had no idea how long he'd been like this.

She turned the oxygen concentrator as high as it could go. No change.

"I Googled 'white foam,' " she later wrote. "Two possible scenarios: seizures or respiratory death. I knew we weren't dealing with seizures and thought, 'This is it. This is the day Kenan dies. What do I do? Do I call his hospice nurse? Do I wake Dann?' "

Her mind raced until she settled on one other possibility. What if there was a hole in the plastic tubing delivering the oxygen? She raced to the closet and searched frantically for new tubing.

"Lo and behold, that was it!" she wrote on Facebook. "Kenan's oxygen goes back up, his respiration relaxes, he stops producing foam, he wakes up to his baselines. Everything goes back to normal, except for me."

Spencer's husband watched Kenan that afternoon. She took Tamsen downtown. They danced at a Chicago Cultural Center exhibit on house music, then went across the street to Maggie Daley Park.

"Surrounded by the laughter and roar of a thousand children, I climbed through apparatuses and went down slides too small for me. One made my stomach drop so much, I screamed.

"Sometimes the only thing you can do for yourself is reset the button."

***

"YOU ARE TAKING TOO LONG!"

Spencer feared her voice would crack as she spoke to Public Health officials responsible for implementing Krabbe testing in Illinois. So she wrote her statement to Burton's subcommittee in advance, using all capital letters for that sentence, though she needed no reminding of the exasperation those words carried.

It was September 2015, and Illinois still wasn't testing its newborns for Krabbe disease, eight years after passage of the law requiring the state to do so. Statewide testing for five other lysosomal disorders had begun that May.

The state lab's machines were testing newborns for the Krabbe enzyme, but the lab wasn't recording the data. Public Health officials said they still needed an outside lab to perform the second-round tests to weed out false positives. Mayo Clinic was willing to perform the confirmatory tests, but nobody had approved that contract.

What's more, money was drained from the newborn screening fund again. The extra charge to hospitals had amassed more than $15 million to fund testing for Krabbe and the other lysosomal disorders. But that year, the legislature passed a law that allowed state officials to raid the newborn screening fund. This time, they diverted $5 million to pay for other state programs, records show.

By then, Dizikes had left Public Health for a job in Tennessee, and it wasn't clear to Burton who was in charge of making the Krabbe screening happen. Illinois had a new governor and a new Public Health director, and Burton felt like she was pushing her boulder up a hill again.

Earlier that summer, Burton had invited Spencer to join the Public Health advisory subcommittee the Lurie doctor chaired when the two shared a taxi to the airport after a symposium on Krabbe disease.

When it came to the impasse in Illinois, Burton thought: Who better to hammer home the urgent need for testing than a mother caring for a child with Krabbe?

Spencer surmised that many of the state employees who appeared before Burton's group mustering excuses for their inaction had never seen a child with Krabbe and knew little of the daily suffering endured.

During Spencer's first meeting, a conference call that July, she sat quietly as a contractor explained that unfilled state jobs might be slowing down the review of the Mayo Clinic contract.

At the September meeting, however, Spencer scolded the group, which included state lab officials and Public Health administrators. "When I hear there is turnover in staff ... delaying this another six months, that is not justification for another child and family to live through a variation of our scenario," she told them.

Spencer asked each of them to open their mouths as wide as they could, then inhale. That breathless feeling— the sensation of drawing air with one's throat muscles— is what Kenan experiences every moment, she explained. She wished she could see whether they were trying this exercise as they sat in their state offices, to know whether her words resonated.

"He can throw me a look when I walk into the room that says, 'Mom, suction me because the nurse isn't doing a good enough job,' " she told them. "And if he can do that, then he is also aware of how difficult it is to breathe."

This shouldn't take eight years, she implored them. Then she repeated it: "YOU ARE TAKING TOO LONG!"

Spencer and Burton both remember the uncomfortable silence that followed.

***

That same month, Spencer requested a meeting with Dr. Nirav Shah, the global health physician and attorney whom Gov. Bruce Rauner appointed Public Health director in January 2015.

In a letter, Spencer invited Shah to step into her shoes for 30 minutes, describing an experience a few days earlier.

The story she told to Shah began happily:

"It was time to leave for physical therapy, a ten minute walk from our house on a beautiful day. Even better, Kenan will go swimming, an activity he loves. His seven-year-old sister, Tamsen, has her shoes on and is ready with her scooter," she wrote.

Spencer lifts Kenan into his Kid Kart, a wheelchair that keeps his body reclined, but then notices that he can't breathe.

"Whatever transition his body just went through from floor-to-chair has aggravated the physical obstruction in his airway. He is making a gasping sound. My adrenaline surges because, now, I feel helpless."

She makes her usual adjustments— moving pillows, changing the wheelchair's angle, propping Kenan's body with rolled-up blankets. Nothing helps.

Should she cancel or plow ahead? If she can just get Kenan to the therapy pool at La Rabida Children's Hospital, she knows he'll be fine. This is temporary, she tells herself.

Spencer stops to suction him— threading the floppy catheter into his throat while the machine connected to it suctions the secretions. As soon as she puts away the catheter, Kenan needs suctioning again.

With Kenan still struggling to breathe, Spencer adjusts the Kid Kart again. A rule of thumb for Krabbe families: What doesn't work one minute might work the next. She notices an improvement— "perhaps only five percent, but enough to get me out the door."

"Across the street I push his cart as fast as I can in between stops to suction. I walk along side, talking Kenan through while holding his jaw so he can breathe. Every single bump, crack and sidewalk groove can be felt in the torque of my waist, shoulder and wrist trying to steer the handle bar."

She dodges the tree branches that the city hasn't cleared and stops short when curious Tamsen stoops to pick up a dollar lying on the ground. Meanwhile, the rubber suction catheter, which has the consistency of a wet noodle, keeps falling out of its protective sleeve.

Spencer contorts her body to hold Kenan's jaw at the same time she propels the wheelchair, which weighs about 100 pounds with Kenan in it and the suction machine attached.

This frenzied routine— stop, suction, start again— turns a leisurely 10-minute trip into a 30-minute ordeal until the La Rabida doors slide open and she wheels Kenan along a smooth hospital floor to the therapy pool changing area.

Kenan is fine. The walk home is uneventful.

"Things are ok. Then they're not. Then they are again. Imagine this same scenario from Kenan's point of view. Without exaggeration, this is an average day."

In her letter, Spencer then explained to Shah that she is a member of Burton's subcommittee, so she has learned from his own employees about the state's failure to implement the law that called for screening every Illinois newborn for Krabbe before Kenan was born.

His department, she wrote, seemed to have everything in place to begin screening newborns for Krabbe "except a sense of urgency."

"Eight years is not being thorough and responsible," Spencer wrote. "It fringes on the opposite."

She explained that Dylan Maubach missed a chance for a transplant and died the prior November. Lives, she wrote, were at stake.

***

Spencer's letter sent Public Health officials scrambling.

Conny Moody, a deputy director in charge of the office that oversees newborn screening, wanted to know why Spencer knew so much about the holdups, records show. In an email she asked Claudia Nash, a newborn screening manager who regularly attended Burton's subcommittee meetings, about Spencer: "How would she be privy to these details?"

Nash sent Moody a list of each of the six times since 2012 that Spencer had phoned, emailed or attended Public Health meetings that discussed Krabbe. Of Spencer, Nash wrote: "She has always been extremely pleasant."

Moody ordered Nash to construct a timeline of events on Krabbe testing "to provide the Director with context." So Nash detailed Public Health's missteps in bullet point after bullet point, including the dates in the past when state employees had wrongly predicted testing would begin.

Nash also included the dates of the 13 meetings Burton's subcommittee had held since 2008 during which the group's medical professionals had devised protocols for Public Health to catch the real cases of Krabbe in newborns while weeding out the false positives.

After sending this timeline to Moody, Nash forwarded it to a co-worker with a more candid assessment of the delays: "Mind-boggling! And that is the condensed version!"

Nash added, "start ... stop ... how many times?"

Her colleague shot back, "I know. With large lapses of time."

Nash later vented to Moody when the agenda for a Public Health managers' meeting included a planned discussion of the second-round confirmatory tests for Krabbe under the heading "should this testing be provided." After nearly a decade of explaining repeatedly why these tests were critical, Nash likened the situation to Bill Murray's 1993 movie about reliving the same day over and over again.

"Groundhog Day!" Nash told Moody. "We had to go over it all again about why this was needed. ... Seems to be going in circles."

***

Spencer wondered whether Shah, Public Health's director, had even bothered to read the story she shared about Kenan.

Shah never granted Spencer a meeting. Instead, he sent Spencer a letter that made no mention of her son and oddly thanked her for "sharing your personal story of supporting families affected by Krabbe disease."

The same passage, records show, previously appeared in a letter Shah sent to an out-of-state advocate for families of children with Krabbe.

The letter bearing Shah's signature told Spencer what she already knew: that Public Health was working to secure a contract with an outside laboratory that could conduct the confirmatory tests.

"This process," the letter said, "will ensure that we identify a laboratory that can perform the molecular test for Krabbe in a timely manner, with high quality, and within cost parameters."

The letter wrapped up by saying: "We recognize the significant impact this disease has on children and their families and assure you that we are working diligently to implement Krabbe screening."

Shah's letter arrived at a time when Kenan's breathing problems had grown so severe that the only way Spencer could help him was to hold his jaw at a certain angle, a position she maintained for hours on end until her arm went numb.

She wasn't going to let Shah brush her off.

In an email to Moody, Spencer explained how disappointed she was with the director's response. "I was hopeful it would include specific information on where we stand now and a timeline moving forward," Spencer wrote.

She asked Moody to tell her where the Mayo Clinic contract stood in the state's approval process.

Moody's reply, which arrived three weeks later, made it sound like Krabbe testing was nowhere in sight.

"Due to the delays in obtaining spending authorization for the current fiscal year, we find it is necessary to conduct a thorough review of options," Moody told Spencer. "We hope to have decisions made as soon as possible. Unfortunately, the state procurement process is an intricate and time-consuming process, exacerbated by the state's current funding situation."

What Spencer hadn't been told was that the future of the state lab's newborn screening program was up in the air.

After Rauner toured the Chicago lab in October 2015, Public Health Director Shah asked his senior staff to explore outsourcing not just Krabbe tests but all newborn screening to a private contractor. A department official warned E. Matt Charles, who oversees the entire Division of Laboratories, to avoid "fearmongering" in his presentation at a strategy session Shah scheduled for senior staff.

Internally, Charles and his colleagues wrote that the cost of newborn screening at the state lab was "not sustainable." They predicted that a private lab would charge $55 per baby for the same testing that cost Illinois $110 at that point, records show.

***

Marshall Wilson, the Oregon boy who gave Spencer her first glimpse of a life with Krabbe, died in a hospital emergency department waiting room at the age of 6.

Every aspect of his death in March 2016 felt cruel to Spencer.

On Facebook, she reflected on the transformative day she met the boy, his little brother and his parents just after Kenan's diagnosis:

"If Marshall, 4.5 years later, my designated, reigning boy champion of outliving Krabbe disease, can die, so will Kenan. If Marshall can be taken out by a stomach virus he would easily have survived a year, 6 months, 3 months, even 1 month prior in an ER waiting room with his mother ill and four hours away, then I am again bleakly reminded that this disease reigns free, void of Kenan's strength or regard for my role as his mother.

"And so I grieve: Marshall, his symbolism, a friendship now transitioning out of the privilege of empathy and into a more distant sympathy and the loneliness I feel because of it."

Marshall's little brother, Michael, remained a symbol of what Kenan's life might have been like if he had received a transplant at birth. Later that year, Spencer posted a video on her Facebook page of Michael Wilson zip-lining.

She had to remind her incredulous friends: "He is four months older than Kenan and likewise, born with Krabbe."

Michael, who just turned 7, still shows no signs of the disease.

***

None of the pressure Burton and Spencer had applied was working. So Burton dashed off another angry email to the latest Public Health official who refused to tell her when Krabbe testing would start.

"I feel like this is a complete runaround," she wrote in May 2016. "... I think it is absurd that Krabbe testing was legislated in 2007 and we have yet to test one single newborn."

Like Spencer, the Lurie doctor tried setting up a meeting with Shah, the director. In a phone call that summer, Burton recalls, Shah blamed the state's byzantine procurement process for the lag time in finalizing the contract with Mayo Clinic.

That system, by design, requires precise steps be followed and builds in multiple layers of review, a time-consuming process that can be traced to the path between Illinois state offices and prison.

Chronic wrongdoing begets rules designed to prevent it. Policy-makers created new regulations and paper trails to thwart unscrupulous employees who would otherwise throw lucrative state business to companies for kickbacks, as one Public Health chief of staff did a few years before Kenan was born. Indeed, former Illinois Gov. George Ryan wound up in prison for steering state business to cronies for bribes.

The new contracting rules, however well-intentioned, increased the time it took to award state business.

A contracting process for confirmatory Krabbe tests that started in 2014 still wasn't settled two years later. The "Invitation for Bid" for the 100 to 130 confirmatory tests the lab anticipated it would need annually to weed out false positives was 40 pages long.

At first, a state purchasing officer rejected the Mayo Clinic bid because "the pricing was entered in the wrong place," records show.

"Must start over on procurement," the chief of the Division of Labs wrote in February 2016.

Six months later, the revived bid was rejected. The reason: Mayo Clinic wasn't registered with the Illinois secretary of state's office, records show.

Nash, who had compiled the bullet points on earlier missteps, emailed Deputy Director Moody to express her frustration: "Well it seems like they could have figured this out from the time the bid was in ... not months later!"

Some Public Health managers, anticipating the precarious nature of the procurement process, had pursued a parallel track that led to a workaround. The state lab would use the University of Illinois at Chicago Medical Center, which already had a contractual relationship with Mayo Clinic, as a go-between.

Public Health first broached the idea in January 2015, but it took more than 20 months to iron out an agreement with UIC. After the back and forth between lawyers came to an end, the agreement sat for weeks waiting for Shah's signature.

"Is your Director planning on signing the Agreement?" a UIC employee asked Public Health in October 2016. "It's been about 3 weeks now. Please advise us what the delay is."

Shah signed the agreement that month. But even then, Krabbe testing didn't begin.

***

The following March, Spencer snapped a photo of Kenan at the Shedd Aquarium. Reclined in his wheelchair, Kenan was in front of the giant Caribbean Reef tank, his eyes barely open.

"For six years now, I've known him better than anyone, yet his inner life remains a mystery. In most respects, he's completely dependent," Spencer wrote on Facebook. "In others, utterly alone."

That longing to understand her son became overwhelming during the rare moments when Kenan unexpectedly behaved like a typical child. Once, as she leaned in to give Kenan a kiss, his lips closed in what felt like a pucker.

"Maybe the nerves were connecting, and it was intentional, maybe it was an involuntary response to stimuli, or maybe I cut him short of a hard earned swallow," she wrote. "Whatever the reason, I'll never forget the feeling. I kiss him all the time, but WE don't kiss. I hug him all the time, but WE don't hug. It's an ache for him as much as for me, Dann and Tamsen.

"Moments like these are emotionally dangerous because they promote this exact thinking, but we have gotten very good at pulling ourselves back, staying in the moment, hovering between wanting and needing."

***

The latest holdup in Illinois involves software.

Public Health officials explained to Burton's subcommittee in April that they were waiting for PerkinElmer, a private contractor, to add Krabbe to the computer program that takes the data from the mass spectrometers, interprets the results and generates reports for pediatricians.

Richard Zimmerman, who is in charge of quality control and regulatory compliance for all state labs, said his department hoped to have everything in place to begin testing Illinois newborns for Krabbe by late summer or early fall of this year.

At a follow-up meeting in June, Zimmerman hedged: "We're at the mercy of PerkinElmer. Initially they told us that was their timeline. But with any development in algorithms of its computer language, sometimes things take a little longer."

He assured Spencer, Burton and everyone else on the conference call that "this is a priority."

"We're trying to push it along as best we can," he said.

***

Just as Spencer feared, at least two more Illinois babies were born with Krabbe after she warned Public Health Director Shah of this danger. Their conditions were not diagnosed until it was too late for a transplant.

Lana Shelton, a North Riverside baby born in July 2016, was diagnosed at Lurie in November, the nerve damage well underway.

Lana's pediatrician sent her to Lurie neurologists after her parents, Laura and Don Shelton, noticed that Lana at 4 months old wasn't holding her head up as well as she had been and didn't smile like other babies her age.

"I just want to see her smile," Laura Shelton says.

Lana never did. Spasms and breathing trouble repeatedly landed Lana in the intensive care unit over the summer, and she got a feeding tube after she lost her ability to nurse.

Hayden Ponce, a Coal Valley, Ill., baby born in January, was diagnosed at Children's Hospital of Illinois in Peoria in June.

Doctors told her parents, Kilie and Nic Ponce, that Hayden's breathing was so shallow they feared that if they intubated her for the feeding-tube surgery, she might spend the rest of her life on a ventilator.

Her parents declined and met the hospice team that would see them through her final days.

***

The July meeting of Burton's advisory subcommittee quickly grew tense.

Just a few weeks earlier, Logan Nichols had died of Krabbe at the age of 2. By the time Logan was diagnosed at Lurie earlier this year and became one of Burton's patients, his disease was in the final stages.

As the conference call began, Logan's death weighed on the minds of Burton, Spencer and Terry Hammonds, another mom who'd joined the subcommittee. Hammonds' son, Liam, died of Krabbe in 2001.

Asked about the "late summer/early fall" projection for Krabbe screening, a Public Health official pushed back the timeline to "sometime in fall."

Zimmerman, the labs' regulatory director, was even more vague. "We're hoping to have everything up and running by the end of the year," he said.

Hammonds told Zimmerman there had been a recent funeral for an Illinois child who died of Krabbe, a reference to Logan. "Time," she said, "is of the essence."

Zimmerman responded, "I can't give you a definitive time and date. We're hopeful, and we're doing our best."

Burton told the Public Health officials on the conference call that their priorities were "messed up."

Said Burton, "It's almost mind-boggling that we're on a call discussing this in 2017 related to legislation passed in 2007."

Zimmerman said PerkinElmer, the private contractor whose software needed changing, was busy working on another project for the lab and would focus on Krabbe after that was done.

A colleague of Zimmerman's explained that if the state put that other project on hold for Krabbe, PerkinElmer would lose six months of its work.

That was the breaking point for Spencer. What was six months of work, she thought, when they had been waiting nearly 10 years for Krabbe testing?

Her voice rose with fury as she addressed the group.

"What if it's not running by 2017 and we're looking at 2018?" Spencer asked. "This is what I've been hearing about since my son was diagnosed in 2011. It's been 'three months,' 'six months,' '12 months,' then years.

"It's infuriating to be told 'maybe fall, maybe 2017.' I realize everyone is doing their job, but at what point does someone do something more than their job? That's my frustration! We've had three new diagnoses these past few months."

***

Hayden Ponce, the baby who was diagnosed in June, died in her mother's arms at her home in Coal Valley on Sept. 25. She was 7 months old.

***

Here's how Krabbe screening began in two other states.

Kentucky's governor signed a Krabbe screening law in March 2015. The state contracted with Mayo Clinic to perform all of the tests needed and had its program running by February 2016.

That December, the screening caught a baby boy with Krabbe. As a result, Tygh DeRossett had a transplant when he was 24 days old.

His family actually lives in a small town in Tennessee. His mom, Amanda, chose to give birth at the hospital 12 miles north— across the border in Kentucky.

Had she gone to the hospital 12 miles south of her home, Tygh's disease would not have been caught because Tennessee wasn't screening for Krabbe then.

DeRossett recently posted on Facebook a video of Tygh, now 10 months old, giggling as he bounced up and down in his "Finding Nemo" jumper. Another post showed him tasting a Dairy Queen ice cream cone for the first time.

Says DeRossett, "Thank God he was born in Kentucky."

In July, Tennessee began its own testing program for Krabbe, joining New York, Missouri, Kentucky and Ohio.

It took two years to implement Tennessee's Krabbe screening law. A state lab in Nashville performs the enzyme tests and uses PerkinElmer and Mayo Clinic for the confirmatory ones.

***

It's hard to surprise Spencer, given all she's been through. But as she was washing the dinner dishes one night this summer, the scene in her living room took her breath away.

Tamsen, then 8 years old, was sitting at Kenan's feet in her pajamas. Kenan's vision and hearing are limited, but his mom says she can tell from his respirations and facial expressions that he loves getting his big sister's undivided attention.

Without warning that night, Tamsen started singing Verdi's "Va, pensiero."

Singing is like breathing for Tamsen, something done so routinely she doesn't think of it as a talent. On the rare occasions Tamsen does something that merits scolding, she has stormed off to her room to cry. Her parents hear the sobs intermingled with singing until the crying turns into words, and all they hear is song.

That Spencer was hearing her daughter sing Italian opera wasn't really a surprise either. Tamsen is a member of the Chicago Children's Choir, which performs numbers spanning genres and languages.

Yet, as those mournful Italian words— Hebrew slaves lamenting the loss of their homeland— filled the room in the dim light, the connection between sister and brother bordered on the sacred to Spencer.

Tamsen has wrestled with the idea of Kenan dying from her earliest days. As a toddler with her baby dolls, Tamsen's play routinely included taking a picture of their brains.

As she got older, Tamsen struggled to understand why she got in trouble but Kenan didn't. When the word "infraction" appeared on her third-grade vocabulary list, Tamsen wanted to know why Kenan never committed any infractions. Spencer had to explain gently to Tamsen that she wished Kenan could, but he couldn't.

One time Tamsen said she wanted to have Krabbe so she and Kenan could sit in connected chairs and watch their mom feed them both through their g-tubes.

She was only 4, her mom recalls, when she first said, "When I grow up, I won't have him, and that makes me sad."

Helping Tamsen work through that sorrow has been among Spencer's biggest challenges. But as Spencer listened to Tamsen sing Verdi's opera to Kenan, the roles had shifted.

She saw Tamsen sharing with Kenan the power of song to release grief.

"She was offering that coping to her brother," Spencer recalls. "What was beautiful about that moment was that my children transcended it for me. I didn't do any work.

"It was Tamsen and Kenan that made the moment for me. I got to be a witness."

When Tamsen was done, Spencer asked her to sing the song again so she could preserve that memory with a video. It wasn't the same the second time.

It didn't need to be.

***

The Illinois Department of Public Health now anticipates it can begin statewide screening for Krabbe by the end of the year.

In a statement to the Tribune, the department didn't provide a specific target date. Through a spokeswoman, Director Nirav Shah and other current Public Health employees declined to comment.

Melaney Arnold, the department spokeswoman, acknowledges that the state is now on "Plan D." "Implementing testing for Krabbe has taken longer than we wanted," she says in a written statement.

Outsourcing all newborn screening to a private company is no longer being considered, she says.

Arnold adds that PerkinElmer is not to blame for the software delay. "While it may sound as simple as a quick software change to finalize implementation for Krabbe, it's actually very complicated with numerous steps and moving parts to coordinate," she says.

A spokesman for PerkinElmer says "states and their labs set their own agendas and prioritize their own projects."

Dizikes, the former regulatory director for Illinois labs, declined to be interviewed.

Nash, the Public Health manager who had likened the bureaucratic process to the movie "Groundhog Day," retired from the department but still works as a contract employee. She says the staff in the lab and the screening follow-up program are dedicated to helping babies.

Many state employees, she says, have been frustrated that launching Krabbe screening is taking so long, but she considers this an anomaly.

"It's a horrible disease," Nash says. "We're moving forward with our target and at this point we're working hard to get things implemented."

***

This is the cost of a decade of bureaucratic dysfunction in Illinois. Kenan, Dylan, Logan, Lana and Hayden were all born after the 2007 Krabbe screening law passed. Each might have been helped by a transplant. None of them got that chance.

Three are dead. The brainstems of the other two are disintegrating. There may be more than those five.

"Our whole state government is such a broken-down horrible mess," Burton says. "What can I tell a parent to do? The sad thing is these parents deserve to make choices for their child. We let them go until there's no treatment option when we've had a law on the books for 10 years. To me, it's a travesty."

She wonders how many more will be born before Illinois starts screening newborns for this disease.

"I've watched all these other states come on after us, and they're doing it, and here we are still waiting," Burton says.

That waiting cost Kenan and his family in ways that only a parent can measure.

"Look at this little boy," Spencer says. "I was counting on him to tell me what it's like to be a boy."

Kenan is lying motionless in his wheelchair, reclined so gravity doesn't restrict his airway. The mere act of sliding elastic-waist pants onto his small frame that morning made his whole body shake in pain. A blanket, decorated with superheroes, is draped over him because he can no longer regulate his own body temperature.

He is 6 years old, and he is dying. Spencer doesn't know what he likes or dislikes. The superheroes on the blanket are just a guess.

This final stage of Krabbe, Spencer says, is like having a short in the wire of a lamp. You can wiggle the cord, and the lamp will sometimes light up. But at a certain point, it won't anymore. The brainstem stops telling the heart and lungs what to do. And no amount of thumping on a chest will help.

She is ashamed of her state government.

"If anyone dares to congratulate themselves when they finally implement this, that's when—" Spencer interrupts herself to tamp down her anger. The words that follow are sharp and staccato: "I'll have something to say."

Spencer's voice softens as she turns to her son. "Right, Kenan?"

Kenan's blue eyes, distant and unfocused, don't move. If he has an answer, there is no way for Spencer to know what it is.

The time between breaths grows too long, so Spencer holds his jaw at a better angle and coaxes him to take in some air.

DIRTY JOHN

LOS ANGELES TIMES

OCTOBER 1-8, 2017

By Christopher Goffard

CHAPTER ONE OF SIX

THE REAL THING

They met on an over-50 dating site. She had money, grown kids and a wounded heart. He had a catchy profile, a killer smile and a talent for knowing what she needed to hear.

Their first date was at Houston's, a restaurant in Irvine, where he opened the door for her and put her napkin on her lap. Candles flickered along the polished-mahogany bar; jazz drifted from speakers; conversation purred.

Debra Newell had taken pains to look good. Her cornsilk-blond hair fell in waves over her shoulders. High black Gucci heels, designer jeans, Chanel bag. At 59, married and divorced four times, she had begun to worry that she was too old for another chance at love. Her four kids were grown, she ran a flourishing interior design firm, and she was looking for a man to share her success with.

Her date was 55, 6 feet 2, with hard-jawed good looks and a gym-sculpted frame. He looked a little weathered, and he dressed lazily— shorts and an ill-matching preppy shirt— but he might have once been an All-American quarterback on a trading card.

His name was John Meehan. He had thick dark hair and a warm, friendly smile that invited trust. His eyes were hazel-green, with the quality of canceling out the whole of the world that wasn't her, their current focus.

It was October 2014. They had found each other on an over-50 dating site, and she thought his profile— Christian, divorced, physician— seemed safe. She had been on three other recent dates, but the men were less handsome than their profile photos, and the talk was dull.

John was different. He showed keen interest in the details of her life and business. He didn't want to talk just about himself, even though his stories were riveting. He told her all about being an anesthesiologist in Iraq, where he'd just spent a year with Doctors Without Borders.

He said he had a couple of kids. That he owned houses in Newport Beach and Palm Springs. That he happened to worship at her church, Mariners. That he would love to meet her grandkids.

And he told her that she stopped his heart, she was so beautiful. She was just his type. Her last serious boyfriend had wounded her, in parting, when he said she wasn't.

John began caressing her back. She thought this was moving a little fast, but she decided to allow it. The intensity of his attention was flattering.

She brought John back to her penthouse, just up the block. They kissed. He wanted it to go further. "This feels incredible," he said, stretching out on her bed.

She thought, "It's just a mattress."

She became uncomfortable. It turned into a fight. He just didn't want to leave, and she had to insist.

She went to bed thinking, "Jerk."

She thought, "Cross off another one."

***

The next day she was back at her office, a little sad, trying to lose herself in work. Over the 30 years that she had built Ambrosia Interior Design, it had been her refuge amid many romantic disappointments. Work was the realm in which her success was unqualified.

She designed model homes and clubhouses. She liked to hire single women and mothers because she could remember how it felt to be alone, with one child and another on the way, after her first marriage broke up.

When people walked into one of her exquisitely arranged rooms, they were invited to imagine their futures in them. She called them "approachable dreams." They were like glossy ads in upscale lifestyle magazines— purged of kids' toys and dirty dishes and other real-world complications.

In her big Irvine warehouse, among the vases and mirrors and other decorative bric-a-brac, stood shelves of color-coordinated hardback books — aqua, navy, gray, brown— because books made nice furniture in perfect homes. She hunted at weekend library sales. The titles didn't matter, as long as they omitted the words "sex" and "death."

Her perfect rooms were like the face you presented on dates, inviting people to fantasize about the piece that may complete their lives. If your eagerness or loneliness or desperation showed too soon, you were done. Maybe that had been John's mistake.

That day he called to say he was sorry. He knew he'd overstepped. He just wanted to spend every minute with her.

***

By the second or third date, he was telling her he loved her, that he wanted to marry her. She didn't mind his idiosyncrasies, like his habit of wearing his faded blue medical scrubs everywhere, even to a formal-dress cancer benefit she invited him to. Some people snickered, but she thought, "Busy doctor."

"So you are the real thing," she texted him after one date.

"Best thing that will ever happen to you," he replied.

He began spending the night regularly at her Irvine penthouse. Her 24-year-old daughter, Jacquelyn, who lived there with her, made it clear she thought he looked like a loser. Maybe even homeless.

She said she didn't like the way his eyes roamed around the place, among their velvet chairs and jewelry and fine art. Or the way he seemed so curious about the contents of her safe, where she kept her collection of Birkin and Cartier bags. Get this creep out of here, she told her mom.

Jacquelyn's reaction didn't shock Debra, since her taste in men often exasperated her children. She thought they'd find something bad to say about anyone she dated. Her friends sometimes joked about her being a "bad picker." Where other people saw red flags, she saw a parade.

***

Soon Debra and John were quietly looking for a place together. They found a $6,500-a-month house on the boardwalk on Balboa Island in Newport Beach. She put down a year in advance. He didn't want his name on the lease. Tax problems, he said. They'd known each other five weeks.

Debra wasn't about to tell her kids that John would be moving in with her. She knew what they'd say— that she was moving too fast, acting with her heart, repeating old mistakes.

What her kids didn't see was how well he treated her. How he brought her coffee in the morning. Got her groceries. Took her Tesla and Range Rover in for maintenance. Carried her purse.

She was convinced that her kids would understand how wonderful he was once they got to know him. She thought that if any of her kids would give him a chance, it was Terra, her youngest.

***

The family's quietest, most docile member liked to daydream about the end of the world.

At 23, Terra watched and rewatched every episode of "The Walking Dead." She spoke of the series less as entertainment than as a primer on how to survive apocalyptic calamity.

She made careful note of why some characters lived and others perished. It had to do with vigilance and quick reflexes and the will to fight. "The world ends," she would say, "and those who are fit to survive will survive."

She was as nonconfrontational as her sister Jacquelyn was assertive. The first word people used to describe her was "sweet."

She was living in Las Vegas with her boyfriend, Jimmy, and studying to be a dog groomer. She knew her mom liked to take care of people, and that she saw the best in men, at times against all evidence. Sometimes they pretended to be sincere churchgoing Christians. Terra had seen her scared, screamed at, hit, taken for money.

She felt protective of her mom and wondered why a guy who sounded as good as John would still be single. Her skepticism only deepened when she and Jimmy drove out to Southern California and met him.

***

John towered over her by a full foot, and a coldness came off him. He barely made eye contact. He cut her questions short. As he helped Debra move into her new house, he huffed and strained and wrestled her queen mattress down the stairs single-handedly, a show of ludicrous machismo.

Terra's three dogs seemed anxious around John. She thought maybe they were picking up on her own unease.

She brooded on some questions. What kind of doctor had no car? Why had no one seen John's houses in Newport Beach and Palm Springs? Why did he seem to spend all day playing "Call of Duty" on the 70-inch plasma TV her mom had bought?

***

Terra and her boyfriend moved into the spare bedroom of the new Balboa Island rental for a few days. This made it hard for Debra to maintain the illusion that John wasn't really living there, though she tried.

Terra discovered the truth the day before Thanksgiving, when she opened a closet and found a nursing certificate bearing John's name. Her mom said she was getting his certificates framed, but Terra knew, and she did something uncharacteristic. She confronted her loudly.

Here came John, instantly transformed by rage. Why was Terra snooping through his stuff? Why was she trying to steal Debra from him? Did she realize that kids should be smacked for this?

Terra screamed at her mother: "How could you let this guy talk to me like this?!"

Terra left, badly shaken, with the sickening feeling that her mother was choosing John over her.

***

"They're jealous."

That was John's explanation for her kids' hostility to him. They didn't want her to be happy. They just wanted her dead, so they could collect.

He had an explanation for why he had a nursing degree but called himself a doctor. He said he had a PhD, which earned him the title, plus advanced training in anesthesiology.

At the big Thanksgiving party the next day, it was impossible to ignore the sudden fissures in the family— impossible to ignore Terra's absence. But others were willing to give John a chance.

Debra's mother, Arlane, thought he dressed tackily, especially for Thanksgiving. But she made allowances for a busy professional. And he was so nice and courteous. "I think he's a great guy," she told Debra.

When Jacquelyn showed up, John asked for a private word with her. She announced that he was the devil, that anything he had to say he could say in public.

***

To John, this was more evidence that Debra's kids were spoiled and out of control. His words tugged at her anxieties.

She wanted a professional's objective advice. She found a therapist, who assessed the family dynamics and told Debra she needed to establish firmer boundaries with her children.

If they wanted to come over, they had to be invited. They couldn't yell at her. They couldn't try to run her life.

They couldn't sabotage her happiness— she had a right to it, just like anybody else. If John was the man she had chosen, it was her business.

Absolutely, John said.

***

Their house on the boardwalk had floor-to-ceiling windows, and from the rooftop deck they could watch the sailboats and the great yachts slide over Newport Harbor. Water lapped against a ribbon of sand yards from their front door, and they could hear the tall, wind-rustled palms and the muted creaking of the boat docks.

They were living inside a postcard. They walked the island hand-in-hand. He doted on passing babies and dogs. He liked to play-wrestle her grandkids. He acted like a kid himself, vulnerable and sweet, and single-mindedly besotted with her.

He liked to pose shirtless and take selfies of his washboard abs. She smiled when he'd stop in front of a mirror and say, "Damn! I'm good-looking."

Wardrobe-wise, she thought he was kind of a mess, with his baggy pants and University of Arizona sweatshirts. He said his clothes had been stolen while he was in Iraq.

"Dress me," he told her. "I want to please you."

She took him to Brooks Brothers. She bought him shoes, dress shirts, slacks, a tweed sport coat, form-fitting cashmere sweaters— deep burgundy, navy blue. He looked good in darker tones and pastels. It felt like having a new doll.

***

He kept begging her to marry him, and she kept resisting, until she couldn't. In early December, she was driving to Vegas on business, and he was tagging along. Why not drop by the courthouse?

The ceremony was in a plain room with a plant-covered trellis. He chuckled a little as he tried to get the ring on her finger. They celebrated with lemon-drop martinis. They had known each other less than two months. No one had been invited to the wedding.

Debra would say, "I felt this was an opportunity to love again."

***

She kept it a secret as the weeks passed and Christmas approached. The family planned to have their traditional Christmas get-together at the Orange County home of Debra's eldest daughter, Nicole.

Jacquelyn refused to go. Terra was torn. She desperately wanted to spend the holiday with her little nieces and nephews, but she didn't even want to look at John.

Terra went to a therapist with her mom. They came to an understanding that Terra and John would keep their distance during the party.

The day came, and John bustled in with his arms full of presents for the children— dozens of presents Debra had bought. The kids surrounded him. Terra began crying hysterically. It became a scene.

"You promised he wouldn't hang out with the kids," Terra told her mom.

Terra's grandmother found her in the family room, trembling and crying.

"I just want to leave," Terra said. "I don't like him. There's something about him."

***

Terra knew what people were thinking: "There she goes again, being overemotional." She was the youngest in the family, her parents split up when she was young, and she'd been looked after by nannies during the years her mom built her business.

She knew some people still thought of her as the little girl who needed attention. It was sometimes a fight to be taken seriously, and she would question the intensity of her own feelings.

In early 2015, Terra was back home in Vegas, with Jimmy and their dogs. Terra wasn't talking to her mom. She just hoped John would go away.

***

Back in Orange County, Jacquelyn was thinking about John's fingernails. They were dirty.

She had spent time around doctors, during the time she worked in sales for a plastic surgeon. Their nails were meticulously clipped and scrubbed.

Plus, the doctors she had known did not go everywhere in their scrubs, as John did. She thought he looked like a man wearing a costume.

Something else was wrong with John's scrubs: the bottoms were frayed around the heels as if they belonged to a medical-office receptionist who ran errands in tennis shoes.

Other things unsettled Jacquelyn, like the slangy, misspelled texts she received from her mom's number that were clearly not from her. And the way her mom kept calling to complain that money was missing from her wallet. Had Jacquelyn dropped by her office to borrow some?

Jacquelyn told her to think about the loser she was dating. She thought her mom, so nice and trusting and naive, had no idea who he was.

Jacquelyn bought a magnetic tracker and put it on her mother's Tesla to monitor John's movements when he left the house. He said he traveled between clinics and operating rooms, doing anesthesiology work as needed, but who knew? Debra would not remember agreeing to the tracker, but Jacquelyn insisted she asked.

From her iPhone, Jacquelyn began studying the strange routes he took around Southern California, looking for patterns and clues. He went to doctors' offices in Irvine and Mission Viejo and San Diego, a warehouse, a post office, fast-food joints, Tesla charging portals.

Jacquelyn knew she had to be careful about what she told her mom— it could get back to John. She didn't want to be dismissed as a meddler. And none of what she found was necessarily incompatible with his story. These were fragments of a puzzle.

When she told Terra what she was doing, Terra asked, "What if he hurts her?"

***

In Debra Newell's family, the question carried a freight of unspoken dread, because the worst had happened before.

In 1984, her older sister, Cindi, had been trying to escape a husband she described as controlling and possessive. One day he pressed a handgun against the back of her neck and pulled the trigger.

It was the reason Debra hated firearms. It was the reason she refused to have one around, long after people began warning her that she needed one.

CHAPTER TWO of SIX

NEWLYWEDS

Debra's family regarded John with suspicion. She knew so little about her new husband, beyond the way he made her feel. Then she went to the mailbox.

After church one Sunday, Debra Newell walked into the living room with her husband to find a woman she did not recognize.

The stranger sat trance-like before the big window that overlooked Newport Harbor, a thin, weathered woman in her late 30s or early 40s. She had just used the shower; her curly blond hair was wet. She was dressed all in white; she had taken Debra's clothes. She held a tiny Bible and sipped Ovaltine. She acted like she belonged there, though she wouldn't meet their eyes.

John pushed her head onto the countertop and pulled her arms behind her back. He ordered Debra to leave the house and call the police. Debra didn't want to press charges. She figured the woman was homeless, maybe a drug addict, and had climbed in through the third-floor skylight.

John denied knowing her, but Debra wondered. Had he said something to the woman before police took her away? Had he warned her not to reveal their connection? Had she been to the house before, and learned of its unlocked entrance?

John announced they needed to ramp up security. Even in a $6,500-a-month bayfront rental they couldn't be too careful about drifters. Soon the home bristled with cameras that he monitored on his smartphone. He also insisted on cameras at the Irvine office of her interior design firm. He just wanted her to be safe.

Is he watching me? Debra wondered.

And she thought: I can watch him, too.

***

She didn't know where he went all day, when he kissed her goodbye and disappeared in her Tesla. He never brought home a paycheck, but that was easily explained— as a freelance anesthesiologist who traveled between operating rooms, he was paid in cash by the uninsured.

One day, she pulled up the security footage and saw that John wasn't going off to work like he said. She watched him leave the house in his blue scrubs, return a little later, climb into bed and go to sleep.

She debated whether to confront him. He could become so volatile when challenged, as he had with her children.

She decided to ask, but not in an accusatory tone that might upset him. Gently.

"The patient failed a treadmill test and they had to cancel the surgery," John explained instantly, nonchalance itself.

She didn't press him any further. Questions might puncture the dream.

***

Debra knew so little about her husband, beyond the way he made her feel. At 59, she'd never been happier with a man.

He ran her errands, the way her assistants usually did. Made sure her bills were paid. Sat beside her at doctors' appointments. Brought her bouquets of peonies, her favorite flower. Held her all night, breathing against her neck, his weightlifter's body draped over hers.

She wondered about the scars that crossed his abdomen and back, legs and ankles. He said he'd been in a chopper crash as a medic in the war zones of the Middle East, just before meeting her. He praised the accuracy of "American Sniper," the film about a sharpshooter in Iraq.

During his time in the desert, he said, he had learned something about himself. Five or six times, he'd had to kill. It was easy, if you had to.

Ruthlessness was in his genes, he explained. He bragged that he was a blood relation of the notorious Mafia hit man who once ran Murder Inc. He didn't show a violent side himself, except the time he grabbed the shirt of a homeless guy who said something rude to Debra on a Seattle street. John screamed in his face, and Debra had to pull him away.

He told her she made him a better man. They attended Mariners, an evangelical megachurch in Irvine, with modern worship music, keyboards and guitars. John always seemed excited to go.

He said he'd attended the church before he met her, though once he slipped up and called the pastor a priest. She thought it was because he'd been raised Catholic.

She watched him inject testosterone. He said this was for his kidneys. She watched him pop OxyContin. He said this was for his bad back.

***

Debra had been telling her nephew, Shad Vickers, all about the handsome doctor who seemed to live only for her, and when Shad met him he thought, "A good, fun guy." He was impressed with John's confidence and tales of battlefield derring-do. Most of all, he was glad to see his aunt happy. She'd been looking for so long.

Shad and Debra had always been close. For years he had thought of her as a second mother. Their bond was forged by a shared experience of unhealable horror. When Shad was a boy in 1984, as his parents were splitting up, his father shot his mother to death and went to prison. The victim was Cindi, Debra's older sister.

Debra treated Shad like one of her own kids. She brought him on family vacations. She paid for his football and track leagues, which gave the traumatized boy some focus and release. She gave him a job in her furniture warehouse. She stuck with him during the years his rage and confusion were at their worst, during the brawls and scrapes with the law.

Now he was a single father in his 40s with three daughters, gregarious and sweet-tempered, with a job at a trucking company, and he loved his aunt and hoped John would make her happy. Shad brought his kids over to the beachfront house, and John was great with them.

Shad knew some people in the family disliked John— Debra's daughter Jacquelyn had sized him up as a con man and been especially vocal in her contempt— but he was willing to give him a chance. He tried not to judge people too soon.

He did have some questions. Like why had he come into Debra's life with only a few old clothes? Why did he play video games all day long? Did doctors really jump out of helicopters with machine guns?

Then John said something that didn't sit right. It was at Debra's place in late February 2015, and John was making margaritas in the kitchen when Jacquelyn's name came up.

"I could take her out from a thousand yards," John said, and Shad would recall that Debra laughed, not taking it seriously.

Shad thought it wasn't a thing to joke about, even if you'd been to a war zone and had a war zone sense of humor. It seemed kind of sick, actually.

He began to fear for his aunt. So when he got word that some of Debra's kids had hired a private investigator to look into John's past— when he learned that a preliminary report had come back— he wanted to know everything.

He studied the report. John had a bankruptcy. A nursing license, not a doctor's license. Addresses in Arizona, Ohio, Indiana, Tennessee and across California, including a recent one at a trailer park in the desert of Riverside County.

His curiosity gnawing at him, Shad called the trailer park. A woman answered. Shad thought up a lie, saying his mother had married John Meehan, and could she tell him anything about him? The woman said

John had lived there. They'd had a relationship. He had disappeared. She hung up.

There was another address linked to John Meehan: 550 N. Flower St. in Santa Ana. The Orange County jail.

***

Shad wanted to warn Debra without telling her too much. What if he was wrong? What if the man in the report was a different John Meehan?

In early March 2015, Shad called Debra and reminded her that he'd lost his mom, and he didn't want to lose her too. He said, "What if he isn't who he says he is? What if he isn't an anesthesiologist? What if I could prove to you he was in jail, and not Iraq?"

Her response would stay in his memory: "Even if it was true, I wouldn't care, because I love him."

And because she loved him, Debra relayed Shad's remarks right to John. And John decided that Shad was his enemy.

"Why don't you simply go away," John texted him. "You're not invited here. You come near and I call the cops. ... Worry about your own miserable life and I'll worry about Debbie, who is a lot closer to me than you can ever imagine. You won't win this."

Shad replied: "You told my grandma and I that you are a doctor. Prove it. You told my grandma and I that you own two properties. Prove it. Once you prove those two, you are good in my book."

John: "I couldn't give a s--- about being in your book."

Shad said he hoped his aunt would open her eyes and dump him.

John: "Boy, are you in for a big surprise."

Shad: "My mom is looking down on me making sure I don't give up on her sister and making sure I know her sister [knows] the truth about your lying ass."

John: "Good thing your mom ain't here. She'd be embarrassed."

Shad: "It's not a good thing. It's not good at all."

John: "You don't have an aunt anymore. Get it? ... I ain't going nowhere and neither is she. Stay away from the house. Accidents do happen. Again, Deb wants nothing to do with you and if you were on fire I wouldn't piss on you to help you out."

Shad: "If I hear of you threatening my aunt or harming her, you will see me."

John: "Please show up. ... And she ain't your aunt anymore. Just ask her."

John got a lot nastier. He insulted Shad's girlfriend and his little daughters.

John: "It isn't about me or what I've done. It's about you harassing her to the point where she fears for her life. ... And by the way, we're married. That makes your threat my threat."

Shad: "I pray you're not married."

Now the whole family knew the secret.

Shad was a former football player, 5 feet 10, a burly 195 pounds. But John had 4 inches on Shad, and probably 25 pounds, and Shad had seen boxing gloves and a heavy punching bag in the garage. Shad thought John would be able to overpower him, if it came to that.

And there was a single-minded viciousness about John, a sense that he'd stop at nothing. For now, Shad decided to keep his distance.

***

The beginning of Debra's own disillusionment came in the mailbox, in the form of a letter from the county jail.

It was addressed to John, from a former jail mate saying hi. Debra tore it open and began reading, there in the walkway.

She stood there frozen for a minute or two, trying to make sense of it, and then she looked up. John was rushing toward her.

She realized that he had been watching her on camera— that maybe he'd been watching her more than she realized.

He snatched the letter out of her hand. She asked him what this meant. She told him she thought he'd been lying to her.

He demanded to know why she was looking at his mail. Didn't she know it was a felony?

John said his jailhouse correspondent was just a guy he was helping out— sending him care packages and a little money. He wouldn't admit he'd been in jail himself.

***

The next day, when John left on one of his mysterious errands, Debra walked into the home office they shared and began hunting. John was messy, and his papers were scattered everywhere.

Who exactly had she married?

The answer, she learned with apprehension that crept up on her and then came in a flood, lay in piles of documents he had made no effort to hide.

They told a story of a former nurse anesthetist who became hooked on surgical painkillers and lost his career. Of a con man who took nasty pleasure in the mechanics of a dark craft he had mastered, and who seemed obsessed with humiliating anyone who defied his will.

From 2005 to 2014— from about the time he got out of prison in Michigan for drug theft to the time he met Debra Newell in California— he had seduced, swindled and terrorized multiple women, many of whom he had met on dating sites while posing as a doctor, court records showed.

"You are my project for years to come," he wrote to a Porter Ranch woman after allegedly suggesting— in an anonymous letter— that he had raped her and taken photos while she was unconscious.

"This I promise. Do you think I joke? Every breath I take will be to ruin your surgically implanted life. Thanks for the pictures!" He described his planned campaign against her as "my masterpiece."

In another case, according to court records, a 48-year-old Laguna Beach woman said she had been recovering from brain surgery at a San Diego hospital when she awoke to find Meehan standing over her bed. He said he was her anesthesiologist.

They dated. She said her family had millions. He suggested she transfer money into his account, to hide it from her estranged husband. She balked. He sent intimate photos of her to her family, and wrote: "You're in way over your head on this one. Make it happen and I walk away. If not, I will be your nightmare."

Police began investigating, and when they searched his Riverside County storage unit, they found a Colt .38 Special. Binoculars. GPS units. Ammunition. Heavy-duty cable ties. Syringes. A pocket saw. A bottle of cyanide powder. Eight cyanide capsules.

"A treacherous, cunning and very manipulative person who uses fear and intimidation as a means to control and coerce his victims," police called him.

As John Meehan awaited trial in the Orange County jail in late 2013, an inmate reported that he was offering $10,000 each for the murders of two Laguna Beach detectives, plus five other potential witnesses against him, including several ex-girlfriends and his ex-wife. His philosophy: "With no witnesses, there is no trial."

To the detectives, one of whom described him as "a ticking bomb, capable of unpredictable violence," the threat felt real enough to request a restraining order. But the jail informant refused to be a witness, no charges were filed for murder solicitation, and the restraining order was denied.

Meehan pleaded guilty in February 2014 to stalking the Laguna Beach woman and being a felon in possession of a firearm. He was out that summer, but jailed again for violating a restraining order against another woman he had threatened.

He walked out on Oct. 8. He met Debra online two days later. By the time they married in December 2014, three separate women around Southern California had standing restraining orders against him; in recent years, at least three others had requested them.

"He threatened to leak nude pictures of me if I did not give him money," wrote one woman.

"He was choking me, telling me if I tell the police anything else he'll kill me," wrote another.

"He told me once he was obsessed with me. And I am VERY afraid of him," wrote a third.

***

Debra thought, "I am going to be killed like my sister."

She took Ativan for her nerves and called a lawyer, who told her to cut her husband out of her will, so he would derive no profit from murdering her.

She knew she needed to get out of the Balboa Island house, even if she lost $50,000 she'd paid on the yearlong lease. She had some time to maneuver, since John had gone to Hoag Hospital for back trouble and — because of vague complications that necessitated painkillers— had checked himself in.

Her family helped her pack. In John's possessions they found papers on which he'd scrawled gun names, codes, phone numbers, jail-inmate numbers, bank routing numbers.

He'd saved printouts from websites on which women posted warnings about scary and unfaithful men. Datingpsychos.com had devoted multiple pages to him:

He conned me out of money ... He is very persuasive. Emotionally needy ... slick liar...

He grabbed me by the throat ...

Do not let this man into your life ...

Don't be fooled by his good looks and prince charming personality ...

He is a parasite, a leech, an infection that festers on anyone he comes in contact with ...

Trust your intuition, ladies. He is a pathologically rotten apple!

Stay away at all costs!

Classic psychopath ...

Times Community News reporter Hannah Fry contributed to this story.

CHAPTER THREE of SIX

Filthy

John Meehan's past was a ledger of lies, swindles and betrayals. In law school, classmates gave him a nickname that seemed to encompass all of it.

He had lavished her with compliments, and now he savaged her looks. He had entered the marriage broke, and now he demanded half her wealth. He had been gentleness itself, and now he threatened her with "long-lost relatives" in the mob.

"Enough," Debra Newell texted him. "You are evil."

"Divide up the stuff and I never see you again," John Meehan texted back. "Your choice."

In March 2015, as Debra studied the paperwork detailing her husband's long record of women terrorized and laws broken, she learned that he had a nickname. It went back decades, to his brief time in law school at the University of Dayton.

Dirty John, classmates called him. Sometimes it was Filthy John Meehan, or just Filthy. But mostly Dirty John.

***

Ask John Meehan's sisters how he became the man who conned his way into Debra Newell's life— ask them where his story begins— and they point to their father.

Their Brooklyn-raised dad ran the Diamond Wheel Casino in San Jose, and imparted to John a series of illicit skills, like how to pull off bogus lawsuits and insurance scams. "How to lie," said one sister, Donna Meehan Stewart. "How to deceive."

Coupled with that was a cold-eyed ethos of leaving no slight unpunished. "If anybody did anything to John, my dad would tell us, 'You go there with a stick and take care of it,' " said Karen Douvillier, his other sister. "It's the Brooklyn mentality of you fight, you get even. If you want to get back at somebody, you don't get back at them, you get back at their family."

At Prospect High School in Saratoga, Calif., in the mid-1970s, John was a great-looking athlete, charismatic, a magnet for girls, an A student who swaggered with a sense of his superior intelligence. He learned that his gifts provided shortcuts.

"I think John thought he was smarter than everybody else, because everybody told him he was, but he had no common sense," Karen said. "He was taught to manipulate at a very early age.

"That's the fault of my parents, especially my dad. Because that's all my dad knew."

In family lore, the Meehans are related to Albert Anastasia, the 1950s-era New York mobster who ran Murder Inc. and was infamous for eliminating potential witnesses. Proof is elusive, but John enjoyed the dark glamour conferred by this supposed bloodline.

John Meehan's parents separated while he was in high school, and it was then, his sisters said, that rage and bitterness began to consume him. Mom had had an affair; Dad tried to win her back with violence; John became a child she'd had with a man she now loathed. He came to hate both parents.

John Meehan modeled himself after Sean Connery's James Bond, suave and beyond the law, and had a customized license plate that read "MEE 007." He liked the ladies, fast cars and easy money. "He was a hustler," Karen said. "Whatever he had to do to get money, he would do."

To win legal settlements, he jumped in front of a Corvette and sprinkled broken glass in his Taco Bell order. Busted for selling cocaine, his sisters said, he testified against a friend and was forced to leave California as part of a plea deal.

He received a bachelor of arts degree from the University of Arizona in 1988, then moved east to attend the University of Dayton's law school that fall.

Kevin Horan, a classmate who lived with him in a house by the cemetery, said John did not stand out as a law student. He made an impression in other ways— for his laid-back, California-guy persona, and for the women he brought back to the house in unreasonable numbers.

His debauchery spawned the nickname Dirty John, though once bestowed it seemed to describe a lot of his behavior. Like the way he took money for roofing jobs he didn't complete. Like the way he rented his housemate a deathtrap truck with no brakes, and claimed not to know. Like the way he used fake names on the credit cards that filled the mailbox, a swindle he would boast about.

"He was basically this strange, lone-wolf guy that did all kinds of scandalous-type things, and it wasn't just with women," Horan said. "I'm like, 'That guy, you can't trust him for nothing. He's rotten top to bottom.'"

In the second year of law school, he disappeared. "Everyone's like, 'What happened to Dirty John?'" Horan said. They got an answer when his report card arrived. They held the envelope up to the light: Ds and Fs.

***

For his next con, John Meehan got married.

Tonia Sells, a nurse, was 25. He was 31, though he led her to believe he was 26, just as he led her to believe his name was Johnathan, not just John. He had shaved five years off his age and added five letters to his name.

"He would tell you story after story about, you know, that he just comes from this family that's just not him," Tonia said. "That he was able to escape them because other people stepped up into his life and helped make him a great person."

They were wed in November 1990 at St. Joseph Catholic Church in Dayton, her family church.

None of John's family had shown up, but he had an explanation: His dad was an alcoholic, his mom a pill-popper, and he didn't want them ruining the special day.

Tonia would keep a tape of the wedding that captured its strangeness. As the harpist plucked and the priest prayed, John sat in his tux fidgeting and smirking, like a boy in a grown-up's costume enjoying some fantastic private joke.

John was still wearing that glib, devil-may-care expression as his friend Phil gave a toast so brief and generic he might have just met him. It included the line, "If you talk to any of his friends, as far as the reaction to his wedding, you'll just find out they're completely shocked and baffled."

John's friends in attendance, some of them former law school classmates, had little to offer in the way of personal anecdote. There was a blank space where the stories should have been. The stories they did have weren't repeatable.

"Let me start by saying that John Meehan's, John Meehan's nickname is 'Filthy John Meehan,' " a guest said.

"Why? Why? Remember when you first heard that nickname?"

"Yes, I do, but it cannot be divulged on camera ..."

After the wedding, watching this video, Tonia was surprised to learn the nickname of the man to whom she had just pledged her life. He laughed it off. Nothing.

Tonia was a practicing nurse anesthetist, and John followed her into the profession.

They had two daughters, and she helped put him through nursing school at Wright State in Dayton and the Middle Tennessee School of Anesthesia.

He struck her as a playful father and a pleasant husband, and they rarely argued. He liked movies and playing basketball and dinner at home, and he studied a lot.

Ten years into the marriage— his degrees secure, his career launched — he wanted a divorce. Maybe, she thought later, her usefulness to him was over.

In July 2000 Tonia tracked down his mother, Dolores, a call John had always forbidden. "I always knew you would call me," she said.

Dolores told her that John's real birthday was Feb. 3, 1959. That his birth name was John, not Johnathan. That he had a drug charge in California.

For Tonia, it was hard to make sense of any of it. She had been enmeshed in a lie the whole time she had known him. She had had a normal upbringing in a good home, and had no yardstick with which to measure this.

"My first experience with evil," she called it.

Tonia searched the house they had shared in Springboro, Ohio, and found a hidden box containing the powerful surgical anesthetics Versed and Fentanyl.

He had become hooked on drugs he was supposed to be giving patients; she knew there was no legitimate reason to have them. She felt guilty that she'd helped John get into her profession. She thought he was a danger to their kids and to patients. She informed police, who began an investigation. It was September 2000.

As suspicions of his drug theft circulated, John lost his job at Good Samaritan Hospital in Michigan and found work in Warsaw, Ind., but fell under suspicion there too. He became convinced that Tonia had notified the state nursing board there, and she secretly recorded his increasingly menacing calls. He was furious that she had called his mother.

"Do you know why I have this big smile on my face?" he told her.

"Why, John?"

"Because, trust me, just trust me. That's why."

"Trust you what?"

"Just trust me."

"That doesn't make any sense."

"It don't have to. You'll understand it all."

"What, the Mafia's coming after me again? Or what?"

"When it happens, Tonia, and you see it in your eyes, remember it was me, OK?"

"Remember what, John?"

"Keep that in mind. It was me."

"Keep what in mind, John?"

He told her he would buy her a Cadillac if he was wrong. He wouldn't say what he might be wrong about.

"Tonia, you enjoy your time left on this earth, OK? Because that's what it's gonna come down to."

Tonia sounded relatively calm, as his remarks grew more frightening. Inside she was not.

"I got a big smile on my face," he said. "You know why? Because it's gonna get done."

"What's gonna get done? You're not making any sense."

"It don't have to. You will understand when the time comes. That's all I gotta say."

"Yeah, and who's gonna take care of your children?"

"I'll take care of them."

He told her he would be enjoying a Cuba Libre with a 22-year-old when it happened— which she took to mean he would kill her or have her killed.

"If there's one thing that happens on this earth, it's gonna be you," he told her.

The court convicted him of menacing and gave him a suspended sentence.

***

Dennis Luken was an investigator with the drug task force of the Warren County Sheriff's Office in Ohio. He began looking into John Meehan in January 2002.

Hospital workers reported that they had seen Meehan bring a gun into the operating room and steal Demerol from a patient he pretended to medicate with it. Of all the criminals Luken studied, hunted and arrested during a four-decade career in law enforcement, Meehan would occupy a singular place in his memory.

"The most devious, dangerous, deceptive person I ever met," Luken, now retired, would call him— a devil-tongued con man with the cold intelligence of a spy, a void where his soul should have been, and a desperate drug addiction that he would marshal his dark talents to feed.

Luken said he found emails showing John had sent drugs to his 44-year-old brother Daniel, who died of an overdose in Santa Cruz County in September 2000. He couldn't make a criminal case on that charge, but his investigation led to Meehan's guilty plea in 2002 to felony drug theft.

Meehan might still have salvaged his career. Instead of surrendering himself to begin a stint at an Ohio rehab clinic, he fled the state and stole an anesthesia kit. He checked into a Comfort Inn in Saginaw, Mich., where police found him semi-conscious, surrounded by drug vials.

The ambulance was rushing him to the hospital when he unbuckled his restraints, grabbed the drug kit and jumped into the road. He fled into a nearby J.C. Penney, scrambled atop a cargo elevator and into the shaft, and kicked a cop in the face. They finally handcuffed him when he tumbled to the ground, covered in grease, and knocked himself unconscious.

Meehan spent 17 months in a Michigan prison, but Luken doubted it would be his last insult to the law. "I knew this case was going to go on until either somebody killed him or he killed somebody," Luken said.

***

His house in Hamilton, Ohio, was ready for him, clean and landscaped and rescued from foreclosure, when he emerged from prison in 2004.

His sister Donna did that for him. She covered his overdue child support and got his car out of impound and handed him a credit card. "There was nothing he would have had to do except to be a better person and go get help," Donna said.

His first night home, Donna saw him logged on to Match.com. She knew what it meant. He was looking for victims.

He followed Donna to California, where she gave him a spare bedroom at her Newport Beach house and a job at her real estate firm. She said he wouldn't show up for work. He kept going to the hospital for drugs, complaining of his back.

"He wasn't going to get better," Donna said. "He was going to do to me what he was doing to everybody else and just suck them dry."

He followed her to the Palm Springs area in 2007. He rented a house and did RV repairs. He was bitterly preoccupied by the past. He told her about visiting their hometown. The old neighborhoods. The family cemetery in Los Gatos.

"Did you go to Mom's grave?"

Yes, he replied. He had pissed on it.

Donna remembered how much John had hated their father, too— how, in the late 1990s, when their father was being consumed by cancer in a Southern California hospice bed, she left John alone with him briefly. And when she returned, their dad was dead.

She could never shake the feeling that John might have injected him with a fatal painkiller, because his slow death was delaying the insurance payout. There was no autopsy before the cremation, no proof.

***

The best glimpse into how John Meehan perceived himself— the best account of how he framed a life littered with self-made disasters— might be in a letter he wrote in June 2012, asking a friend to help him get his nursing license back.

In it, John cast himself as the brave, often-betrayed, long-suffering victim in his life's twisted narrative. He was the victim of his parents, who used him as a pawn in their divorce and treated him coldly. Of his ex-wife, who called police on him and kept his daughters from him. Of his mother, who fed damaging information about him to his ex. Of false accusations that he supplied prescription drugs that killed his brother. Of a herniated disk, which necessitated drugs to escape his pain and depression.

"To be honest with you, I was abusing this stuff not to get high or feel good but because it allowed me to sleep," he wrote. "My job— putting people to sleep."

He explained that he checked into the Saginaw hotel room with the intention of killing himself, and had taken a shower with the aim of leaving "a good-looking body." He injected himself with Versed and Fentanyl, he said, but didn't get the fatal dose right — a farfetched claim for someone who put people to sleep for a living.

In state prison his suffering continued. "You don't even want to know what being in a Michigan prison is like. One guy came at me thinking I was going to be easy. They found him in the shower the next morning. I did what I had to do ... several times. And they finally figured out I was not worth the effort of the trip to the ER. I learn fast, and always had that ability to turn it on when needed."

The letter had the trappings of a confession, but at heart it was a long snarl of self-justification. It was stingy with insights into what created its author.

***

In the end, he turned against his sister too.

When she asked him to remove his trailer from her RV lot in Cathedral City, he insisted the lot was his. He complained to the district attorney. He wrote to the Department of Real Estate.

In 2014, she got a court judgment against him for $90,000 she had lent him. "I knew I'd never see that money, but I did it to protect myself, because John left me alone after that," Donna said. "It was all I had. To me, that was stronger than a gun."

***

Debra Newell did not know all of this about her husband in March 2015. She hadn't talked to John's law school classmates, or his ex-wife, or the Ohio cop. Nor did she get a detailed history of his life and crimes from his sisters. But she did have a stack of documents outlining a history of arrests and restraining orders— more than enough to scare her.

His threatening texts, sent from his bed at Hoag Hospital, amplified her fear. Then, abruptly, his tone became conciliatory. Repentant.

"I still love you and simply can't live without you. I don't want this. I want us without anyone else," John wrote. "I am flawed. But I'm not so easy to give up on you. When I met you it was simply you. I helped you to get back on your feet and stood up for you."

He begged her to see him. He wanted to explain everything.

"I love and need you. Please."

CHAPTER FOUR OF SIX

FORGIVENESS

Debra was afraid she might end up like her sister, who was killed by her estranged husband. So why would she consider returning to John?

The private investigator told Debra Newell how to make herself a difficult target. Change hotels every few nights. Study the crowd before she entered a room. Ditch her stylish clothes for bland ones. Get a wig to cover her conspicuous blond hair. Blend in.

She dreaded that she would meet the fate of her older sister, Cindi, dead 31 years earlier at the hands of her own husband. The deepest trauma in her family history seemed to be replaying, as if in a nightmare loop, and she feared her mother would have to bury a second daughter.

She had more than 300 pages of documents she'd taken from her husband's home office, and during late winter and early spring of 2015 she pored over them, trying to determine the scope of his criminal past.

John kept texting her, pleading with her to visit him in the hospital. She wanted to look him in the eye and ask why he had lied to her. Also, she felt guilty about just abandoning him. "For better or for worse," she had pledged. So she went.

***

He had explanations.

He had hidden his criminal record because he knew she would never have given an ex-con a chance.

He had pretended to be an anesthesiologist because he had been so eager to impress her — she was such an impressive high-powered businesswoman herself.

He could explain why police had found cyanide capsules in his desert storage unit. He had multiple sclerosis, and kept the poison in case he needed a quick exit.

He could explain his cruel, threatening texts to her. It was the hospital drugs.

The restraining orders? Those were other John Meehans.

His arrest for stealing surgical drugs in the Midwest? His then-wife was trying to frame him and get custody of the kids.

The claim that he solicited the murders of cops and witnesses from the Orange County jail? The fantasy of a jailhouse snitch.

His nickname, Dirty John? A mistake. He had no idea where that came from.

***

The idea of returning to him seemed crazy, and then less crazy, and finally a real possibility. He had her doubting what she had read — it seemed so at odds with the repentant, vulnerable John who kept writing to her in late March 2015.

"I will do whatever it takes to make your life easier," he wrote. "I can travel with you and be there for you. No more lonely nights and no more being alone. I am your husband. That means forever. There is nothing to debate. This is going to work. Forever means forever."

And: "When you are near me I want to protect you and be certain you are safe. It's a good feeling. It's just a bit odd feeling dependent on someone. Even married I never did. Bad habit I guess. I love you Deb. Nothing can take that away."

And: "God put me here for you. You can't see that?"

And: "I love you more than the entire world. Come with me to the four corners of the world."

John told her he needed her. He had multiple sclerosis, after all. She wouldn't abandon him to his illness, would she?

Debra made sure John understood that one day her children would inherit all her money. That was fine, John told her. All he needed was her. He liked to say that he would rather be with her, broke, living under a bridge, than living in a mansion without love.

***

She didn't tell her family. She knew they'd be furious. She didn't tell her employees. She knew they would look away. But she began sneaking away to see him. And she began quietly looking for another place with him. Their Balboa Island house was full of bad memories.

By June 2015 they were living in an apartment near the Irvine Spectrum shopping-and-entertainment center. He put up photos of their wedding and their travels. "He treated me so well," she would say. "It was as if I was the only thing on Earth."

To explain why Debra Newell returned to John Meehan, in the face of so much evidence, is not easy. He had deceived accomplished women before. A PR professional. A gynecologist. A nurse anesthetist who said it was not about the brain, and added, "The heart is a different organ."

Maybe part of the explanation lay elsewhere, in the peculiar dynamics of Debra Newell's family. It was a family steeped in Christian faith and the concept of forgiveness, even taken to extremes.

***

Debra's older sister, Cindi, was still in her teens when she married Billy Vickers. She was beautiful and vivacious and headstrong. He was a balding supermarket manager who loved football. They had two boys and lived in Garden Grove.

Cindi told her mother, Arlane Hart, that he had become possessive, that he wouldn't let her go shopping or wear a bikini to the beach— he feared another man might pick her up.

She met a professional football player in Palm Springs. She was flattered by the attention. He would send his limo by to pick her up. The marriage foundered. She wanted a divorce. Hart remembers her son-in-law saying, "I can't let her go."

On March 8, 1984, Cindi was writing out checks at the house they had just sold. Her husband pulled out a chrome-plated .25-caliber pistol with a black plastic handle. He stood behind her, raised the gun and pressed it against the back of her neck.

He fired one bullet into her and another into his own stomach, just below the belly button. He called an emergency dispatcher and said, "I shot myself."

Later that day, Hart's doorbell rang. Police stood with their hats on their chests and told her the news. This is her description of what happened next:

"I lifted my hands toward heaven and I just said, 'God, you've gotta help me. I cannot do this alone. You've gotta help me, God. Help me, God.' I'd been a Christian since I was a little girl. I knew God personally. And all of a sudden I felt a sense of peace come over me, and it drifted down all through my body, and I breathed a deep breath and I looked at the policeman and I said, 'I'm gonna be OK.' "

Her 11-year-old grandson Shad was in another room, watching TV. She told him that his dad had killed his mom. "He looked up at me right then and he said, 'You know, Abraham Lincoln didn't have a mother.' And I said, 'Yes. That's right. You're right, Shad, and look what he turned out to be.' He said, 'I know I can get through this too, like you, Grandma.' "

Billy Vickers recovered from his self-inflicted wound and apologized to Hart for killing her daughter. She told him she still loved him. "And he said, 'How could you love me? How could you?' And I said, 'God has given that love to us for you. We love you, and we forgive you.' And he just sobbed and he cried."

Vickers was charged with first-degree murder and could have gone to prison for life. At a preliminary hearing, a witness named Carol Planchon testified that he came by her house to borrow her husband's gun about two weeks before the shooting. She joked, "Don't hold up a liquor store."

Planchon's husband testified that he never gave Vickers permission to take his gun and worried that Vickers would harm himself. He called Vickers repeatedly and asked to have it back, and Vickers replied, "I don't have it anymore. I got rid of it."

As the trial approached, the defense attorney, James Riddet, received a call that astonished him. The victim's mother wanted to testify on behalf of her daughter's killer. She didn't believe he had been in his right mind, and she loved him.

Her testimony stunned the prosecutor, Thomas Avdeef, who regarded it as a cold-blooded execution. As he interpreted it, the mother's testimony— and that of other family members whose names he doesn't recall— portrayed Cindi as having mistreated her husband.

"They threw her under the bus," Avdeef says. "I don't know the dynamics of the family. I could never understand that. Why say bad things about the victim?"

The defense attorney called on psychologists to make a case that Vickers had killed in a state of temporary unconsciousness. Jurors acquitted Vickers of murder but deadlocked on lesser charges. The prosecutor planned to retry the case, but then Vickers pleaded guilty to voluntary manslaughter.

In exchange, he got a five-year sentence. He got credit for time served, credit for good behavior, and he was out before Christmas 1986. The consequence of forgiveness was this: Billy Vickers spent two years, nine months and nine days in lockup for shooting his wife in the head. Vickers did not respond to requests for comment.

***

Debra disagrees with the prosecutor's interpretation of her mother's testimony. She says her parents taught her to see the good in people, always. Her dad was a youth pastor, her mom a piano teacher. They made it a point to take in troubled kids and give them another chance. They taught that it was important to see the good in everyone, even when it was hard. They believed that none of God's children was irredeemable, and enough love could work wonders.

Her sister's killer remarried and stayed in Orange County, not far from the scene of his crime. For years she'd see him in the bleachers at her nephews' football games and at family functions, and people were careful not to bring up Cindi.

Now and then Debra ran into him at Mariners church, and she'd say hello, she'd try to be polite, but she didn't want to be around him.

Forgiveness might have brought her mother peace, Debra says, but she was never able to do it herself. Her inability to do so made her wonder if something was wrong with her, so deep did the idea run.

***

And now John was the soul of repentance. He wept in church. Debra thought it showed a real desire to change. The Father's Day sermon seemed to hit him particularly hard. He said he missed his two daughters, who were being raised by their mother in another state, and thought about them every day.

He was still recovering from his hospital stay, trying to gain back the 20 pounds he'd lost, lifting weights, chugging protein shakes, frustrated at the slow pace of rebuilding his big frame.

Her kids thought it was lunacy that she had returned to John. And Meehan wanted her kids— particularly her oldest ones— out of her life. He blamed them for the troubles in the marriage, blamed them for hiring a private eye to probe his past, blamed them for temporarily turning his wife against him.

John's hatred for Debra's family did not seem to extend to Terra, Debra's youngest and quietest daughter, even though she had clashed with him. He found her the least troublesome of his stepdaughters.

So he didn't object when Debra drove out to Vegas to console Terra when she broke up with her boyfriend that summer. In the breakup, Terra got Cash, their miniature Australian shepherd.

Terra moved back to California and started applying for jobs. She found one as a kennel attendant and dog groomer. She loved the company of animals.

Terra feared and disliked John— he was the reason she sometimes carried a pocketknife.

She said she was willing to sit down with him and try to work things out, believing he would never take her up on it.

Her sister Jacquelyn was upset with Terra for seeming to give John a chance.

"Terra's a lot more like my mom, where she wants to believe the best in people rather than see any of the bad things," Jacquelyn would say. "I could probably be a little bit more like them, it would do me some good, but I just couldn't see anything good in him, just all bad."

Much of Debra's family was in disbelief. They pulled away from her. In some cases, they wouldn't let her see her grandkids. It was the price of having John in her life. Even her mother had trouble understanding why she stuck with him.

"It totally, totally wrecked the family for many months. The family was just torn apart. We didn't get together because of that," Hart said. "Everyone was talking about it. Why is Debbie staying with this guy?"

In the months to come, Hart would become terrified another daughter would be killed. "I kept praying, 'God, I don't want to lose another daughter. Not another one.' I just say, 'God, help, I didn't know how to pray.' Whatever God needed to do, I just wanted that man out of our lives."

Shad, the 11-year-old who had lost his mother to his father's bullet, was now in his 40s and estranged from the aunt he had cherished as a second mother.

When he tried to reach Debra, John menaced him with texts and emails. Shad tried to block his phone number, and John found him. Shad got off Facebook, and still John found him.

He thought, "I'm done." If Debra wanted to be with John, she wouldn't see Shad or his daughters anymore.

Shad stopped trying to reach her. John left him alone.

***

Debra had cut John out of her will months back, for fear that he might kill her, and though she went to sleep beside him and woke up beside him, it was impossible to completely banish that fear.

He keep getting sick and needing to go to the ER. Maybe it's drugs, Debra thought. She couldn't be sure of anything anymore. She just wanted it to work. Her estrangement from her kids and grandkids was breaking her heart.

Her sister had been killed trying to flee a bad marriage. What was John capable of doing, if she tried?

"I realized," she would say, "that he's not going to be that easy to leave."

CHAPTER FIVE OF SIX

ESCAPE

John insisted he'd been a victim, in case after case. To prove it, he planned to unleash lawsuits against his accusers. The attorney he approached had other ideas.

This couple is all wrong, the lawyer thought.

There sat the husband, John Meehan, glowering wrathfully as he plotted legal mayhem on his enemies.

There sat the wife, Debra Newell, soft-voiced and love-struck and helplessly in his grip.

As he gazed across a conference-room table at his newest clients in April 2015, attorney John Dzialo sensed that Debra was in danger.

The lawyer had not wanted to take this case, though Debra had paid an upfront $25,000 fee. His paralegal had been chilled, looking into Meehan's background. Extortion. Stalking. Harassment.

And now Meehan wanted the lawyer to prove that he had been the victim, in case after case. His plan was a salvo of lawsuits. Against an ex-girlfriend whose accusations had put him in prison. Against cops. Against another woman he swore had cheated him.

Debra wanted help too. She wanted to fix her fractured relationship with her kids, who believed her husband only wanted her money. Could anything be done?

A post-nup, Dzialo explained. If they got divorced, it would cut John off from Debra's money.

Meehan did not erupt, but he crossed his arms. He sank into his seat. His lips tightened. His eyes were hazel, but they filled with a fury so intense that Dzialo would recall them as "black as coal." Dzialo sensed a "seething cauldron" in the man's brain, a rage that looked as if it would split his forehead.

There are tales of encounters with religious personages so holy that their aura persists in memory, years later. It was like that for Dzialo, only inverted. Meeting Meehan would stay with him as a glimpse into some kind of human abyss.

"Scariest man I've met in my 70 years," he would say.

He took the case; maybe he could help her.

***

John Meehan didn't begin screaming until Dzialo called to say he had looked into his allegations and didn't see the basis for lawsuits.

"I'm done! You're fired!" Meehan yelled.

Dzialo had predicted this. He said he'd figure out his bill and return the remainder of the money.

Meehan demanded every penny. He would expose him as a cheat. He would tell the bar. He would tell prosecutors. He would ruin him.

Dzialo had put some time into the case, he had bills to pay, and he hated the thought of surrendering to threats. No way. Then he remembered those bottomless-pit eyes and thought, "This is a guy who would do anything." He cut the check.

It did not stop Meehan from complaining to the bar. Because he couldn't get through to Debra by phone, Dzialo drove out to her Irvine business and left her a note. What did she think of this? Soon Meehan was screaming through the phone:

"If you ever contact my wife again, you are going to regret it!"

***

John told her he wanted to die in her arms, that the world was a dark place without her. He got Debra's car washed, ran her errands, dropped off packages at the post office. He brought her flowers constantly.

It was strange to be in love with someone and fear him at the same time. She came home from work anxious about finding him with another woman. When they went to the dog park with their golden retriever, Murphy, she noticed a woman who kept smiling at her husband. Had they shared something?

She had wanted so badly for this, her fifth marriage, to work. It was hard to accept another failure. She didn't think she could endure another divorce. She thought, "How can I keep getting this so wrong?"

But the size of her mistake was dawning on her. And now she was wearing a mask, trying to buy time, trying to figure out how to escape.

At times, John seemed to sense that something had changed. "You don't look at me the same way," he would say. "I know you're going to leave me."

She told him it was just his imagination. She was busy at work; she was stressed; she was sorry. To pacify him, she'd make him one of his favorite meals: pork roast with vegetables or jambalaya.

Sometimes they had the semblance of a normal domestic life. At night he'd watch TV while she sat reading beside him. He liked "Lockup," the documentary series about life behind bars, and "Intervention," the show about addiction— two subjects with which he had intimate experience.

His favorite show was MTV's "Ridiculousness," which specialized in the mockery of people who did stupid things and got hurt. It always made John laugh.

***

In December 2015, for their one-year anniversary, he typed out a two-page love letter. It was a treacly bonbon with an arsenic center. It reminded her that between her family and her husband, there was room only for him.

One year ... and forever means forever. It's been an interesting year to say the least. We've been through some hard times ... complicated times. But at the end of the day I have you to myself. No family and no issues that we can't work out. I love you. You have the kindest, most forgiving heart I have ever known...

I want to grow old with you. Hear you breath[e] in the middle of the night. Feel you reach for me when there is nothing else between us. I can't imagine living without you ... and your absolutely nutty family. I hope to get over what they did ...

You are simply the best person I have ever known with the biggest heart imaginable. I wish I was more like you ... I wish I knew you when we were both younger. I can only imagine how ditzy you must have been and how you could have made me laugh until I couldn't see straight. It would have been a dream to have a child with you ...

I love you. I love the way you smell and the way you drift off to la-la land while I'm talking to you. I love the feel of you. And needless to say ... making love to you is about as close to a religious experience that I have EVER had ...

I hope I am a better husband than the others. I hope I am a good man and that you are proud to hold my hand. I hope you look at me the same way you do now but in twenty years ... I hope you love me and we grow old together. I hope ...

***

She was no longer thinking about forever. She was hiding money. She took $2,000 from every paycheck and gave it to a daughter or a friend. She didn't want him to have access to all her money, for fear he'd take it. And she didn't want him to know she was still giving money to her kids.

He didn't even want her seeing her kids, particularly Jacquelyn, who had been so vocal in her contempt for him. One day he caught Debra sneaking away to see her and said he'd throw Jacquelyn in the ocean if it happened again.

When he discovered that Debra had been paying for Jacquelyn's real estate classes, he called the school to malign her. He sent Jacquelyn lewd messages. She sent him a Googled image of a pile of feces.

"Mommy wants nothing to do with you and that will kill you," he texted her.

And: "Jumping off a tall building would make me smile. Head first will work."

***

This is sick, Debra thought. In March 2016— after a year and three months of marriage, after threats and lies and the blind, desperate hope that everything would turn out if she just loved hard enough, after taking him back when everyone said it defied all sense— she decided it was over.

She withdrew $120,000 from her bank account, hoping he wouldn't notice. She had $30,000 stashed in the bottom drawer in a closet— banded stacks of hundred-dollar bills— but he found it and dropped it in front of her.

She told him it was hers. He said, everything yours is mine.

He told her to hit him. He would make sure she never got up again. She grabbed some makeup, just one shoe, and left.

***

They had been dividing their time between Orange County and Henderson, Nev., where she had bought a house in the hope of keeping John away from her children.

Now she and Jacquelyn hurried out there to pack her stuff into a moving truck. Debra put tape over the camera lenses, in case John was watching.

She found a family-law attorney, Michael R. O'Neil, who filed to annul the marriage in April 2016. If Debra had glimpsed a frightening side of him during their first separation, John now seemed a creature of pure malignancy.

"You get your family," he wrote. "I got the dog. I got the better deal."

He demanded money. He would drain her accounts through the divorce courts if she fought him.

"For once in your holier than thou life, listen to me," he wrote. "You are going to have to pay both sides. Which could easily take a year."

And: "We had a good run except for your family. There is no trust. But the last thing I want to do is break you."

He sent her a photo of himself with a provocatively posed ex-girlfriend, taunting her. He threatened to ruin her.

"Make yourself available or I ruin a family. There are children involved, Deb. This is bigger than you," he wrote. "You're selfish to allow this. You'll never forgive yourself but I am doing it."

He called her a crook on Yelp. He had once coaxed naked photos out of her, and now he posted them to her nephew's Facebook page. He texted her that he knew where she was when she picked up her grandchild.

He lectured her. "You don't know how to live. Sex is not love. Get help."

He accused her of assaulting him. "It's pathetic it's come to this point, but you leave me with no options after your storm of lies."

"Storm of lies!" she replied. "Wow. You are the expert in that area."

He had entered their marriage with only a few boxes, mostly old clothes, and now he accused her of stealing $120,000 in cash and gold coins from him.

He complained that he shouldn't have to live on the $558 monthly disability checks he received for his bad back. He demanded $7,000 a month in spousal support and $75,000 in attorney's fees.

"It doesn't matter that paying support isn't what a 'real' man demands. It's what the court feels is equitable. That's all that matters. Think Deb. There is no alternative to this unless you start thinking. That, or you will eventually get bled dry," he wrote. "Be smart Deb. You have no idea of the mistakes you made. Be smart and you'll save a fortune."

He had posed as her soul mate, the answer to her longings after four failed marriages, and now he used her past as a barb.

"You think I'm going to allow your family to continue. Look in the mirror. Five times and still making the same mistakes," he wrote. "Now you're getting yours. Pray Deb. Pray hard."

He had turned himself into a churchgoing Christian and wept during sermons, knowing God mattered to her, and now he used her faith as a cudgel.

"Everyone is a better Christian than you," he wrote. "Paybacks are costly and a bitch."

He had rhapsodized endlessly about her beauty and promised she would never know loneliness again, and now turned her vulnerabilities into points of attack.

"You lying old bag," he wrote. "You'll grow old alone."

He sent her a list of her clients— builders who used her interior design business— and threatened to call them twice a day.

"I don't trust anything you say," she replied. "You're evil."

"Face it Deb, I'm smarter than you."

"Stop! Don't contact me again or I will go to the police!"

***

She began wearing a wig, living and working out of hotels, checking in under the names of her assistants. In a request for a restraining order, her lawyer laid out John Meehan's long, ugly history. How the Indiana nursing board had yanked his license and called him "a clear and immediate danger to the public."

How he'd jumped out of a moving ambulance in Michigan. How he'd swindled multiple women and done prison time and been slapped with restraining orders. How Laguna Beach police, who had also asked for a restraining order against him, had found cyanide capsules in his belongings.

An Orange County judge decided there was no immediate threat to Debra's safety. Her husband lived in another state; he had never physically harmed her.

***

If there was any chance of trying again, Debra undermined it when she visited John at the Henderson house soon afterward. She thought she could talk him into an annulment. She suggested they might even try to start fresh, afterward, with no lies— it was the only thing she could think of to say.

He looked terrible. He said he had terminal cancer. He wouldn't hear of it. Hadn't she promised "Till death do us part?" How could she leave him to die alone?

Trying to buy time, she wrote him a $10,000 check to rehab the Henderson house and told him he could stay there while they figured things out. She slept on a mattress on the floor that night.

"I'm dying Deb. Slowly dying. Please just come up with something so we can move on," he texted her when she got back to California. "I'm doing horrible without you. I need you."

O'Neil knew what a judge would say. How scared of him could she be?

***

O'Neil thought, "Just a sick son of a bitch." He believed his threats were probably idle. He thought this until June 11, 2016, when Debra's $64,000 sport-model Jaguar XF disappeared from in front of her Irvine office.

Grainy surveillance footage showed John, in jeans, crouched behind the bushes, watching the car that morning. And it showed him coming back about an hour later wearing gloves and a painter's uniform to steal it.

The car turned up a block away, reeking of gas, with fire damage to the seat and doors. As arson, it was a display of incompetence. The windows were rolled up, the doors closed, so the fire had extinguished itself for lack of oxygen.

June passed, then July. Now it was the third week of August, and Irvine police still hadn't charged him.

Debra was living with Jacquelyn at the Carlyle Apartments in Irvine, near the airport. Jacquelyn liked that there were security cameras.

Debra had cut John off. She wasn't taking his calls or texts. She and her kids were looking after John's golden retriever, Murphy, which he'd left at a pound. And she had the Buick Enclave he'd been using, which had been impounded after he ran it into a gate.

***

On Friday, Aug. 19, 2016, Terra was working at Rebel Run, a Newport Beach dog kennel. A man called with what sounded like a French accent.

The man made it sound as though they had met at some point, and wanted to know if she would be working tomorrow; he wanted to bring in his Rhodesian ridgebacks for her to groom.

She did not recognize the voice, or remember having met him, or think too much about the fact that most of the grooming requests came from women, not men. She told the stranger her work schedule. Yes, she would be there tomorrow until about 5 p.m.

***

Around 11:30 that night, Jacquelyn was returning from dinner with a male friend when she saw John in a car, in the dark, waiting outside her apartment gate.

She saw him reflected in the glow of his smartphone, and they locked eyes. John ducked his head. She told her friend, "Follow him!"

Jacquelyn watched John head onto the 405 Freeway. John had smashed or removed the lights on his car, as if to improve his ability to move furtively in the dark.

Jacquelyn believed John was there to kill her or her mom. That he had been hoping to catch one of them alone, an easy target, and the presence of her male friend scared John off.

Debra was skeptical of her daughter's account about seeing John. She thought the guy probably had just looked like John, that Jacquelyn was overreacting. They didn't call police.

Jacquelyn wanted to know: What if he goes after Terra? Debra didn't share this fear; a psychologist had told her the danger was to her, not to her children. Plus, what had Terra ever done to him? She thought he even seemed to like her, sort of.

But Jacquelyn told her friend to drive to the Coronados, the sprawling apartment complex in next-door Newport Beach where Terra was living.

Jacquelyn circled her sister's apartment complex. She checked her sister's door at Apartment W304, to make sure it was locked. She listened for the reassuring jingle of the collar of her sister's cat. She didn't want to wake her.

She called Terra at 6 a.m. and said, "John's in the area. He's in a white Camry."

In the dark, Jacquelyn had misidentified the car John was driving. Terra would be watching for the wrong one.

CHAPTER SIX OF SIX

TERRA

She always sensed John was dangerous. Her sister told her to keep her pocketknife handy. But her mind was elsewhere that day, and she was on the lookout for the wrong car.

John Meehan bragged frequently about his supposed ties to organized crime, and claimed to trace his bloodline to the prolific East Coast hit man who had run Murder Inc. itself. It had the ring of empty boasting from a man who lived by lies.

What is believable is that he approved of the mob's way of doing business, particularly when it came to dealing with enemies. Over and over, he spoke approvingly of a cold-blooded ethos: A dead enemy couldn't suffer, so you went after their loved ones. You went after their families.

***

Terra Newell was 25. Everyone described her as "sweet." Her voice, a soft singsong, forced people to lean in. As a kid, the smallest on the team, she was so uncompetitive in softball games that she didn't bother swinging at pitches.

Terra was a child of the upscale Orange County suburbs but adored country music, and she liked the songs about drinking beer, having a good time and loving God. It had started with a high school crush on a boy from Oklahoma, in the same way her current obsession with "The Walking Dead" had started with her ex-boyfriend Jimmy.

Like the company of dogs, music made her forget her anxiety. For years, Terra had lived with a vague sense of dread. When she was around 6, she woke up screaming, believing that someone had climbed through her bedroom window to snatch her. Her parents didn't call police.

Her mother thought maybe it was a dream, the function of Terra's distress over what was happening in the house. Her parents were fighting a lot, and were soon divorced. Terra had frequent nightmares at that age. She'd see dark shapes and become convinced they were ghosts or aliens.

Over the years, she said, she wondered whether she was a little bit crazy. In therapy she questioned whether the abduction memory was a real one, but became convinced it had actually happened.

When she was a teenager, a guy she'd been dating flipped out and rammed a car into her leg; she said he was on meth. She got a tattoo on her foot that said "Psalms 23" — the Lord is my shepherd— with a heart she'd seen in a Taylor Swift video.

***

Early on, even before John became her stepfather, Terra sensed he was dangerous. She had sobbed uncontrollably at a Christmas gathering, saying, "There's just something wrong about him. I don't like him." But not everyone felt what she felt; for the longest time, her mother certainly didn't.

She sensed that John was somehow watching her. She liked to have friends crash at her Newport Beach apartment so she would not be alone.

Once she had a dream that John was attacking her, and she had to stab him to save herself. She wrote out a note and put it in her drawer. If anything happened to her, it said, she wanted Jimmy to get Cash, the miniature Australian shepherd.

She was not a brawler and had no martial arts background except for a long-ago self-defense class in PE. She did, however, study television violence with uncommon intensity.

In "The Walking Dead," she absorbed the first axiom of combat with zombies: They will keep trying to kill you until you destroy the head, by blade or screwdriver, machete or gun. She regarded the show as a fount of survival tricks. When a favorite character extricated himself from a bad spot by biting into an attacker's jugular, she thought, "My teeth are a weapon."

More than technique, she said, she took a certain mind-set from the show:

"Kill or be killed."

***

Keep your pocketknife handy, her sister Jacquelyn warned her on the morning of Saturday, Aug. 20, 2016. She had spotted John in town last night.

Terra acknowledged the warning, but her mind was elsewhere. She and a girlfriend had $100 lawn-seat tickets to see Jason Aldean, one of her favorite country acts, who would perform that night at Irvine Meadows.

She put on her rain boots and drove to work at the Newport Beach dog kennel. She greeted the Labs and terriers and Dobermans and poodle mixes. She unlocked the cages. She carried the big bag of dried, high-protein pellets to the bowls. She hosed out the cages and the concrete dog runs. She had strong, round shoulders, strengthened by years of working with large, aggressive dogs.

The French-sounding guy who was supposed to bring in his Rhodesian ridgebacks never showed, but she didn't think much of it. She left work in her Toyota Prius just after 5 p.m. for the three-mile drive home. Cash was in the back seat. It was still full daylight.

***

John Meehan had removed the license plate from the gray 2016 Dodge Dart he had rented.

Inside the car, he had his passport, a vial of injectable testosterone, and what police called a "kidnap kit."

An Oakley backpack.

Camouflage duct tape.

Cable ties.

A set of kitchen knives.

***

Terra pulled up to the Coronados, the sprawling block-long complex where she lived. It was not Newport Beach's choicest ZIP Code. People who lived there said it was common to overhear domestic fights and common to look the other way.

Now she drove up the ramp and through the sliding gate to the elevated outdoor parking lot. She always parked in the same stall, SR 423. She saw the Dodge Dart backed into a nearby stall, a man fidgeting in the trunk with a tire iron. She brushed it off, even when Cash growled. She was eager to get to the concert.

She had Mace in her car, pepper spray in her purse, a pocketknife in her apartment, and no weapon in her hands when she climbed out of the car.

***

He had been formidably big, 6 feet 2 and 230 pounds of steroidal muscle, a survivor of jail or prison cells in at least three states. He had lost serious weight— he was down to 163— but Terra was still a foot shorter and 33 pounds lighter. He had the element of surprise. He had a long silver knife, concealed inside a Del Taco bag. It bore no resemblance to a fair fight.

***

She was crossing behind her car with Cash, and suddenly John Meehan's arm was enwrapping her waist, his eyes cold. "Do you remember me?" he said.

He clapped his hand over her mouth. She bit down. She screamed. Cash lunged for his ankles.

Meehan jabbed at Terra with the taco bag. She realized there was a knife inside. She threw up her forearm to protect her chest. Her arm opened. They wrestled. They tumbled to the pavement.

***

Blond, small-boned Skylar Sepulveda, 14, who didn't know Terra but looked as though she could have been her little sister, had just pedaled home on her beach cruiser from junior-lifeguard training at the Balboa Pier.

She was in apartment T302, wearing only a T-shirt-covered swimsuit, when she heard the screaming and went to the window that overlooked the parking lot. She saw Terra struggling on her back, and Meehan above her, the knife raised over his head.

Skylar told her mom to call police, grabbed her beach towel and said, "I gotta go." Barefoot, she rushed out the door, rushed down the apartment stairs, rushed toward the parking-lot stairs.

Scores of balconies overlooked the lot, and she saw people standing on them, grown men and women, just watching. She saw others walking their dogs, as if the blood-curdling screams weren't splitting the air.

"Going on with their daily lives," she would recall. She saw some people get into their cars. She felt what she called "total disgust with people."

Skylar— a girl with wrists so thin a grown man could have encircled them with one hand— did not pause long enough to worry that the attacker might turn the knife on her when she got to the scene. She just knew she would blame herself if something awful happened that she could have stopped.

***

Now John Meehan's long silver knife was free of the taco bag, and he was striking downward.

The rain boots Terra wore that day were her sturdy pair, with thick tread.

She was on her back, pedal-kicking, trying to save herself, when she clipped his knife hand.

The blade flew from his grip.

It fell to the pavement.

It fell with the handle pointed toward her.

It fell inches from her right hand.

She was right-handed. She didn't think. She began flailing, looking for targets. She connected, again and again.

His shoulder. His shoulder blade. His triceps. His shoulder blade. His upper back. His shoulder blade. His upper back. Between his shoulder blades. His forearm. His triceps. His shoulder. His chest.

His left eye— and through it— into his brain.

***

When she reached the top of the steps, Skylar Sepulveda found John Meehan face-down, bleeding and convulsing. Terra was crawling away, shaking, screaming about how he had stalked her and tortured her family.

Skylar could see exposed muscle in a gash on Terra's forearm, like a surgeon's incision.

Skylar wrapped it with a beach towel and tried to calm her down. She asked her questions: "What is your birthday?" It happened they had the same July birthday. Terra was terrified that her attacker would get up and come at her again. Someone else had arrived and was checking on him.

"He can't get up," Skylar said. "He can't hurt you."

Terra picked up her cellphone and called her mom. "I'm really, really sorry," she said. "I think I killed your husband."

John Meehan was not breathing when the police arrived, and had no pulse. They administered CPR, and soon his pulse was back, and he began to take small, short breaths as they rushed him away in an ambulance.

In another ambulance, Terra Newell asked if she would be done in time to get to the Jason Aldean concert, and they said no, but they turned on some country music. They let Cash ride with her.

***

Shad Vickers thought of how many times John had done evil and escaped the law, and how if anyone might rise from the dead to hurt them again, it was him. Even now, he seemed larger than he was, like a horror-movie villain.

Meehan's sister Donna heard the news and didn't rule out the possibility of some trick. Her brother knew every kind.

His other sister, Karen, was summoned to the Santa Ana hospital where he lay unconscious with 13 stab wounds. She had long ago come to accept that her brother would die unnaturally. Maybe of an overdose, maybe in a confrontation. Not like this.

Debra Newell did not want to be responsible for pulling the plug. She let Karen, a nurse, decide. Karen looked at the brain scans and gave the OK. A transplant team tried to harvest his organs, but years of drug use had ravaged them.

John Meehan— drug addict, failed law student, disgraced nurse anesthetist, fake doctor, prolific grifter, black-hearted Lothario and terror of uncountable women— was declared dead at age 57 on Aug. 24, 2016, four days after he had attacked Terra Newell.

Debra was numb. She and Karen were led to a room in a Santa Ana funeral home where his body lay in a long, plain cardboard box. They watched the lid go on the box and the box go in the oven. The door closed, he turned into black smoke, and that was all. There was no memorial service.

***

News of Meehan's death made the local papers, with scant details. "I just wanted to hear he is really dead," said an ex-girlfriend who called police, then cried in relief.

People were trying to reckon the improbability of the outcome. "Impossible," said Shad. "The last person on Earth I'd ever think would send John to hell would be Terra."

Detectives told the prosecutor, Matt Murphy, that it looked like a clear-cut case of self-defense. In such scenarios, the killer usually wound up on the run, the victim dead, dumped off a freeway or in the desert.

Blind luck, the gift of adrenaline, Meehan's drug-weakened condition, Terra's instinctive refusal to comply with his script— all of them had helped to save her.

"Ninety-nine times out of 100, the nice person is the one that is dead," Murphy said. "Every once in a while, good guys win."

***

She was not going to take any chances, and so her last strike had been through the eye.

"I guess that was my zombie kill," Terra said. "You need to kill their brain. That's what I did."

Had she killed a man loved by someone, somewhere? This bothered her. Then Donna came by with flowers and told her, "You did a good thing." Her brother had hardly known his daughters. He was as isolated a man as ever lived.

Terra went back to the dog kennel, but barking triggered memories of the attack, and she had to quit. Sometimes she'd see a man roughly John's age, and she'd struggle to breathe. For a while she smoked pot to get to sleep, but it made her paranoid and irritable. So she gave it up, but then nightmares flooded her sleep.

She found a therapist, who helped her build a place in her mind where she could go when things felt overwhelming. She thought of a lake in Montana where she used to go with her dad. She put dragonflies in the picture, and, as her protector, her dog.

***

Debra Newell still struggles with guilt that she brought John into her family's life.

She's close with her kids again. She recently bought her daughters stun guns, pepper spray and rape whistles. They talk every day, sometimes just to say "I love you." She doesn't need a boyfriend or a husband, a year later, and said she has no desire to date. She works constantly.

She said she feels she's over John. At the Nevada house where he'd been living, she found a clutter of drug vials and syringes. She found some 200 women on the laptop he used, some of them described with references to their anatomy. She found that he was flirting on three dating sites on the day they were married.

She has concluded that he was some kind of sociopath. But for months she tormented herself, trying to figure out what was real. On her side, the love was genuine and deep, and it was hard to imagine that he had been lying every second, every minute, every day.

Not long after the attack, she took out her iPad and called up footage of their Las Vegas wedding. She watched as they exchanged rings and he smiled down at her tenderly.

She turned away from the screen. She had a catch in her throat, and a question.

"Doesn't he look happy?"

Twelve Seconds of Gunfire

THE WASHINGTON POST

June 11, 2017

by John Woodrow Cox

In Tiny Townville, S.C., First-Graders Are Haunted by What They Survived—And Lost—on a School Playground

Recess had finally started, so Ava Olsen picked up her chocolate cupcake, then headed outside toward the swings. And that's when the 7-year-old saw the gun.

It was black and in the hand of someone the first-graders on the playground would later describe as a thin, towering figure with wispy blond hair and angry eyes. Dressed in dark clothes and a baseball cap, he had just driven up in a Dodge Ram, jumping out of the pickup as it rolled into the chain-link fence that surrounded the play area. It was 1:41 on a balmy, blue-sky afternoon in late September, and Ava's class was just emerging from an open door directly in front of him to join the other kids already outside. At first, a few of them assumed he had come to help with something or to say hello.

Then he pulled the trigger.

"I hate my life," the children heard him scream in the same moment he added Townville Elementary to the long list of American schools redefined by a shooting.

A round struck the shoulder of Ava's teacher, who was standing at the green metal door before she yanked it shut. But the shooter kept firing, shattering a glass window.

Near the cubbies inside, 6-year-old Collin Edwards felt his foot vibrate, then burn, as if he had stepped in a fire. A bullet had blown through the inside of his right ankle and popped out beneath his big toe, punching a hole in the sole of his Velcro-strapped sneaker. As his teachers pulled him away from the windows, Collin recalled later, he spotted a puddle of blood spreading across the gray wax tile floor in the hallway. Someone else, he realized, had been hurt, too.

Outside, Ava had dropped her cupcake. The Daisy Scout remembered what her mom had said: If something doesn't feel right, run. She sprinted toward the far side of the building, rounding a corner to safety. Nowhere in sight, though, was Jacob Hall, the tiny boy with oversize, thick-lensed glasses Ava had decided to marry when they grew up. He had been just a few steps behind her at the door, but she never saw him come out. Ava hoped he was okay.

Standing on the wood chips near a yellow tube slide, Siena Kibilko felt stunned. Until that moment, her most serious concern had been which "How to Train Your Dragon" toy she would get for her upcoming seventh birthday.

"Run!" Siena recalled a teacher shouting, and she did.

Karson Robinson, one of the biggest kids in class, hadn't waited for instructions. At the initial sound of gunshots, he scrambled over a fence on the opposite side of the playground and briefly headed toward the baseball fields where, as a Townville Giant, he had gotten his first recreation league hit. Karson then turned back to the school and found his classmates banging on a door.

"Let us in," Siena begged, and the kids were hustled inside.

The gunfire had stopped by then, and, in a room on the other side of the school, Collin had discovered the source of all that blood.

Sprawled on the floor was Jacob, the boy Ava adored. At 3½ feet tall, he was the smallest child in first grade — everyone's kid brother. On the green swings at recess, Collin would call him "Little J" because that always made Jacob cackle in a way that made everyone else laugh, too. But now his eyes were closed, and Collin wondered whether they would ever open again.

"Press, press, press," an automated defibrillator repeated as the school nurse pushed on Jacob's chest, trying to keep him alive. "Give breath. Give breath."

"Look at me," a teacher urged Collin, but the boy couldn't stop staring at his friend.

On a gray wall inside Townville Elementary's front lobby hangs a framed dreamcatcher, and beneath its blue beads and brown feathers is a Native American phrase: "Let Us See Each Other Again."

It was among hundreds of items — letters, ornaments, photos, posters, plush toys — that deluged the school of 290 students after the Sept. 28 attack. But the dreamcatcher held special meaning. It had been sent to four other schools ravaged by gun violence, and the names of each were listed on the back: Columbine High in Colorado, Red Lake High in Minnesota, Sandy Hook Elementary in Connecticut, Marysville Pilchuck High in Washington state.

It is slated to travel next to North Park Elementary in San Bernardino, Calif., where in April a man killed his estranged wife, who was a teacher there, and fatally wounded an 8-year-old before taking his own life.

In each shooting's wake, the children and adults who die and those who murder them become the focus of intense national attention. Often overlooked, though, are the students who survive the violence but are profoundly changed by it.

Beginning with Columbine 18 years ago, more than 135,000 students attending at least 164 primary or secondary schools have experienced a shooting on campus, according to a Washington Post analysis of online archives, state enrollment figures and news stories. That doesn't count dozens of suicides, accidents and after-school assaults that have also exposed children to gunfire.

"A meaningful number of those kids are going to have significant struggles," said Bruce D. Perry, a psychiatrist who worked with families from Columbine and Sandy Hook. "It's stunning how one event can have this echo that will impact so many more individuals than people realized."

Every child reacts differently to violence at school, therapists have found. Some students, either immediately or later, suffer post-traumatic stress similar to that of combat veterans returning from war. Many grapple with recurring nightmares, are crippled by everyday noises, struggle to focus in classes and fear that the shooter will come after them again.

Because of the lasting damage, Townville's teachers, administrators, first responders, counselors, pastors, and parents and their children agreed to speak to The Post about what the community of 4,000 has endured over the past eight months.

They'd always felt safe in this swath of countryside, a place 40 miles southwest of Greenville that claims a single stoplight but at least six churches. Gable-roofed chicken houses stand among cow pastures and rolling fields of hay, wheat, corn and soybeans, and everyone shops at Dollar General, nicknamed the "Townville Target."

Overwhelmingly white, it is home to families that have farmed for decades, retirees with lake houses, college-educated professionals who commute up the road to Clemson University and hundreds of people in mobile homes living from one paycheck to the next.

What connects them is a beloved two-story, red-brick school where generations of children have gathered to learn and play and grow up together.

The gunman paced the sidewalk, a cellphone in his hand.

Moments earlier, as he had shifted his aim from the green metal door to the playground, his .40-caliber pistol jammed, ending his rampage 12 seconds after it began. Now Townville Principal Denise Fredericks and some of her staff congregated at the end of a second-floor hallway to keep track of him until help arrived. From behind a sign on a windowsill that read "Dream," they peered down as he walked beside the school.

Then he looked up.

"That's Jesse Osborne," a teacher gasped.

He was 14 years old.

Jesse had attended Townville — walked its halls and romped on its playground — through fifth grade, before he transferred and was later home-schooled. Not once, Fredericks said, had his behavior prompted concern. He was quiet, earned good grades and almost never got into trouble. He played catcher in the recreation league. He got invited to birthday parties.

Jesse had called his grandmother, Patsy Osborne, just minutes before he'd driven to the school that afternoon. He was screaming, she said. She couldn't understand him.

Patsy and her husband, Thomas, sped to his house, where they discovered their son — Jesse's father — slumped on a couch, eyes still open. He'd been shot to death. And Jesse had disappeared.

Then Thomas's phone rang.

It was his grandson.

"I told him not to," he recalled the teenager saying. "I told him not to do that."

His grandfather asked where he'd gone.

"I'm behind the school," Jesse said.

Thomas pulled up moments after Jesse had been subdued by an armed volunteer firefighter, arriving in time to see his handcuffed grandson loaded into the back of a patrol car.

Inside the school, 300 children and teachers cowered in locked classrooms, bathrooms and storage closets. Siena remembered someone covering up windows with paper. Karson remembered playing with markers and magnets. Ava remembered a teacher reading a story about sunflowers. They all remembered the sound of weeping.

By then, Townville's fire chief, Billy McAdams, had hurried through the first-grade door with the shot-out glass. In the classroom, he saw an alphabet rug soaked with blood.

Down the hallway, he found Jacob, whose femoral artery had been sliced by a bullet that struck his left leg. Eventually, the 6-year-old was loaded onto a gurney and taken to an awaiting helicopter, and Collin would never see his friend's eyes open again.

A week later, on a Wednesday morning in October, Jacob lay inside a miniature gray casket topped with yellow chrysanthemums and a Ninja Turtles figurine. He was dressed in a Batman costume.

Ava couldn't bear to look at him, so she sat on her mother's lap near the back of Oakdale Baptist Church and turned away.

She called him "Jakey." He was the only boy she'd ever kissed.

Nineteen days before he was shot, she had written him a note.

"Come play with me please," she scribbled in pencil. "You can play with my cats. Do you want to get married when you come? My mom will make us lunch."

At the bottom of the page, she'd drawn herself in a pink dress standing next to a bespectacled Jacob, who appeared about half her height. "I love you!" she added beside a red heart.

After the shooting, Ava realized she'd forgotten to give Jacob the letter and crumpled it into a plastic bin in her bedroom. Now she was at his funeral.

"He's not really dead, is he?" she whispered to her mother.

"Yes," Mary Olsen told her. "He is."

Jacob's family had asked that people attending the service dress like superheroes because of the boy's infatuation with them. Ava wore a Ninja Turtles top with a purple cape. Siena and Collin, who was still in a wheelchair, both dressed as Captain America.

Karson had also come, his shirt displaying a "J" within a Superman logo. But he'd hesitated in the parking lot.

"Mama, that looks like that boy's truck. Is he here?" Karson had asked, motioning toward a dark pickup.

From their seats, the children listened to the same pastor who presided at the funeral for Jesse's father three days earlier. They watched as, midway through the service, Jacob's mom staggered to his casket, then collapsed to the floor. They stared as his body was wheeled up the center aisle at the end of the memorial.

Then, just hours after their friend's funeral, they returned for the first time to the place he'd been shot.

The school, scheduled to resume classes the next day, hosted an open house that afternoon. No one knew how the kids would react, but Fredericks, the principal, believed the small step of a brief return might help with the big step of a permanent one. In Townville, where nearly 7 in 10 of the school's students live in poverty, it wasn't viable to construct a new building or bus them elsewhere.

They had to go back.

When they did that afternoon, some kids even returned to the playground. Collin rolled out on his light blue medical scooter. Siena climbed a play set.

But Ava lingered behind with her mom.

"Please don't make me go out there again," Ava said, before they eased onto the sidewalk, holding hands. With each step, the girl's fingernails dug deeper into her mother's skin.

"What if he gets out?" Siena asked her parents in the days after the shooting. Then she never stopped asking.

They explained that Jesse was in jail, that she was safe. But still, Siena obsessed over him coming for her again. Next to a sign beside her top bunk that read "Night, Night, Sweet Pea — Sweet Dreams," she relived the shooting in her nightmares.

Fredericks and her staff did all they could think of to ease the kids' dread on that first full day back, Oct. 6, when all but 10 students showed up for class. They were welcomed by uniformed officers, therapy dogs, volunteers in superhero costumes, more than 20 counselors, a line of signs — "Have a Great Day at School!" — in the parking lot.

For Siena, though, each morning included a negotiation with her parents.

"I don't want to go to school today," she would say. "I don't feel good."

At drop-off, she would search the parking lot for the cruiser of the police officer assigned to Townville Elementary after the shooting. She needed to know he was there.

One day, Siena announced to her mother, Marylea, that she couldn't go to summer camp anymore: "They don't have a police officer."

Like many of her classmates, loud, unexpected sounds petrified her. Once, outside a Publix, a car backfired, and she dropped to the ground before dashing inside. Another time, after a balloon popped at a school dance, the entire gymnasium went silent as the principal rushed to turn the lights on. Fredericks later banned balloons at the spring festival.

"Noises are different now," she said.

Siena and her friends began carrying stuffed animals as a form of protection. In those first days back at school, she would slip a tiny pink teddy bear named Lovie into her pocket and squeeze it when she walked onto the playground.

Even at home, she'd lost her sense of security. Siena, whose mom is earning a master's degree at Clemson and whose dad runs a business, lives on a peaceful cul-de-sac in a two-story house that overlooks a lake.

Siena would deadbolt the front door when no one was looking, and at the sight of unfamiliar cars, she'd scurry inside.

One afternoon, she stood in her bedroom as Marylea ran her fingers through the girl's shoulder-length brown hair. Siena again thought of Jesse as her dark eyes fixed on a pink heart taped to the wall.

"Are they going to let him out?" she asked, her finger picking at the decoration.

"Nope," her mother said.

"Ever?"

Marylea didn't want to lie. She searched for the right response, still stroking her 7-year-old's hair.

"Not any time when you're still a kid."

A month had passed since the shooting, and Karson was beginning to sleep and eat normally again, but a sense of guilt still haunted him.

"Maybe I should have waited on Jacob," he told his mother, Kayla Edmonds. "He could have jumped over the fence with me."

She insisted that he couldn't have saved Jacob's life, but Karson wouldn't be convinced. He'd stood half a foot taller than his friend. The big kids were supposed to help the little ones.

The trauma had left him with intense separation anxiety — he'd follow his mother, who works at Subway, when she stepped out for a smoke — and profound grief. He'd known Jacob since they were toddlers. They'd bounced together for hours on a trampoline. They'd giggled together playing "Grand Theft Auto," the video game with the bad words in it.

When Jacob died three days after the shooting, Karson's mom didn't tell him right away. It was his seventh birthday, and they were celebrating at Chuck E. Cheese's. On their way home, he asked, yet again, if Jacob was getting better. In that moment, she told him his friend had gone to heaven, and Karson began to cry.

After that, he didn't like it when people mentioned Jacob's name. For Valentine's Day, Karson wrote a card in his memory: "I loved him but he diyd but he is stil a life in my hart."

In the corner of his room, behind a bunk bed covered in Paw Patrol sheets, Collin rummaged through a blue plastic toy bin. His medical boot had come off months earlier, and the bullet wound had healed, leaving a dark, nickel-sized splotch on his ankle. He could run again, too, though sometimes he had to take breaks because of the pain.

Now the boy picked past a T. rex figurine, a Burger King crown, a black Franklin baseball glove, the Captain America mask he wore to Jacob's funeral.

Then Collin found what he was searching for and held up a plastic pistol with an orange cap on the barrel.

"His gun looked like that," he said, his tone matter-of-fact as he explained how the Dollar General toy from China resembled the weapon that had nearly killed him.

Of all the children who survived that day, Collin seemed the most vulnerable to psychological damage in the eyes of many Townville parents and teachers. Before learning to tie his shoes, he'd been shot and seen his friend covered in blood. But he didn't have nightmares, and he didn't think much about Jesse. At school, as long as one of his stuffed animals was within reach, he felt fine.

His father, a 200-pound construction worker, broke down about what had happened more often than Collin did. It wasn't that the boy didn't care, because he did, especially for Jacob's 4-year-old sister, Zoey, whom he'd often hug when he saw her at school.

But Collin, now 7, can discuss that day with clarity and composure.

About the bullet: "It was moving through the air super fast."

About how much it hurt: "I didn't even feel the exit hole. It was just the enter hole that had the most pain in it."

About Jacob: "He wasn't even moving."

Researchers who have studied kids for years still aren't certain why they react to trauma in such different ways.

Perhaps no one understands that better than Nelba Marquez-Greene, whose son survived the Sandy Hook massacre but whose daughter did not.

"That's a factor you can't predict — how your child is going to deal with it," said Marquez-Greene, a family therapist for the past 13 years.

She warned, however, that parents can't assume their kids have escaped the aftereffects, which sometimes don't surface for years.

"We still have this tendency to want to say, 'Okay, it's done. He's good. She's good,'" Marquez-Greene said. "That's not where the story ends."

Ava sat on the edge of a brown exam table, her eyes on the floor. It was mid-February, five months after the shooting, and her pediatrician kept asking questions.

Did she still feel scared a lot?

"Yes," Ava's mother recalled her answering.

Did she feel safe at school?

"No."

What did she not like about school?

Ava, clutching a stuffed Ninja Turtle that had once belonged to Jacob, didn't answer.

Three weeks later, the doctor filled out a state form recommending that she be home-schooled. His diagnosis: "Severe PTSD/depression, exacerbated by school attendance."

Ava — the only student pulled from Townville this school year because of the shooting — alternated between long stretches of quiet anguish and explosions of rage, her mother said. She started hitting herself and yanking out her eyelashes, and she once clawed her nails so deep into her elbow that it became infected.

Ava had mastered a cartwheel days before the shooting but no longer talked about becoming a cheerleader. Instead, she began repeating what the shooter had screamed on the playground: "I hate my life."

She stopped watching "Frozen" because Elsa's parents die. She erupted when her mother took off the necklace with the vial of Jacob's ashes his family had given them. She couldn't look at the pistol her father, a former police officer, kept in the house. She snipped glittery green and red stickers into tiny pieces, then used them to cover up scary words in "Little House on the Prairie": gun, fire, blood, kill.

The shooting had lasted just 12 seconds. Ava's parents worried it would torment their daughter for years.

They didn't know what to do, in part because their son, Cameron — just 10 months younger — had also been on the playground that day, but he fared far better in the aftermath. They sent Ava to two therapists, took her to doctors who gave her medication for anxiety, encouraged her to record her thoughts in a leopard-print journal.

"I miss Jacob," she wrote one day in March.

"I can't stop feeling mad," she scribbled one day in April.

"No one ever listens to me," she confided a few days later.

"I hate guns," she scrawled a week after that.

Ava had made progress, her parents thought, until the day before Easter, when she and her brother were playing "boat" in the bed of their dad's Chevrolet pickup outside the family's home. Suddenly, Cameron frightened her. She pushed him and he fell backward, hitting his head against a stone well. Blood trickled down the back of his neck.

"Oh, my God," she screamed.

Their parents loaded the kids into the car and rushed to the emergency room.

"I don't want to die," Cameron cried. Then Ava, fearing what she'd done to him, said:

"I'm just like Jesse."

Forty miles away, the 14-year-old at the center of it all sat inside a juvenile detention center on a recent evening and considered his future.

"I don't want to go to hell," he told Patsy, his grandmother.

Jesse, who hasn't entered a plea but could serve decades in prison if he's tried as an adult, spends most of his time reading, particularly about Mars, his family said. He wants to fly there one day.

They don't dispute the accusations against him, but they've struggled to understand why their "baby," who stands taller than 6 feet, would harm anyone.

His mother, Tiffney Osborne, remembers the wild rabbit he once rescued from the jaws of a family guard dog. Jesse kept it alive for five days in a cardboard box.

His grandmother remembers his reluctance to work with his father, Jeffrey, in their farm's chicken houses because he didn't like to break the birds' necks.

His grandfather remembers camping trips to North Carolina and the day they saw "Frozen," one of Jesse's favorites.

The teen had handled guns since he was young, but so had many other kids in Townville. His family said he was enamored with Airsoft, a paintball-like game in which players shoot one another with pellets, and that he liked to fire pistols at hay bales with his dad — just as they did the weekend before the killing.

They've all heard the theory that he shot his father because he thought Jeffrey had killed a pet bunny, Floppy. Maybe, his grandfather said, that's what Jesse meant in the call — "I told him not to do that." But maybe he fired the gun for some other reason. Father and son, Tiffney said, sometimes had heated arguments.

Jesse, his mother said she'd learned, had retrieved the pistol from her husband's nightstand and shot him from behind. After his arrest, he confided to her that he didn't want his dad to suffer, so when Jesse realized Jeffrey was still moving after the first bullet, he kept firing.

The teen told the firefighter who restrained him that he'd lost faith in God and didn't know what else to do, said McAdams, the fire chief. Jesse also told the firefighter that he was sorry.

His mother and grandparents insist they didn't see that bloody day coming, but Jesse may have offered at least one sign he was capable of violence. In seventh grade, his family said, he was kicked out of school after bullies harassed him and he snapped. A fellow student, Patsy said, had spotted something frightening in his backpack: a hatchet.

On another balmy, blue-sky afternoon, seven months to the minute after a stranger with angry eyes pulled up and pointed a gun, the first-graders rushed onto Townville Elementary's playground.

Some kids headed to the swings and others to the play sets. Collin, wearing a black T-shirt with a green smiley face, talked to a friend at a picnic table near where the truck had careened into the chain-link fence, since replaced by a shiny new section. He held his stuffed turtle, Tortle.

A game of tag broke out, and Karson chased a friend, just as he used to when he played the Joker and Jacob played Batman.

Collin darted by the green swings where he used to call out "Little J" to make Jacob laugh.

Siena, gripping a stuffed purple cheetah named Glamour, wandered past a pink metal ladder with a hole, probably the result of rust, that she believed had come from a bullet.

Four miles away, Ava's mother said, the girl lay in bed next to Jacob's old Ninja Turtle, her eyes still watery from another outburst.

As recess neared its end, a half-dozen of the kids carefully placed their stuffed animals atop a green metal bench.

Siena leaned down and pointed at Glamour.

"Stay there," the girl said, racing to the monkey bars to see who could swing the farthest.

A pair of teachers — each holding red bags packed with first-aid kits — watched while their students ran, jumped, climbed and laughed.

When it was time to go back to class, the playground grew quieter as the first-graders returned to the bench. Then they picked up the stuffed animals and disappeared inside their school.

His Heart, Her Hands

The Oregonian

April 16, 2017

By Tom Hallman Jr.

A Lifelong Pianist Struggled to Play As His Memory Began to Fade. A Professional Musician Brought His Songs to Life Again

All his life, Steve Goodwin had been a private man. No matter the circumstances, he'd say he was doing just fine. But as he sat in his Wilsonville home that Monday morning, he wasn't fine.

Over the weekend, he'd argued with his youngest daughter, Melissa. The blowup ended when his daughter, her voice shaking and tears in her eyes, opened the front door to her home and told him to leave.

As is the case in all families, they'd had minor disagreements before. But Saturday's battle had been raw. Steve knew he needed to set things straight. It was time to reveal his secret.

With paper and pen, he retreated to a quiet place in his home. He struggled to find the right words, to explain why he'd been so different these past months. When finished, he told his wife, Joni, he was ready.

She called Melissa, who lived three blocks away. After she arrived, they gathered in the living room and made small talk. Then, from a shirt pocket, Steve pulled out his handwritten notes.

Mom and I saw a neurologist. I have a spot in my brain. I am being honest. If this progresses into Alzheimer's, I know what it is like. I saw my mom. I experienced the pain of her personality changing, her being unkind to me and saying hurtful things.

If I ever do or say anything hurtful, I want you to know that I am sorry.

No matter what I do and say, you are my little girl and I love you.

***

Tears and hugs. Questions with no answers. Fear and doubt bubbling below the surface as each grappled with dark thoughts, knowing the family would be forever changed.

For Melissa, the bitter news explained so much.

The argument, so out of character for her father, started after her parents came over to help take down her Christmas tree because Melissa's husband wasn't home.

While Melissa removed ornaments and lights, her parents kept an eye on the boys, 2 and 4, who ran through the house, loud and wound up.

Melissa noticed her father, always so easygoing, was clearly irritated with the boys. She figured he hadn't yet had his morning coffee. She climbed off the ladder and made him a cup. It didn't help. Within the confines of the living room, the tension built.

And then he snapped at the boys.

Melissa, feeling protective, confronted her father. She didn't know what was wrong with him. She yelled, then cried and said it was time for her parents to leave.

What was happening with dad?

Now she knew.

But the real change, she realized, began the previous summer. She'd been at her parents' house, and she'd asked her father to play his piano, something he'd done all her life. Steve was a software engineer by profession, but music was his true passion. Growing up, Melissa and her sister fell asleep each night to his music. Decades later, the music allowed Melissa, now in her late 30s, to forever be the little girl who so loved her father.

"My father expressed himself through his music," Melissa said. "That's how I knew what was in his heart."

On that summer day, she watched in confusion as her father, always so smooth and proficient, fumbled and stopped. He said he hadn't been practicing. Now she knew the truth.

After writing the one-page letter, Steve and his family refused to accept the diagnosis that the spot on his brain was causing forgetfulness. He was healthy. He ran marathons, hiked and rode a bike. He worked in the garden. He ate salmon and kale. More extensive tests in 2015 revealed Steve, then 65, had early-onset Alzheimer's, a disease passed genetically from his mother. Even with hard proof, the Goodwin family denied the inevitable.

"I'm into alternative health," Melissa said. "I convinced my father to leave no stone unturned: yoga, oils, meditation."

Melissa's husband, and her sister's husband, were doctors who certainly could reach out to researchers, experts and specialists. The rest of the family may have waited for a miracle, but Steve knew.

By the time his mother died, at age 74, she spent her days, in silence, staring out a window. She didn't recognize her son. Once an accomplished musician, she didn't know what to do with a piano.

Now, it was his turn.

A grim fear took hold within Steve.

The piano, once Steve's friend, now mocked him. He'd sit at the keyboard, waiting until he was alone so others wouldn't witness the loss. He'd start a song, get a bar into it and then. ...

He'd forget.

***

I had a business with lots of clients. I had to retire. I couldn't serve them.

Worse was what happened with my music. It became torture for me to play the piano.

My mother played the piano and sang. I had three siblings. None were interested. My mother made me play. I was stuck going to lessons for years. My friends would be playing outside, and I'd be inside practicing to make my mother happy.

But I ended up liking it. The music became a part of me. When I was 8, I met a girl my same age in Sunday school. For the first few years, we teased each other. Then we realized we liked each other. When I was 15, I wrote my first song to her. When we were 20, we got married. Been together 46 years.

My music is my soul.

At first, I could play fluently.

Then I struggled to play the song.

Then I struggled to remember that I used to play the song.

Then I struggled to remember I was the person who wrote the song.

***

The disease, Melissa knew, would block out all her father had ever been.

"This wasn't cancer where radiation and chemotherapy could offer a glimmer of hope," she said. "A murderous fog in his brain would take my father away from us."

When he forgot, what would she remember?

Her father's essence was his music, the soundtrack to her life.

She'd taken it for granted.

And now the music was dying.

"My father would disappear," Melissa said. "I had to save his music."

She knew it was next to impossible.

***

All those years, I never wrote my songs down or recorded them. Everything — every note and phrase and chord progression — was in my head. All my life, I could remember every song and how to play it.

Then I couldn't.

I felt like my fingers and my heart were doing everything they were supposed to do. But the result wasn't coming out the way it was intended. There was a gap between my head and the piano. I can absolutely hear the music in my head. That's what's so frustrating. I know how it's supposed to sound, but I can't make it happen.

I'm angry.

I'm sad.

I'm scared.

It's all in my head.

***

The music and the source of Steve's inspiration remained a mystery. He was the only musician in the family. No one else spoke, or understood, his language.

Melissa thought about hiring a professional pianist to work with her father. But she figured most would require a musical score. Her father had none. She needed someone who could pull the music from him, and also respect and treat tenderly the composer's vulnerable soul. A proud man, Steve hadn't told anyone outside the family about his diagnosis.

Whenever Melissa approached her mother, Joni changed the subject: Let's not ruin this good day. Please, we need positive thoughts.

"Discussing the music meant accepting the outcome," Joni said.

Instead of looking to the future, she focused on the present, protecting Steve and his dignity. He used to cook dinner, but now he didn't remember if he'd added salt, or whether the recipe called for salt. He tested her patience by asking the same question repeatedly.

She missed hearing him at the piano. His music represented a life together: Courtship, marriage, family, buying a house, grieving over the death of a pet, empty rooms when the girls left for college and, now, the joy of being grandparents.

Steve's life, as is the case with many men, had been defined by what society calls success: money, power and an impressive résumé.

"Steve was a freelance software entrepreneur," Joni said. "He made a comfortable living, but we weren't rich. But he always believed he had it in him to create something special with his software. He talked about his ship coming in."

But before his projects launched, she said, a big player in the competitive industry would beat him to the punch.

"Poof," she said. "Poof."

Joni had always told her husband his true gift, even if no one outside the family heard it, was his music.

"He'd say 'Sweetie, thank you very much,'" Joni said. "Then he'd get back to his software to pay the bills."

And now it was just too damn late.

"I lived in fear of losing the music," Joni said. "When it was gone, a bit of me would be gone, too."

***

Just like her father, Melissa had told no one what was going on. Not even her closest friend, Naomi LaViolette,who knew only that Melissa's father was dealing with a medical issue. Nothing more was offered, and Naomi, respecting Melissa's privacy, didn't pry.

They became friends three years earlier in one of those strange and fortuitous moments where two unrelated lives become so intertwined. Their kids attended the same preschool and they'd see each other in the parking lot.

One day, Naomi, a deeply private woman, surprised herself when she began crying after Melissa asked how her day was going. Instead of saying fine and getting in her car, she said she was going through a divorce and was afraid.

"It's hard to do things on your own," Naomi recalled. "You can, but it's so much better when we help each other. I realized I needed help."

They went on walks, talking about life and struggles. When Naomi had to move, Melissa found her an apartment near her own home.Over the years, the two women had family dinners and outings. Melissa watched Naomi's kids when Naomi needed time alone or had to work on her career.

She was a pianist.

Naomi started piano lessons at 4. Blessed with perfect pitch, a genetic trait some researchers say is found in only 1 in 10,000, Naomi could identify a musical note by hearing it played once — without using another note as a point of reference. At 7, she discovered she could learn a piece of music by listening to it. As an adult, she earned a master's degree in classical music and could play anything from jazz to pop to gospel. She performed in clubs and festivals, released her own music and was featured on CDs with other musicians. In addition to being in demand as a session player and accompanist, she was also the pianist for the Oregon Repertory Singers.

In the summer of 2015, the two women met for coffee. Naomi casually asked Melissa how she was doing. This time, it was Melissa who cried. She told Naomi about the diagnosis and the music, how her father no longer played the piano, and how the music would be lost. Naomi, who had no idea that Steve was a pianist, wanted to help.

"I told her that I could learn his music, even by listening to parts of it," she said. "If he could provide anything, we could work together."

The difficulty would be the Alzheimer's. She'd never been around anyone with the disease.

"If I did this," Naomi said, "I'd be dealing not just with music, but the emotional component. When I was going through my divorce, I needed Melissa and her incredible skills of empathy. And now she needed me to help her family."

Music, she believed, was a spiritual language, conveying deep emotions, different from other art forms. She would find the music deep inside Steve Goodwin's failing brain.

And then she would save it.

***

While grateful, Melissa declined Naomi's offer. She told Naomi her father had never played for anyone outside of family and friends. With his skills now fading, she doubted he would subject himself to such embarrassment. As the disease had progressed, Steve grew more defiant.

He didn't want special attention, certainly not anyone feeling sorry for him.

Music was no longer talked about. Joni banned Melissa from raising the subject.

But during a phone call, Naomi brought up the music once more. She asked Melissa to reconsider. Melissa wasn't sure. She knew time was running out and told Naomi she'd think about it.

A month later, Melissa learned her father was scheduled to take a test to see if he was sharp enough to receive an experimental drug that might slow the pace of the disease. Steve had taken the test twice. Both times, he had failed. This was his last chance.

To help her father relax, she took him on a hike the day before they had to be at the doctor's office. As she drove him back home, she thought about Naomi's offer.

If she told her father, he could get anxious and fail the test. Her mother might be furious. She pulled into the driveway, turned off the engine, still not sure what to do.

"Screw it," she said. "I went with my gut."

Melissa told her father she wanted nothing more than to save the music.

"I told him that I saw him struggling with the piano," she said. "He didn't say anything. We just sat there in the car. I said I had a friend who was a talented pianist. She'd offered to work with him to preserve his music."

For a long while, Steve was silent.

"Then he asked me why she'd want to work with him," Melissa said. "He said it would be a waste of her time."

Why do this?

Because, his daughter said, she cares.

Silence.

Dad?

And then ...

"Yes."

Steve Goodwin said yes.

And then he began to cry.

***

After dropping her children at school, Naomi drove to the Goodwin home, where Steve, Joni and Melissa waited. They talked honestly about the future. Although Steve had passed the test and received the experimental drug, his brain was not responding.

Naomi told Steve she'd love to hear him play. Steve moved to the piano and sat at the bench, hands trembling as he gently placed his fingers on the keys.

"I understood," Naomi said. "I told him to play anything he could remember."

Naomi discreetly slipped a small recorder near the piano. She knew nothing about his skills. She had no idea what she would hear. Starts and stops and mistakes. Long pauses, frustration surfacing. But Steve pressed on, for the first time in his life playing for a stranger.

That night, Naomi pulled out the recorder. She listened, just as she had as a child and later as a student to transcribe the jazz solos of Horace Silver, Bill Evans and Thelonious Monk. She understood Steve's music. She found hints of themes, counter themes, harmonies and rhythms.

"It was beautiful," Naomi said. "The music was worth saving."

Her responsibility, her privilege, would be to rescue it. The music was still in Steve Goodwin. It was hidden in rooms with doors about to be locked.

The task would be unlike anything she'd ever attempted. Steve would have to play what he could remember. She'd fill in the blanks, interviewing him, playing for him, trying to understand the music he heardbut could no longer bring to life.

In many ways, she decided, the project was a spiritual calling. Shebelieves every human has the ability to create and bring beauty into the world. Within each of us is something worth preserving.

"I found myself, at the age of 41, wondering how I'd fare in the face of a degenerative disease," Naomi said. "Would I face it with such grace? As much as I don't want to think about death and dying, we all are taken from this life someday, somehow. I am gradually finding peace about it."

And so began the partnership.

Naomi would be the fingers.

Steve would be the heart.

***

Every other week, Naomi and Steve met in his home to spend hours together. He'd fumble at the piano, then she'd take his place. He'd tell her what he remembered and tried to answer her questions. He struggled to explain what he heard in his head. He stood by the piano, eyes closed, listening to his own work, for the first time being played by someone else.

"It amazed me how positive he stayed," Naomi said. "He always, always focused on what he was thankful for. He did not let the disease determine how he saw his life."

Steve and Naomi spoke in code: walking bass lines, playing just off the beat, intervals, moving from the root to end a song in a new key.

Steve heard it.

All of it.

He just couldn't play it.

Once, when Naomi played one of his songs, she noticed Steve and Joni were both crying.

"When she sat down and played," Joni said, "I can't describe the moment. She literally played like he played. In that moment, she became Steve."

The disease, though, took a toll on Steve. One afternoon, he could remember how he began and then ended one of his compositions. But the middle, no matter how hard he concentrated, was lost. Without it, the entire song would be lost.

At the next session, Naomi asked Steve iftheycould work together on the middle section to save the song. He agreed. With Steve's input, she created the passage. Steve loved it, said it was what he would have played if he could. He insisted that she be credited as a collaborator on the piece. On another piece, because Steve could no longer improvise, she added a blues solo. She suggested lyrics, which he loved. Again, he insisted she be listed as a collaborator.

And, then, another miracle.

Working with Naomi had stirred within Steve the belief he could compose one last song.

One day, Naomi received an email. Attached was a recording of this final song, a testament to loss and love, to the fight. Steve called it "Melancholy Flower."

Naomi hit play.

She heard multiple stops and starts, Steve struggling, searching while his wife called him "honey" and encouraged him. The task was overwhelming, and Steve, frustrated and angry, said he was quitting. Joni praised him, telling her husband this could be his signature piece.

Keep going, she said, keep going.

He did.

It would be the last song Steve Goodwin would ever compose.

***

Through 2016 andinto 2017, Naomi LaViolette figured out how to play 16 of Steve Goodwin's favorite, and most personal, songs. She memorized them, and scored the music for future musicians.

With Naomi's help, the Goodwin family found a Portland sound engineer to record Naomi playing Steve's songs.

Joni knew the day would come when Steve did not recognize her, but the music, the beautiful music, would remain.

She could play the CD for her husband. Deep within his brain, he'd find comfort and peace in hearing what he had created.

Joni thought that would be the end.

But it wasn't.

In the months leading up to the 2016 Oregon Repertory Singers Christmas concert, the director asked Naomi, the group's pianist, for song choices. She said she had a special one in mind: "Melancholy Flower."

She told the director about her project with Steve, the song's composer. The director agreed to add it to the repertoire. But to make it work, Naomi would have to take Steve's piece and add lyrics and a choral arrangement for the singers. She asked Steve's permission. He considered it an honor. For the first time in his life, a professional musician had recognized the beauty of his work. He was no longer a software engineer, but a fellow musician.

After the concert, Naomi told the family Steve's music was beautiful and professional. It needed to be shared in public.

The family agreed. They rented The Old Church on the Southwest edge of downtown Portland and scheduled a concert for April 7. They told friends. Word got out. By the day of the show, more than 300 people had said they would attend.

By then, Steve said he was having a hard time remembering the names of some of his friends. He knew the path his life was now taking. His daughter and her friend had saved his music.

He told his family he was at peace.

Steve arrived at the church and sat in the front row, surrounded by his family.

The house lights dimmed.

Naomi took the stage.

Her fingers.

His heart.

***

This has been an absolute miracle.

Naomi crawled up into my brain and found the parts and pieces, all of them broken, and brought them back to me.

I don't dwell on the negative. I try to be grateful for everything that is positive. My heart is happy. I know what is happening. I know what my mother went through.

I know what is ahead.

But research is beginning to figure out what all this is about in the brain. I believe that neither of my daughters, and none of my grandchildren, will experience this.

My wife sits at her desk and listens to the CD of my music. I hear it every day.

It's strange the music will be shared at the concert. I'm a bit embarrassed by the attention.

I was just a man who learned to play the piano as a little boy.

And I loved it.

The Last Refugee

The Boston Globe

By Jenna Russell

Story 1 in an ongoing series

It took a moment, when they woke up in a strange new place, to remember where they were and how they'd gotten there.

Framingham. A town near Boston. In America.

Abdulkader Hayani walked through the clean, bright rooms of his family's new home, reaching out to touch the things that had been left there for them. The four small beds for his four children. The ceramic plates and baby bottles in the kitchen. The soft brown couch; the brand-new toys; the overflowing fruit bowl with a pineapple beside it.

The 29-year-old Syrian refugee knew what he'd been told, arriving here last night: This house was theirs to live in while they started their new life. But everything last night had been a blur; he had been so overwhelmed by strangeness and exhaustion. Seeing it now in the wintry morning light, he could not help but wonder if he had misunderstood.

It was so beautiful, so much. Had they only dreamed that it was theirs?

The family had been searching for a new home since fleeing their own in Aleppo in 2012, amid the bloody civil war in Syria. They had hoped they would one day go back. Then it became clear that they could not. It took years of waiting, living in limbo in Jordan, to be cleared for travel to the United States. The war was still raging five years later when they finally boarded a plane in Amman. By then, more than 4 million Syrians had fled the country. An estimated 400,000 had been killed.

Abdulkader had fastened his seat belt and begun to cry. He cried all the way to Germany, for the country he loved and might never see again.

When they stepped off the plane at Logan Airport on Jan. 18, it had seemed at first that no one was there to meet them. The children had collapsed in sleep on a bench, the four of them draped over their mother, bent like flowers in need of watering. Abdulkader stood apart, a name tag looped around his neck, listening to the bland, staccato security announcements he could not understand. He gazed around the half-deserted terminal, wondering what to do next.

All at once the Americans appeared, concerned and apologetic, after rushing from the wrong gate where they had been waiting. They carried signs that said "Welcome" in Arabic — listing the family's names — and as soon as Abdulkader saw them, everything felt different.

Somebody knew them. They were not alone here.

When the smallest child — 2-year-old Ameeneh — began wailing from exhaustion, one of the American women picked her up, swaying her from side to side until she quieted. Another American had brought a football. He tossed it playfully with the older boys on the long walk from baggage claim to the garage.

The relief of having someone there, showing them the way, carried Abdulkader through the last leg of their journey: the harsh shock of January air; the cumbersome, unfamiliar buckling of carseats. On their drive, ice sparkled faintly on the highway, under pine trees silhouetted black against mauve sky.

It was after midnight when they made it to the house. The children started playing, their fatigue magically gone, while the Americans showed Abdulkader how to use the oven and call 911.

Then their guides gathered up their coats and paperwork and said good night, leaving the travelers to a long-awaited rest.

The family could not fathom, yet, what their arrival meant to those Americans. An unlikely coalition of Jewish leaders and synagogue members, local Syrian-Americans and Muslims, philanthropists and refugee experts, they had worked for months to bring the Syrian refugees to Boston. With determination and persistence, they had convinced the State Department and its partners that the families could succeed here, in spite of the city's high cost of living. They'd asked to receive families with children, making those young lives a focus of their mission. They'd woven a safety net, flexible and strong, to make certain that it turned out right.

The support they got along the way had overwhelmed them — housefuls of donated furniture, stacks of donated gift cards, scores of enthusiastic volunteers lining up to offer child care and English lessons. Congregants at a dozen synagogues pledged to sponsor Syrian families at varying levels. At one, supporters donated $100,000 in a month and arranged to help two families pay rent for a year.

Then came the US election, and a stunning threat: The new president might stop refugees from coming.

A dozen families, or more, were supposed to make new homes near Boston. Abdulkader's was only the second to come. No one knew if the rest would make it — or how those who did might be affected by the turmoil.

Starting over would be hard enough, even with help. They would have to learn to navigate a new culture and a new language, and they would have to do it fast; they were expected to find jobs and start supporting themselves within six months, a year at the outside. At the same time, they had to reckon with the past, come to terms with losses they had suffered. They would have to do it all without their extended families near — in a country where they knew some people did not welcome them.

Sometime soon — maybe today, maybe tomorrow — this family would dare to start unpacking, hanging up the remnants of their past in empty closets. In one suitcase lay the coats made by Abdulkader, a tailor who had honed his craft since he was 9 years old. These were high-end garments, elegantly cut, every inch engineered by his expert hands. In them, he saw everything his life had been — and, perhaps, a way to make a future.

Everything was uncertain, and everything was at stake. Tomorrow Donald Trump would be sworn in as president.

America, like this family, faced a new day, and no one could be sure what it would bring.

The next morning, Bonnie Rosenberg drove to the cream-colored house with the black shutters where the Hayanis now lived. The Newton retiree was hopeful and excited: Today she would finally meet the Syrian family. For months, Bonnie and the other volunteers from Temple Beth Elohim in Wellesley had prepared for the family's arrival. They had collected donations of cash and clothing and furniture; they had shopped for soap and pillows and umbrellas. They had pondered questions that could not be answered yet:

What will they be like? How will they feel about us? How will we communicate with no common language?

Bonnie, an expressive, youthful-seeming grandmother of eight, had been to the house two days earlier, just before the family arrived. The volunteers had met there to make plans for the family's first days: A walk to the playground. A trip to buy winter boots. A first visit to the grocery store. They waited outside in the driveway until the caseworker came, found the key and opened up the door. Then, just inside, they all had fallen silent, overwhelmed by the sight that greeted them.

The morning light revealed the loving preparations of another team of temple volunteers who had turned the tidy house into a cozy haven. There were toothbrushes and towels in the bathroom, child-safety latches in the kitchen cabinets, notecards taped above the appliances, providing instructions in handwritten Arabic. Two matching baby dolls lay near the front door, for the two little girls who would be soon be here.

A word came into Bonnie's mind unbidden: *sacred.*

She, like many of the others who stepped up to help, strongly felt that Jewish history demanded it. Jews had suffered and died by the millions in World War II, in part because other nations wouldn't take them in. The United States had been among those who refused. How could they now ignore another displaced people? Bonnie had volunteered eagerly and with conviction, but still, the practicalities were worrisome. She could not speak their language; did not know their customs. How much help could she really offer?

But standing in this house so carefully, tenderly readied, she saw that they would give these strangers the most basic things: Warmth. Acceptance. A place to feel safe.

All of the volunteers felt it. Several were in tears. They were moved to pray, but they hesitated — the family coming to live here was Muslim. Was a Jewish prayer appropriate? They turned to the caseworker, the only Muslim there.

"We say 'Amin' at the end of a prayer; you say 'Amen.' There is so much that is the same," the woman told them.

They sat in a circle on the floor and said a well-known Hebrew prayer of gratitude: "Barukh ata adonai elohenu melekh ha'olam, shehecheyanu, v'kiyimanu, v'higiyanu la'z'man ha'zeh."

"Blessed are you, God, who has granted us life and sustained us . . . and allowed us to reach this occasion."

Now, returning to the house on her first day as a volunteer, Bonnie carried that same sense of gratitude. On this morning, she would drive with the family to a government office in downtown Framingham, the first of many bureaucratic errands. There, the family's resettlement caseworker would help Abdulkader and his wife apply for food stamps and other temporary benefits, aid that would sustain them until he found work. Bonnie's job, with another volunteer, was to entertain the children — two boys and two girls — while their parents were occupied.

She thought of all the family had gone through to reach this day. She did not know much about their journey, but she knew it had been hard. She resolved to be, with the children, the calmest, gentlest version of herself. She had worried about driving their father downtown — unsure if he would be at ease in the car with a woman — but his grateful smile reassured her. The awkward silence on the drive quickly dissolved, as Bonnie taught the boys what the stoplights meant — "Green, go! Red, stop!" — and they happily chimed in from the backseat.

Bonnie had deliberately chosen this day to spend with the family. It was Jan. 20, Inauguration Day. She had been heartbroken by Trump's victory; she could not bear to think about the midday ceremony. It was the first inauguration she would ignore since college, where she'd majored in political science and been caught up in the passions of the 1960s. Now she focused on the things she could hang on to, the values she believed in.

She knew the road ahead would not always be smooth, for the family or the people helping them. At a training session for the temple volunteers, she had listened to a stream of anxious questions: *What do we say if the families are scared of being sent back? What if we're out with them somewhere and someone harasses them? What if we don't agree with them about the role of women?*

The concerns were real, but with the children near, Bonnie felt it in her gut: Good had to prevail. They arrived at the government office and settled into a large, uncrowded waiting room lined with plastic chairs. Bonnie emptied the bag her grandchildren had helped her pack, full of books and stickers, paper and markers to play with. The boys, Mustafa and Ali, were 9 and 8; whip smart and beautifully behaved, they had warmed to Bonnie's fond, straightforward manner right away. Their little sisters, 2 and 3, looked almost like twins, their big, dark eyes inquisitive and friendly.

The children's attention anchored her in place. She forgot, for a time, what was happening elsewhere.

Just after noon her Apple watch flashed an update: It was done. America had a new president.

Bonnie held the child in her lap a little tighter.

Now it's up to us, she thought.

***

A few days later, in her tiny kitchen in Framingham, a young Syrian woman raised a shaker of mixed spices above a pan of chicken. She breathed in the familiar scent: cinnamon and cardamom; cumin, ginger, pepper. This simple food would mark a milestone: Late tonight, if all went well, another family of Syrian refugees would arrive at a nearby apartment. They would carry in their suitcases, lay their children down, and sit at last to eat their first meal in America.

The young woman had been here since November; her family had been the first to come to Boston. Fearing possible repercussions for family members in Syria, she asked that her real name not be used and that she be identified instead as Um Alnoor, or mother of Alnoor, her son's middle name. Hers had been the only family here for two months, but three more had just arrived, including the Hayanis. She knew there was a chance the next one wouldn't make it; at any time, the brand-new president might block more Syrian families from coming. Already she had seen one arrival canceled, a pregnant mother abruptly deemed unfit to travel. It had been a sharp reminder that uncertainty remained — and she knew how quickly uncertainty could become chaos.

Her family had left their home in Darayya, a suburb of Damascus, in 2012, after her husband, Abu Alnoor — the father of Alnoor, as he asked to be called — was badly hurt in a brutal militia attack. The 30-year-old had ventured out in search of diapers for his baby son and medicine for his mother when he found himself under fire in the street. He had tried to duck into a building but couldn't find a way inside. When he went to help an injured teenager lying in the open, his arms and legs were ripped by shrapnel. Seriously wounded and in need of treatment, he fled for the border with his family within weeks.

Just before the crossing, the family was caught in an ambush, cowering on the ground with their 18-month-old. "No child was allowed to cry," Um Alnoor recalled. "No cellphone was allowed to light. . . . They were shooting at people, and if you fell, no one came to get you."

Over the border, they spent five hard years in Jordan, their freedom to work tightly restricted, before they were approved to go to the United States. Um Alnoor had been unnerved by Trump's election — like so many, she had not expected him to win — but she tried to set aside concern. They flew first to Germany, with a large group of refugees, then on to Miami. There the family parted from the others. On the nighttime flight to Boston, they were alone: surrounded by Americans, submerged in a choppy tide of English words.

Their flight landed after 11 p.m., the lights of the city they had never seen beneath them. They knew no one in this place that would be their home; they had never met or spoken to the strangers who would meet them at the airport. They filed slowly up the ramp behind the other passengers, some wearing shorts and flip-flops in the chilly air.

As Um Alnoor emerged into bright fluorescence, she saw a woman in a white head scarf straight ahead, beaming at her and holding her arms open. Then Um Alnoor was enveloped in her embrace, both of them crying, swaying back and forth. The woman who held her — resettlement caseworker Nermin Helaly — murmured in Arabic: "You're OK now. This is the end of your journey."

They stood that way for nearly a minute, the other passengers streaming around them. Leaning into Um Alnoor's side was her 5-year-old son, his expression somber, his gaze cast down to the floor.

She stepped back and wiped the tears from her cheeks. She felt over-powering gratitude and relief — and she felt another, less familiar feeling.

For the first time since the war started, she felt safe.

Since then, nearly every day had felt like progress. Their son had gone off to kindergarten. Her husband had found a job in a small grocery. Um Alnoor was learning English, proudly greeting the caseworker with an easy "Hi, how are you?" There was even time now, here and there, for dreams: about buying their own house one day or opening a restaurant like they'd had in Syria.

And there were, at last, other Syrians here. One family was living with Americans in Needham; another was in Boston. The largest — the Hayanis, with their four young children — were close by, in the rented house in Framingham. Each had help from members of a different Jewish temple.

Now, in the kitchen that had come to feel familiar, Um Alnoor finished cooking for this night's arrival, sprinkling golden raisins onto the baked chicken. She emptied a large bowl of yellow basmati rice — flecked through with chopped onion, tomato, and peppers — into a tinfoil platter and snapped on a plastic cover. Then she did the same with a chopped salad. Later, she would take the food next door to the new family's apartment, in the same brick residential complex.

She knew they, too, would feel uncertainty and fear, walking off the plane and into the unknown, and she hoped that familiar food would be a comfort. More than that, she hoped they all would be OK, in this place where hope was real, but so much was unknown.

That night, just before the next family arrived, the bad news they had all been dreading finally broke: President Trump planned to sign an executive order choking off the flow of refugees to the United States.

In the cavernous Delta terminal at Logan Airport, the Americans were on their way to greet the family at their gate. They carried the usual gifts — stuffed animals for the children, flowers for the mother, warm coats for them all to wear on the way home. The head of the resettlement agency held up his phone to show his staff the breaking news. Gathered around him, they stood silent for a minute, reading the words on the screen and absorbing the impact. The murmur of travelers echoed through the space around them, under a giant American flag that hung from the ceiling.

No one had to say it — it was understood: Tonight might be the last time they performed this ritual. This family would make it, just in time. But this family might be the last to reach them.

Only a few months had passed since the State Department had agreed to send Syrian refugees to Boston. Getting the green light had not been easy, given the high rents seen as an obstacle to refugees' success. But outcry over the Syrian crisis was growing, as was pressure on the US government to help.

Back then, everyone thought Hillary Clinton would win the election, and more Syrian refugees would follow. Then Trump won, and the clock started ticking on his promised immigration crackdown.

There was a window, before the inauguration, when a handful of families could get through. But what would happen to the others they had planned for?

The answer meant more to them than they had ever expected. For Marc Jacobs, the leader of the team, it was a chance to revitalize a core mission of his agency, Jewish Family Service of Metrowest, which had helped to resettle Russian Jews in the 1990s. For his partner in the venture, Ed Shapiro, it was also deeply personal. The 52-year-old investment manager had recently retired from daily work to spend more time on philanthropy. He had aimed, with this project, to show his children the power individuals had to make a difference.

Ed had been at the airport when the Hayanis arrived; he had tossed the football with the boys while his wife, Barbara, cradled one of the weary toddlers in her arms. They had also welcomed the first family, in November. One week later, on Thanksgiving Day, Ed drove to Framingham with his teenage son and daughter and delivered a hot turkey dinner to Um Alnoor, her husband, and son. With it they brought a page of Arabic writing, translated from English, that explained the meaning of the holiday.

It said, too, how thankful their family was that the Syrians had made it to America.

Ed had recalled the visit often since that day. To stand with people whose lives you had helped change, whose child's fate you had helped to shape, was the rarest privilege he had ever known.

He held the memory close as the borders closed.

***

The volunteers couldn't talk with Abdulkader, but when they visited his family in their new home and saw the coats he'd made, they understood: This man had a calling. He needed to sew. A machine was found, a basic Singer, collecting dust in one of their back rooms. One week after the family's arrival, on Jan. 26, volunteers arranged to bring it to the house and surprise him.

They carried it inside and placed it on a table. The tailor pulled up a chair, switched on a light. His wife appeared with a ripped pair of pants. Abdulkader flicked the machine on, it hummed to life, and then, leaning in, he began to sew.

His family fell silent, seemingly transfixed. The sight of his slight frame attending to the bobbin and the steady sound were so familiar, after all these days of unrelenting strangeness.

They knew Trump was poised to restrict immigration, barring other Syrian refugees from coming. Abdulkader assumed, when he heard about Trump's order, that it would mean his family would have to leave. *Where can we go now?, he asked himself. Will we have to go back to Syria?*

The Americans reassured him he was safe. Abdulkader listened and tried to believe. Soon enough, the courts would intervene, placing a temporary hold on the president's action. The door reopened, just a crack; only time would swing it wide, or slam it shut.

Outside, the pale winter sun was sinking through the trees. Pinkish light came through the curtains in the living room. He finished sewing the red pants and held them up.

He could not explain how much the gift meant, after everything he'd lost before he came here. It was a small machine, but it was a start, and the kindness of the gesture from these strangers stunned him.

He stood up, barefoot on the rug, and turned to face them. "Thank you so much," he said in English.

STORY 2 IN AN ONGOING SERIES.

Threads of new life

The tailor waiting in the lobby of the menswear factory — his eyes on the floor, his heart pounding in his chest — had already known the blackest depths of doubt and fear. Abdulkader Hayani was 29 years old, a refugee from Syria. He had escaped the war that had ground his country to dust, lost the career he'd spent a decade building, and somehow, despite the odds against it, steered himself, his wife and their four children to safety in the United States.

Yet the trial before him now felt like a test he could not pass: his first job interview in America — his first job interview ever. In a country where he had been for less than one month. In a language he could not speak or understand.

Abdulkader carried two long, tailored jackets, draped over one arm. He had made them by hand, while working in Jordan after fleeing Syria. They were elegant garments, beautifully cut, and he prayed that they would say what he could not: that he knew and loved this work; that he would do it well.

The lobby of the menswear company was busy. Other job candidates waited there, too, on sleek, black furniture by a coffee table stacked with fashion industry trade journals. This gleaming new facility in Haverhill housed Southwick Apparel, where 500 employees from 40 countries stitch Brooks Brothers suits. Abdulkader stood apart from the other applicants, clutching his jackets, half wishing he could disappear. He peered down a hallway, where a glass door revealed a vast factory floor bustling with workers. A steady, muted buzz and clatter drifted from within it.

The young tailor recognized the rhythms of the room, and the jolt of the familiar gave him sudden hope. He turned to Danny Woodward, the young American caseworker who had brought him to the interview. "I worked in a place like this," Abdulkader said in Arabic. "In Lebanon."

Danny was new in his job assisting several families of Syrian refugees who had recently been brought to the Boston area. Tall and reserved, with a degree in Arabic studies, he had been hired by the Framingham agency resettling the Syrians because he was fluent in their language. The rest of the job he was learning as he went.

Settling Syrian refugees here was an experiment the State Department and its partners had been reluctant to approve. The area's high cost of living was considered risky for people already facing obstacles. Nevertheless, a small army of volunteers and community leaders was determined to try and make it work. They helped with most everything in the families' lives — guiding their search for work, paying much of their rent. It meant the Hayani family could stay afloat for now. But the aid would eventually end, and when it did, Abdulkader knew he could not afford the house their benefactors had rented and furnished for them, at $2,200 a month. It was the looming problem he could not stop thinking about.

A woman came into the lobby and led the job applicants to a large room, where she asked each one to introduce himself. When she came to Abdulkader, he answered the best way he could: He held up his jackets for everyone to see.

Lay them out here on the table, the woman told him. She called in a supervisor to look. Did you do all this, they asked, pointing to the stitching.

Yes, he told them. Yes, I did it all.

Abdulkader didn't need to understand the words they spoke. He could hear it in their voices: There was hope for him.

They brought him to the sprawling factory floor he had glimpsed from the lobby, and sat him down at a machine to watch him sew. The young Syrian looked around the room in awe. He had never seen a plant so impressive. Then he turned his focus to the task before him.

The tailor was totally absorbed, any trace of nervousness now indiscernible.

When it was over, they took Abdulkader to a room overlooking the manufacturing floor. Across a long table, a manager offered him a job and laid out the details: $11 an hour, minimum wage, while he trained, then a likely raise to $15. She offered help with moving expenses if he wanted to relocate his family nearby; there was an Arabic-speaking community here, she assured him, and grocery stores with familiar food.

On the drive home, Abdulkader felt triumphant: He had found a job in America. It might not pay enough for them to stay in the house where they now lived, but it was a leap toward possibility, a future. For the first time in weeks, he felt like he could breathe.

Beside him in the driver's seat, Danny struggled to find the right tone. He knew how much this first taste of success meant, and he worried it would lead to disappointment; the job was far from Abdulkader's home.

"You should be happy," he told Abdulkader. "We just have to think about it."

***

Abdulkader's wife could see how much he wanted the job. She tried to find some way she could embrace it, but the idea filled Asmaa with trepidation.

The company that wanted to hire her husband was 60 miles away from the small, cream-colored house where they lived with their four young children. Abdulkader had no car and no driver's license. He might find another commuter to ride with, but it was unlikely. He could look for a cheap room to rent in Haverhill, but that would leave his wife and children — two boys and two girls, all under age 10 — completely on their own during the workweek.

The thought of being so alone, in a place where she knew no one and could not speak the language, was more painful than Asmaa could bear. The prospect of leaving Framingham was almost as bad. It wasn't home yet, but it was the closest thing she had.

They had taken the children to the playground down the road, and begun to figure out how to walk to nearby stores. They had propped a few photographs on a shelf, and found a spot for Abdulkader's sewing machine. He had plans to make new curtains for the sunny living room. One day, another Syrian family had walked over from their home to visit, bringing a housewarming gift, a mixer they had purchased on the way at Target. Their kids all played together as the parents chatted in Arabic.

Their schedules were surprisingly busy: hours of intensive English classes and appointments with doctors and dentists to catch up on years of missed health care. They relied heavily on help from Danny and other staff at Jewish Family Service of Metrowest, and on volunteers from Temple Beth Elohim in Wellesley, who provided rides and child care and daily guidance on life in America. Most important, there was a school nearby with an Arabic-speaking aide, who could help their children navigate the scary leap into their new classrooms and new country.

They both knew it was not a good time to relocate. But if it was his dream, Asmaa told him, then she would accept it.

"If you can find a place in Haverhill where we all can stay," she offered, "then OK."

"I would rather lose the job than lose the people we have here who help us," Abdulkader answered.

He tried to make it seem easy. But it was crushing.

As a tide of noisy children poured from the cafeteria into the school hallway, Abdulkader's two young sons, Ali and Mustafa, stepped back from the fray. Quiet and wide-eyed, the boys kept near their father as they and a cluster of others — a caseworker from the resettlement agency; a volunteer helping the family; another Syrian dad and his 5-year-old daughter — followed close behind a guidance counselor who was showing them around.

The children would be starting school here the next day. They were 7 and 9, heading into first and second grade. Abdulkader knew they were afraid; everything was strange and intimidating. They knew no one. They could not speak the language. The games and rules that mattered here were mysteries to them.

He laid his hands on Mustafa's shoulders as they filed into the boy's new classroom. He thought of things he might tell his sons later, at home. Advice for making friends without a common language: Show your classmates who you are until you learn the words to tell them. Make your expressions, your eyes and hands, spell out your empathy and kindness.

All of this was new to Abdulkader, too — the school, even the idea of a tour for parents. There was no such practice in Syria. He had left school when he was 9 years old, to learn the tailor trade beside his older brother. He had never mastered reading and writing, and he knew his world was smaller for it. Everything this move demanded of him — learning English, finding a job — was so much harder because he had left school. His children would not suffer the same fate. For him and for Asmaa, that was most important. And that meant they had to find a school where their children could thrive.

Was this school such a place? The early signs were promising.

The guidance counselor leading them around stopped in a bright hallway by an indoor garden. Panels of sunlight glazed the beige tiled floor, streaming over basking racks of potted plants. Their tour guide gestured at the slender shoots in the smallest pots.

"These plants are new," he told the Syrian children, as he did each time he welcomed new immigrant students, 40 or 50 each year. "Those big plants, last year, were like these small ones."

The children listened intently as their caseworker repeated his words in Arabic.

"This is your school, and you will grow here and become big plants," the counselor continued. "You will speak English, you will learn, but just like these plants, it will take time."

The boys looked thoughtful, their faces lit by the sun, wondering if the promise was one they could believe in.

It was March, six weeks after the job offer in Haverhill. Since then, there had been no solid progress. Abdulkader had met with tailors all over Framingham and beyond, but the conversations went in circles.

Advice was plentiful, as was freelance work that would pay him by the piece. But no real jobs, with regular paychecks, took shape.

The resettlement team brainstormed and networked, calling old connections, consulting employment experts. Their goal for Abdulkader's family, and all the families, was self-sufficiency within a year. That was when their financial support would be phased out, and they would be expected to pay their own bills. Bolstered by tens of thousands of dollars in private local fund-raising that supplemented the basic funding the government offered, it was a much more generous timeline than the 90 days most refugees around the country get. Just two months had passed since the Hayanis had arrived. There was still plenty of time, the Americans kept telling Abdulkader. But with each week that passed, he grew more anxious.

Every Monday, he shared an Uber ride with the other refugees to downtown Boston, where, in a Financial District high-rise, home to the nonprofit Jewish Vocational Service, he learned skills to help him find a job. Every week or two, it seemed, the students' numbers dwindled, as another one among them started working. One had found a position in a grocery store. Another, who had been a shoemaker in Syria, got hooked up with a paid internship at Reebok. Two more were taking jobs at a hotel in Natick.

This time, at their weekly session, it was only Abdulkader and one other refugee in the classroom. Their instructor stood at the whiteboard, his black marker a blur as he scrawled important phrases for job interviews:

Why should I hire you?

I will be on time.

Abdulkader, carefully and slowly, copied each one down on a sheet of paper.

If he tried hard enough, he told himself, maybe he would be next.

***

Their life was fretful and unsettled but radiant, too, with unexpected discovery.

These weeks since coming to America were the most time Abdulkader and Asmaa had ever spent together. They had been teenagers, strangers, when they married in Syria, in a transaction brokered by relatives. They had barely spoken before they became husband and wife. In the dozen years since, Abdulkader had worked day and night, sometimes far away from his family. "Will your children even know you?" one of his bosses had joked.

Now they had only each other, and it had brought them closer. "We got to know each other, and it turns out we like each other," Abdulkader said with a smile.

Sometimes after the children were in bed, he would sit down with Asmaa and try to soothe her worries. There were plenty of those. One concern was Mustafa, their older son, who sometimes said he wanted to leave school. Sensitive, and old enough to see his father's burden, the second-grader spoke of finding work to help the family. His parents coaxed him to focus on the future, a possible career in medicine or engineering.

When she saw her husband struggling, Asmaa tried to help him gain perspective: You have worked hard all your life, she said. It's OK if it takes a month or two to start again.

***

The tailor's shop sat on a busy corner, in a yellow brick building topped with an enormous sign. Inside, it was crammed with racks of formal dresses in a rainbow of colors, each awaiting custom alterations. Every few minutes, a customer carrying another ill-fitting garment came through the door. Two employees — a pregnant woman from Albania and a young Syrian man — labored on sewing machines in opposite corners, while the owner dealt with customers.

Abdulkader had met the owner of this shop at a mosque in Worcester where he and the other Syrian men had gone to pray. The owner was an older tailor, also from Syria, who had been in business here for 25 years. Come and try it out, the older man had urged him. So a volunteer had driven Abdulkader 30 miles west to see if a job might be had in Worcester.

The shop owner gave Abdulkader a pair of pants to hem. "I want to see his experience," the older tailor explained. "I have very expensive things here, and I have to be able to trust someone."

Abdulkader worked carefully, his expression solemn as he marked the fabric with white chalk. He laid down a ruler to ensure the hem was straight.

In Syria, where tailoring was an important and respected craft, it was Abdulkader who had been in charge. In Aleppo, before the war, he had owned his own business. There, he was the master dressmaker, overseeing six employees and 10 sewing machines. They made stylish, high-end dresses and abayas — robe-like garments often worn by Muslim women — from the designs of his older brother.

He'd had the shop for just a year when the war began. Overnight, the city he loved began to disappear, its homes, hospitals, and historic monuments devastated by bombs, fires, and looting, and he understood with dread that he and his family would have to leave. In another country, Jordan, he began again. For a time, before his family joined him, he was homeless, sleeping at night in the workshop where he labored. When he saved enough to send for Asmaa and the children, they moved into an old refugee camp, its stark, stone housing units cheap and rough and bare.

Now, five years later, in America, he was crouched over the starting line once more. In two days, Abdulkader would turn 30. How many times would he have to start from nothing?

The shop owner leaned in to examine the hem he had sewed. "Good, good job," the older tailor murmured. He invited Abdulkader to come back a few days later.

Abdulkader left the shop with hope. He would return a few more times, for what the owner called training. But a job, with a regular schedule and paycheck, remained a mirage.

***

At night, when the world outside grew still, Abdulkader slipped out the front door to walk. It was the best way to clear his head — steady motion through the quiet, hilly maze of suburban streets.

He walked to the edge of the neighborhood and back, counseling himself silently as he went:

Patience. Remember to be patient. Everything will happen, God willing, in due time.

The dark felt comforting, a cloak that made him invisible, broken by the occasional orange glow of a street light.

At the house, the staff and volunteers who were enmeshed in the Hayanis' lives stopped by almost daily. There was Bonnie Rosenberg, the exuberant Newton grandmother who took Abdulkader shopping for fabric to make curtains, and Jessica Lasser, a lawyer and Kentucky native who comforted the wailing little girls, Ameeneh and Fatimah, when they got their first shots at a doctor's office. Lina Musayev had been a refugee herself, arriving in America at 9 years old from Azerbaijan, and now helped the Hayani boys with their homework. Stephanie Juma grew up in Jordan. She spoke Arabic and interpreted patiently for the others.

These Americans had come to care deeply for the family, and to treasure their deepening bond, the little girls running to greet them at the door. They could see the toll unemployment was taking on Abdulkader, and they shared his ratcheting impatience.

Some of them had tailoring work they needed done. In their longing to help, they hatched a plan: They could hire Abdulkader to sew for them. And all of them admired Asmaa's cooking. Whenever they visited, she served the volunteers steaming tea or strong dark coffee, and, often, plates of homemade food: stuffed grape leaves; kibbeh, a baked meat dish made with cracked wheat, almonds, and spices; heaping bowls of sweet rice pudding topped with pistachio nuts. Why not pay her to teach them cooking? But this, they knew, was complicated territory.

Making food and fixing clothes were ways this couple showed their gratitude. Would an offer of money take something from them, or even offend?

They decided to risk it. One of the American women asked Asmaa to try teaching a lesson. But the volunteer said nothing about the plan to pay her.

Asmaa squatted on the kitchen floor, a large metal pot on the white tiles in front of her. Above her, the American women stood in a circle and watched. The Syrian woman was showing them how she made lentil soup. Staying in her crouch, she poured the creamy liquid through a strainer, scraping away the mushy residue with a spoon.

Asmaa had never had a kitchen counter in Syria. The floor was where she'd learned to cook, and it was where she was most comfortable.

It was a Sunday afternoon in early April. Bonnie, the volunteer who had organized the trial lesson, was taking notes for a keepsake book of recipes shared by the refugee families. Jessica, another volunteer, was down on the floor, taking a turn straining the soup. Asmaa looked at ease in leggings and a sweater, her long dark hair pulled back in a ponytail. With only women present, her head was uncovered. Before lowering the soup pot to the floor, she had simmered the lentils with ground garlic and mint, and dumped in a cup of lemon juice squeezed by Abdulkader.

He watched them happily from a distance. Near the end of the lesson, he called his mother in Turkey — conjuring a grainy video feed on his tablet — so she could see, from 5,000 miles away, the Americans learning the soup recipe. It was his mother's lentil soup they were studying; she had taught Asmaa to make it after the couple married and Asmaa moved in with his family.

They ate the soup together at the big kitchen table, the children seated at a smaller table beside them, and talked about the garden they would plant in the backyard. The Hayanis refused, as expected, to take any cash for the soup supplies. But when the volunteers insisted, they reluctantly gave in and accepted a Stop & Shop gift card.

Later, as they cleaned up the kitchen, Asmaa made what was, for her, an unprecedented request: She wanted the Americans to show her, 10 weeks after her arrival, how to use the dishwasher she had never touched.

The volunteers exchanged excited looks: This was a milestone. Together they filled the racks with brightly colored plates and showed her how to push the square start button.

Her soup was made the old Syrian way, on the floor. For the cleanup, though — modern convenience.

Abdulkader had another interview soon after. At a clothing store that did in-house tailoring, he demonstrated, yet again, what he could do. The store was close to home, and they liked his skills. But they did not have a position open.

If a job comes up, they promised, we will call you.

When his employment coach suggested he apply for a dishwashing job at an Olive Garden restaurant, he agreed at once. "The important thing is that I work," he said.

This time, he felt confident. It was April, a season for beginnings; the spring colors here, deeper and greener than in Syria, heightened his sense of optimism. His job coach from the Boston employment center, Aseel Sharif, was there beside him. But the first question the manager asked flattened their hopes: "How much English does he understand?"

Aseel launched into his pitch: Abdulkader lived nearby; he was a fast learner; he badly wanted to work. How much English did he need to wash dishes? But the interview was over in five minutes.

Back at home at his kitchen table, the unemployed tailor gave in to despair. If he could not even wash dishes, then what could he do? Darkness settled into his expression, a look in his eyes like a trapped animal's.

Seeing him from across the room, his wife was startled. I have never seen his face like this, she realized.

He wondered again if they should have stayed in Jordan. He said it out loud: Perhaps we should go back.

Aseel, his employment coach, tried to reassure him. There were jobs in other kitchens; they would find one.

Abdulkader's gaze was stony.

When? his eyes asked. When?

***

Two weeks later, Abdulkader's phone rang. It was Danny, the caseworker from Jewish Family Service who had helped him with his job search since his first interview in Haverhill. "I have good news," Danny began.

"I haven't heard good news in a while," said Abdulkader, his voice cautious.

The clothing store where he had interviewed — where they liked his skills but had no openings — had called Danny back. Now it looked like they would need someone in May.

The job was Abdulkader's if he wanted it.

"You are kidding," Abdulkader said.

No, Danny assured him. I am not.

Shokran, shokran, Abdulkader told him. Thank you. Then he didn't know what else to say, or how to say it.

The struggle that had brought him to this moment was behind him.

This is where it starts, he told himself. My life in America begins right now.

STORY 3 IN AN ONGOING SERIES.

Letting go, taking hold

The Voice of Fear

Through other eyes, it was a summer paradise that lay ahead, glittering in the morning sun: a curve of golden sand where people in bathing suits sprawled beneath a flawless sky, kicking off sandals, anointing themselves with sunblock, wading into the cool, rippling water. But the Syrian woman, Asmaa Hayani, covered in a headscarf and long, tailored coat, gazed out at the view and tried to cast away her dread.

"Isn't it pretty?" asked the easygoing, blue-eyed woman who had organized this outing and driven Asmaa and her family here to Walden Pond. Jessica Lasser, 38, was one of a small, close-knit team of volunteers and resettlement caseworkers that looked after this young refugee family.

For seven months now, it had been their responsibility to ease the family into a country and a culture where virtually nothing was familiar. They had settled the Hayanis — 27-year-old Asmaa, her sweet-natured 29-year-old husband, Abdulkader, and their four young children — in a little house in suburban Framingham that they had scrubbed and furnished. They drove the family to doctor's appointments, escorted Abdulkader to job interviews, and helped to enroll the two oldest children in school.

One frigid day during the winter, when Jessica took the family sledding and they marveled at the cold, she promised the Hayanis a trip to the beach when summer came. The children counted the days. Abdulkader, too, was game. But Jessica worried about Asmaa.

Asmaa had been wary of going out in public almost from that first rainy night in January when the team from the resettlement agency,

Jewish Family Service of Metrowest, met the family at the airport under the shadow of a looming presidential travel ban.

In this alien world, Asmaa felt conspicuous, especially when wearing the clothes that covered her body according to her faith. She was paralyzed by the possibility she would encounter someone who hated her because of it.

The volunteers had tried to make her feel safe. They went to the house to keep her company when Abdulkader was away at night English classes, when the dark seemed to deepen her discomfort. Asmaa eventually told them she would be OK without the visits, that she would rein in her fears on her own. But the problem didn't go away. Jessica had seen Asmaa's delicate face cloud with panic, just at finding herself in a crowd of people. The volunteers told her the anxieties weren't uncommon or unreasonable; her family had been forced from a country eviscerated by war, after all, places they loved bombed to rubble, friends and loved ones killed. Asmaa explained to them that she had always had a fearful nature. When she landed someplace new, it could overwhelm her. What she feared most was to be unwanted.

Worried, but trying to project a cheerful calm, Jessica kept an eye on Asmaa as they crossed the parking lot toward the pond, toting their children, a cooler, stroller, and bags stuffed with towels. She'd gotten them there early to beat the throngs, but groups of beachgoers were steadily arriving. As the boys ran ahead, Jessica directed them past the busiest stretch of sand to a protected nook, backed up to a steep embankment, that would give Asmaa some shade and privacy. There, they spread two blankets side by side under a canopy of leaves, one for Jessica's family and the other for the Hayanis.

At first, Asmaa stayed anchored there, but eventually, as the sun rose higher, she ventured from their refuge and walked toward the children as they laughed and splashed in the shallow water. Jessica watched, pulse quickening. Asmaa hitched up her long coat, took off her shoes, and stepped in, wavelets lapping the tops of her feet.

The tension they all felt seemed to dissipate after that. They lounged on the blankets, eating the tabbouleh salad, stuffed grape leaves and kibbeh meat cakes that Asmaa had made and packed in grocery bags, and the bagels and zucchini bread Jessica had brought. Leaning back on the blanket, Abdulkader spun an inflatable beach ball, a map of the world on its surface, and planted a kiss on the tiny shape of Syria.

When one of the girls needed to go to the bathroom, Abdulkader and Asmaa walked her there together. A time later, when her other daughter tugged at her, Asmaa took her hand and repeated the trip on her own. Asmaa's gait looked freer, it seemed to Jessica, her steps lighter, even as her coat swung around her ankles. Exhilaration surged in Jessica. Asmaa had braved the beach. It was a turning point.

Asmaa was happy, too. The glow of it stayed with her on the drive home, and later that evening, while she and Abdulkader hosted another newly arrived Syrian family for dinner at their home, Asmaa offering them advice and comfort.

Four days later, though, Asmaa fell ill, and a volunteer took her to the emergency room. It was crowded and chaotic, and as they sat waiting, Asmaa could feel someone staring at her. A man nearby was glaring, his gaze steady and unfriendly. Every time she looked up, his eyes were fixed on her. Then he got up and came walking toward her.

He addressed her angrily and loudly. *Children are not allowed in the waiting room*, was what he said. But he did not scold the other people who had children with them. Only her, a mother wearing a hijab.

This was what she had feared all along, what she had braced for. The day at the beach had been a dream. Now she was awake, and her fear had a voice, and a face.

She couldn't shake it from her mind, even when she was safely back at home. Even after days had passed, she still felt threatened. Would the man come find her? Would he try to hurt her?

One day, she thought she heard knocking at the windows. Certain it was him, she called Abdulkader, and later told her caseworker at Jewish Family Service. All offered comfort, but the worry stayed. Nothing could dislodge her feeling that, despite their sunny, spotless home and all the kind people who helped them, she was stuck in a place that might not want her. And she was so very far from home.

2. Dancing Memory

Abdulkader's memories came in fragments, bright flashes from a dimming past. The village of small stone houses where they came from. Asmaa's father tending his pistachio trees on a shared plot of land. The family weddings where Abdulkader danced the dabke, kicking and stomping side by side with his brothers, a tradition as deep as any he knew.

Often when he slept, Abdulkader dreamed of home.

One night he saw himself on a balcony. As he stood there in the open, someone started shooting.

In another dream he was on the road to his old house. Elation swept through him at each familiar landmark, until he turned a corner and saw the Syrian army. Stricken with terror, he turned and ran away.

Even in his dreams, he could not go home.

He tried not to dwell on the things he had lost. He willed himself into the present, for the sake of his family, their future. The only way forward was to make a life here.

The volunteers from Temple Beth Elohim in Wellesley came to the house almost daily, drinking tea, reading with the children, driving them all to appointments and errands and playgrounds. The Hayanis socialized with a half-dozen other Syrian families who had been resettled in Framingham at the same time, and attended English classes several times each week.

Abdulkader rode his bike to the full-time job his caseworkers had helped him find, as a tailor at the menswear store Jos. A. Bank. In Syria, he'd had his own shop, with six employees, after leaving school at age 9 and laboring for a dozen years. Still, he'd been elated to find steady work in America, in the trade he'd practiced and perfected all his life. His employers were just as pleased with him, his skill and precision and eagerness.

On his days off, he pedaled to a small family-owned fur shop not far from the house, where he refashioned vintage coats beside an older Greek tailor as a crackly radio played 1980s ballads.

The second job provided a little more much-needed money — his constant worry — and it was teaching him new skills, fueling his dream of one day owning his own shop again.

But it was becoming apparent to him that there were obstacles he had not foreseen. Abdulkader was a devout, conservative Muslim, whose religious practice forbade him to touch women he wasn't related to. In Syria, it had not been a problem; men and women went to separate tailors. Here, it was different. Men and women routinely shook hands; male tailors measured female clients. How could he run a business if he could not do those things? He tried not to despair, but he worried that he would have to find a new career.

At home, he and Asmaa exulted in the children, who seemed to thrive. The boys, Mustafa and Ali, 9 and 7, twirled fidget spinners, sang along to Justin Bieber, and played soccer in the backyard with other neighborhood kids in a noisy, happy pack that reminded them all of life in Aleppo.

The boys already could speak and read English and were getting better by the day. It made Abdulkader gleeful — they would be doctors and engineers — but it also tugged at a thread of unease. He and Asmaa were much slower to learn the language, even with dedicated practice and YouTube tutorials. He did not want to lose his children in that gap, and he did not want them to forget the place they came from.

In July, Abdulkader was sitting in an English class when his teacher extended an unexpected invitation. Her friend Joanie Block ran a local professional dance company, and she was planning a special show, Muslims and Jews dancing onstage together. She wanted Abdulkader and the other Syrian men to perform the dabke.

Curious and excited, the Syrian men in the class all began talking at once, arguing about what music they should dance to. Abdulkader felt a rush of emotion: This would be his reason to teach his sons the dance, to pass on the tradition his brothers had handed down to him.

When he had time between work and English lessons, Abdulkader sat at his sewing machine in the playroom, carefully cutting and stitching swaths of fabric, making traditional Syrian costumes for the boys: the wide-legged sirwal trousers dabke dancers wore, with matching tunics and snug wraps to go around their waists. The night he finished, he was so excited he went to their room and shook the boys from sleep to show them.

One day shortly after, he summoned them and told them it was time; he would teach them the joyful dabke steps. But his feet felt rooted to the floor. Abdulkader had not danced in seven years, since before the war, before everyone he'd known then had been killed or scattered around the world. The dance was so entangled now with grief and loss.

He turned to YouTube again, and called up a video of dabke dancers. The quick pulsing beat of the music filled the room, and all at once the boys were dancing, or trying to, laughing and tripping and spinning without yet knowing how.

Abdulkader stood to join them and willed his feet to move.

3. To Live
Asmaa reached for the bottle of laundry soap. It was empty. It had been two months since the terrible day in the hospital waiting room.

She'd made a fortress of her home since then; if she needed something, she called Abdulkader and asked him to bring it home.

You can't give in to fear, Abdulkader often told her.

Her husband had said something else, too: *There are good and bad people everywhere. That man in the ER knew only what he heard on TV about Muslims. He doesn't know us.*

She looked outside at the pretty autumn day.

Come on, she called to the girls in Arabic. She took them by the hand and started walking, determined, down the hill, from their quiet neighborhood toward the busy shopping complex.

The detergent aisle at Stop & Shop was dizzying, a visual assault. Asmaa pulled a jug from the shelf, and carried the heavy bottle all the way home before she realized she had purchased bleach by accident. Down the hill they went again.

By the time Abdulkader got home, the laundry was clean. Quietly, proudly, she told him what she had done.

4. We Welcome You

"We were strangers in a new land," the rabbi said, standing in the center of the crowded temple. "Egypt, 3,000 years ago."

It was late September, Yom Kippur — the holiest day in the Jewish calendar. Asmaa and Abdulkader and their children sat in the front rows with the other Syrian families.

The rabbi had invited them here, to Temple Beth Elohim in Wellesley, to receive a blessing and meet their benefactors.

Asmaa and Abdulkader could not have imagined such a thing, or even conceived of it, nine months earlier. In their first days in this new country, they had been shocked and afraid when they learned that many of the people helping them were Jewish. They lay awake at night, trying to reconcile what they had been taught — what they had thought of as truth — with the love and generosity they saw. They had been raised to believe that Jews were their enemies.

They had learned that a man from this temple, Ed Shapiro, had fought to bring Syrian refugees to Boston. He had partnered with a Jewish resettlement agency, JFS, to convince the State Department, and then people from this temple and others had gone to work. They were the people who met them at the airport and made them a home — Jessica and all the rest, who had waited in lines with them and walked their boys to the bus stop and played endless games of peekaboo to make their daughters laugh.

They listened now to the rabbi's history lesson, an Arabic interpreter translating his words. "Because of that experience, for 3,000 years, it has been important to us to welcome people," he said.

He called for all the volunteers and all the Syrian families to step up on the bimah, the podium that holds the Torah, for the blessing. They crowded close together, shoulder to shoulder, looking out at 800 upturned faces. The rabbi asked God to grant them health and peace.

Outside the sanctuary's glass walls, it was stormy, trees whipping in the wind. Inside, on the bimah, some volunteers were crying.

"We are very happy we have met you, and that our lives are shared," said the rabbi, Joel Sisenwine. "I did not want all of these people at the airport," — he gestured at the massive congregation — "but they wanted to say 'Welcome to America.'"

When the service ended, the Syrians were besieged. Crowds of congregants pressed in around them, blocking the aisles, waiting for a chance to greet them. Asmaa felt someone take her hand, and looked down startled; a man was holding it, his face full of kindness. This touch from a man was *haram*, forbidden. Then another hand was on her arm, and another. Nearby, Abdulkader was also surrounded with men and women patting his shoulders and taking his hand.

This new life, this new country, demanded so many things of them they had never imagined, compromises, tiny steps and giant leaps into the unknown. It was terrifying, disorienting, and thrilling at times, to wrench themselves from their own past, agonizing over what fragments to hang onto, without knowing where they were going or who they would be when they got there.

Now, in the crush of warm smiles and embraces, they surrendered.

Later, in the hallway, Abdulkader turned to Asmaa. "There was a lot of touching today," he said. She looked back at him, her expression understanding. "Yes," she said, "it happened to me, too."

"I hope that you will pardon me," he said in Arabic.

"And that you will pardon me," she answered.

Wrong Way

Tampa Bay Times

August 16, 2017

By Lisa Gartner and Zachary T. Sampson

At 15, Isaiah Battle was the county's No. 1 car thief

Isaiah Battle believes in heaven. When he pictures it, everything is gold, everyone sitting on couches among clouds. He is not sure if people in heaven have to share rooms. But if they do, he hopes he can share one with his sister, Dominique.

They shared one on earth, in St. Petersburg, back before she drowned in a stolen car in a cemetery pond. Two beds where they'd lie side by side and joke about their boyfriends, girlfriends, school. Smoke weed and watch whatever was on TV. Tell each other *I love you* before lights out each night.

The many things they shared also included the backseat of a police cruiser. In the year before his sister died, Isaiah was the kid arrested the most for stealing cars in Pinellas County: a Camry from a driveway, a Porsche from a man pumping gas. He did donuts in a silver minivan and took his hands off the wheel of a Hyundai, holding them above his head like he was on a rollercoaster, laughing.

And she did it, too. When Isaiah was first caught driving a stolen car, Dominique was one of his passengers. She laughed as police handcuffed her, told them it wasn't a big deal.

Isaiah went to her wake in shackles, sentenced for his own crimes. He cried over his sister's body. He swore he'd never steal a car again.

But nine months later, Isaiah took an Acura. He sped through the St. Pete night with his headlights switched off, blowing stop signs and running red lights.

Why did he do it? After everything that happened, how could he keep stealing cars?

Isaiah and Dominique shared a world very far from heaven, where fathers disappeared and houses burned down, where men choked their mother and boys shot their friends. That, Isaiah said, is "a normal life." Strangers' cars were an escape from it.

"I did everything everybody else did," said the boy, now 16. "I ain't never had to do nothing out of the ordinary."

Stealing cars had taken so much from him. It had taken his sister. But this life was the only one Isaiah knew. Speeding in the wrong direction on St. Pete streets, he would let it take even more still.

***

Isaiah was 6 weeks old when his father went to prison for selling cocaine. His 20-year-old mother, Yashica Clemmons, was alone with three children under the age of 3: Isaiah, his older brother Jovontae and his 1-year-old sister, Dominique. Yashica worked at Winn-Dixie. She wore clothes and shoes with holes in them so that her children, growing fast, could have new outfits.

Their father got out of prison three years later. He'd come by on weekends, take the kids out to eat or to St. Pete Beach. Isaiah liked to play in the waves, the bigger ones pushing him back to shore. But their father was still selling drugs, and this time, the judge gave him 30 years. He went back to prison the summer after Isaiah turned 6, and the boy remembers thinking, "Okay, I ain't going to have him, he's not going to be a part of my life."

They haven't talked since.

There was no one else he'd call "dad" among the rotating cast of men who moved into his house and beat up his mom. When he was five, he told police that he watched as one of these boyfriends shoved her into a bunkbed. Dominique was too shy to tell the officers anything.

They broke up three years later, after another baby and a fight over the paternity test, when he followed her to the park where Isaiah was playing football. Yashica had to lock herself and Dominique and the baby in a Kentucky Fried Chicken bathroom until the cops came.

Isaiah started getting in fights at recess and P.E., throwing punches when a friend got jumped, sometimes taking on a kid who looked at him the wrong way. He and his sister went to Melrose Elementary, a school on its way to becoming the worst-rated in the state. Fighting made him feel good, alive.

Their mom started dating a new man and they all moved in together, to a 400-square-foot house a couple blocks from Melrose. Neither Yashica nor her boyfriend had a job. The six of them shared two bedrooms and one bathroom. They didn't pay for electricity, snaking an extension cord in from a neighbor's house.

They got a puppy, a pitbull that Isaiah loved. He took it on walks and let the dog chase him all around the backyard.

One evening Isaiah's mother got in a fight with her boyfriend. She was afraid of him. So she packed up the kids — Isaiah was 10, Dominique was 11 — and took them to their grandmother's house for the night.

That's when someone burned their house down. Flames completely engulfed the front as the roof collapsed onto the porch. All of Dominique and Isaiah's things — her clothes, his Nerf gun, their bicycles and backpacks — were lost in the fire.

Police found two gas cans by what used to be the porch. Their mother was sure it was the boyfriend, but a jury acquitted him.

Isaiah spent a week walking the neighborhood, calling for their puppy.

***

If nothing else, they had each other: Isaiah and Dominique were like twins. Where he went, she went. They walked their little sister to school together, then stole a little girl's bike, pink and white, off the rack. Isaiah posted photos of Dominique on Facebook, sticking her tongue out, riding the school bus, sitting on the trunk of a car. Everything made her smile, her brother says. She wanted to be a pharmacist, maybe even a doctor.

One night, their mother's new boyfriend came home drunk, Isaiah remembers. He said his cell phone charger was missing, and that he was tired of the kids disrespecting him. He shoved Yashica, even though she was holding their 6-month-old baby.

And he went after Dominique.

He hit her in the face and Isaiah shot out of the bedroom, yelling at this man to leave his sister alone. Isaiah was 5-foot-7, 14 and skinny. The man pushed him against the wall, punching him in the stomach three times. The boy ran out of the house. Isaiah remembers the man following him down the street with a knife.

Isaiah and Dominique tried not to be home much, especially after their family moved into the Mosley Motel. Six of them shared one room. The last stop before homelessness, it was a haven for drunks and addicts.

Dominique shoplifted from Walmart. She skipped school and hung out at the Tyrone Square Mall. Isaiah started skipping too, bored in his classes, bubbling in random answers on tests. He walked the neighborhood around Azalea Middle, looking for bicycles to take.

When he found one he'd head to Childs Park, the neighborhood they had lived in when they were younger. Isaiah had hated it as a kid, the drive-bys and the murders and the noise. He would go to the park in the heart of the neighborhood when he was mad, playing hide-and-seek and tag and talking to friends until he felt better.

Now, he went there to play basketball with other boys playing hooky. He met older kids who had dropped out of school.

Police would call some of them gang members, but Isaiah says they took care of him. He took showers at their houses and ate dinners at their tables. If he needed money, they could lend him some.

"We won't let nobody be broke," Isaiah explains. "I don't call it a gang. I just call it a family."

And everybody in this family stole cars.

***

Kids say it's fun to take cars. They brag to each other about how many they've stolen and the sleekest models they've sped away in. They say they are bored and that it's easy, sharing videos of themselves driving at 120 miles per hour. They smile with key fobs, offering rides on Facebook.

But all of the biggest car thieves had something to run from.

Tampa Bay Times reporters analyzed the lives of the most chronic kid car thieves in Pinellas. Using a database they built of every juvenile auto theft arrest in the county, reporters identified 14 kids who were arrested for stealing five or more cars between January 2015 and June 2016. Reporters then read thousands of pages of court documents and police reports from more than a dozen agencies before knocking on doors and writing letters to prisons.

All 14 of these prolific offenders are male. Twelve are black, one is Asian, and one is white. At least nine live in St. Petersburg — though they're rarely in the same house for long — and the others live in Clearwater, with stops in Largo and Pinellas Park. The majority were evicted at least once; a few families, like Isaiah's, faced eviction three times.

All 14 of them come from fractured homes. Their parents sued each other over paternity and child support. Some of these kids went to live with guardians. One ran away from a teen shelter.

Eleven experienced domestic violence in their homes, their mothers roughed up by their boyfriends, sometimes in front of them. Six were the subjects of child abuse or neglect cases; investigators came into their homes with questions about black eyes and burn marks.

One of the car thieves was just a baby when his mother tried to run him over with a car. Another was molested while playing football in the neighborhood. He was eight. Yet another future thief stood in the doorframe to the kitchen and watched a man choke his pregnant mother, pressed against the dinner table. The boy hid in a corner, 6 years old and too scared to see what happened next.

They attended some of the worst elementary schools in the state, Melrose and Lakewood, then went on to Azalea and John Hopkins, the most troubled middle schools with the highest truancy rates in Pinellas County.

Nine were listed as "suspects" on police reports by their 14th birthdays; one had just turned eight when neighbors saw him slamming a stolen tricycle into the ground at a nearby park. Most of them were caught for gateway crimes like this before they ever got charged with grand theft auto: They stole bicycles, or they were lookouts first; before the cops ever found them in a car, they found them testing door handles, or with strangers' key fobs in their pockets.

Nearly all of them were 15 or younger when they were first arrested for stealing cars.

Four of them are now in jail or prison.

For Isaiah, that first grand theft auto charge came at 14 years old. Over the next year, he'd be caught seven more times. He'd become the most arrested kid car thief in Pinellas County, topping the list of 14.

If Dominique hadn't died in the pond that night, she likely would have been arrested over the Honda Accord. It would have been her fifth grand theft auto arrest, enough for her to make the list, too. That would have been one more thing the brother and sister shared on earth.

***

Isaiah was acting as a lookout one evening around 8 p.m. His friends were "car-hopping" on 10th Avenue N, looking for unlocked cars with keys left inside to steal. Isaiah was supposed to shout if he saw someone coming. But as his friends tried to get into a Saturn, then a Nissan, Isaiah failed to notice a woman sitting on her porch. He heard her yell: Should she call their mothers or the cops? Isaiah ran.

He made it only five blocks before police put him in handcuffs. They took him to the Pinellas Juvenile Assessment Center. The state rarely holds a child for a "property crime" like grand theft auto, or in this case, vehicle burglary. Within hours, Isaiah says, he was sent back home.

That was easy, he thought.

So was his sister. Dominique hadn't been caught yet. But she was running away. She was taking rides from strange men. One of her friends would later tell police that two of these men took them to hotel rooms. They gave the girls ecstasy, and charged other men $50 to have sex with them.

Two months after this report, Dominique was arrested for stealing a Dodge Ram.

***

A few weeks later, Isaiah put his hand in his T-shirt as he opened the door to a Toyota Camry. It was a trick his friends had taught him, to avoid leaving fingerprints. He climbed into one of the passenger seats, and they all took off through Childs Park.

Soon, police were behind the stolen Camry. Isaiah was arrested at gunpoint, his hands up as he got on the ground. He called the cop "sir," thinking if he was polite enough, the officer wouldn't shoot him. "It was scary," Isaiah says.

Once again, Isaiah was taken to the assessment center.

Once again, he went home. *That was easy*, he still thought, even though a gun had been trained on him.

Riding around in another stolen car, he told his friend at the wheel, "Let me drive."

"You don't know how to drive," the friend said.

"Yes I do." But he didn't, and that's how Isaiah taught himself to drive.

On March 16, 10 days after his first grand theft auto arrest, police stopped Isaiah driving a stolen Volvo. Dominique was one of his passengers. He says she told him it was a friend's car. He didn't know, he says, that she was stealing, too.

But she had taken it from a man who had asked for her number, then agreed to give her a ride to Bartlett Park. When he stopped for gas, she took off in the Volvo.

The cops handcuffed Dominique and Isaiah and put them in the backseat of the same cruiser. She laughed and said she wasn't scared. She asked the officer to take her to the McDonald's drive through.

Maybe Isaiah should have been worried for her then. But he was still just a 14-year-old boy. He was more concerned about being locked up for spring break. He didn't want to miss all the fun.

***

There's always a kid at the top of the list. One thief gets caught enough times, gets sent away for a few months to a juvenile program, and another kid takes his spot. He steals everything on four wheels and speeds around town. He's all over Snapchat, everyone's posting about him on Facebook and, to them, he becomes the biggest name in stolen cars.

For one long, hot stretch of 2015, that name was Isaiah Battle.

On April 6, 2015, he lifted a Dodge Stratus a few blocks west of the Walmart near Central Avenue, his fingerprints left on the rearview mirror. "Well you have to adjust things to see good when you're driving," he told officers.

In the second week of May, he chased a school bus in a green Hyundai Santa Fe, trying to impress a girl he liked who was on the bus. His friends cheered him on from the backseat. One of his friend's mothers ratted him out: "She told her son that she didn't want those 'cars' around her home," the police report noted.

He took another Sante Fe on June 5, this one white. He got tired of walking, he told the police.

They found the car abandoned in an alley, bullet holes in the back. Isaiah's mother said she hadn't seen him in a week. Isaiah said a kid named T-Man was with him when he stole it.

A week later, on June 12, he took a Ford Escape from a church on Central Avenue while the owners were donating items for charity.

His victims were usually able to identify Isaiah, taller and thinner than most of the other kids at it, says Tim McClintick, a St. Petersburg police officer who handcuffed Isaiah several times that summer. One person even noticed the shape of Isaiah's ears, wide and low-slung on his head.

He was playing football with his friends on July 7 when kids in a stolen Toyota drove by and shot at them. A bullet struck the foot of one of Isaiah's friends, also 14. "It happened so fast. I turned around, I see guns." Isaiah took off running. He thought, "I don't want to get shot."

Three days later, July 10, a man saw a stolen Toyota Sienna minivan doing donuts in a parking lot. Isaiah took a corner too fast and busted the tires on a curb. Black smoke poured down the street, but he kept driving.

The minivan crashed. He ran.

***

It was like this all summer long, mostly stealing cars in the dark from victims he rarely saw. But as time wore on, Isaiah became more reckless. On the afternoon of August 30, a week before his 15th birthday, Isaiah dove into a Porsche while a man pumped gas on Central Avenue. His friend at the wheel, they drove off with tires screeching and almost hit a group of children.

He says what happened on Sept. 26, 2015, was an accident.

Isaiah was walking around Childs Park, itching for a car. He spotted a woman cleaning her Chevy Cruze in the driveway, all the doors wide open. Isaiah walked back and forth on the sidewalk, waiting for the woman to go inside for a drink or a bathroom break. Gospel music from the car radio cast across the street.

She walked into the house. He thought she was gone. Isaiah ran to the Chevy. It took him a minute to close all four doors.

And she saw him.

When the woman reached into the Chevy to pull him out, Isaiah put the car in reverse. She was halfway in the driver's seat. He dragged her down the driveway, into the neighbor's yard.

Isaiah could hear her screaming. He abandoned the car straight away. He sent a friend to walk by the house, to make sure the woman was okay. Her leg was scraped up and gashed.

The police came for Isaiah the next day. They found him in a friend's yard in Childs Park, sitting on a toddler's battery-powered toy car. "A little Hot Wheel," Isaiah remembers.

This time, they charged him with carjacking.

***

The judge sentenced him to nine months at a program in Okeechobee County, the farthest he had ever been from home. It was a quiet place, Isaiah says. "Everybody had one thing on their mind: going home."

Dominique was still stealing cars in St. Petersburg. In November, police caught her driving a Chevy Impala, bailing from the car and running from officers until her friend, a passenger, was hit with a Taser.

Dominique asked the officers how they knew the car was stolen. Then she laughed and said, "Never mind."

Six weeks later she took a Nissan Murano, hitting parked cars as she tried to get away.

She came to visit Isaiah at Okeechobee with their mother, baby brother and sister in the first week of March. Isaiah told his mom he was going to change.

He was so happy to see Dominique, now 16 to his 15 years. Isaiah missed staying up talking with her in the room they shared, watching TV and laughing.

She caught him up on everything that was going on back home, who was doing what. The kind of nothing, normal stuff that Isaiah wishes he could remember now. It was the last time he saw her alive.

***

Dominique and two of her friends hitched a ride in a Honda Accord on a Wednesday night three weeks later. The driver says he ran into Walmart to buy a television, and the girls took off in his car. They drove around all night, drinking strawberry-flavored alcohol, eating McDonald's and texting a friend with plans to meet up.

Police began tailing them around 3:30 a.m. The girls switched off the Honda's headlights and wove through a cemetery, pitch-black but for the distant glare of the highway. They must not have seen the pond. The car sank to the bottom, all of them trapped inside.

The dive team found Dominique in the driver's seat, draped over the center console. Her friends were in the backseat. The keys were still in the ignition.

It was late afternoon when another kid from St. Pete came running up to Isaiah in the yard at Okeechobee. The boy had just received his weekly phone call.

"Hey Isaiah," he said. "Your sister died."

It was rec time. Isaiah had been playing ball. The clouds had been drumming them with rain all week, but that day was dry.

"For real?" Isaiah asked.

"For real, bro."

Isaiah doesn't remember everything that happened next. He knows he was taken to the program therapist's office. He dialed his mother's number into the phone, but she didn't answer. He reached his friends, back in St. Petersburg.

He remembers leaving the room and being back outside. He cried there, out in the yard, alone but for his jailers.

***

He went to the wake in shackles. He shuffled up the aisle of the funeral home. She was alone, in a black casket.

Isaiah had never seen a body before.

Dominique was wearing a black dress. Her makeup was done too neatly.

"That's not my sister," he kept saying.

It hurt him, how much the girl in the casket did not look like Dominique.

Then he noticed something he hadn't seen before. She had gotten a new tattoo, in large looping letters on the inside of her left arm:

"Isaiah."

He cried.

He leaned into the casket.

He kissed his sister on the forehead.

***

When Isaiah was released from Okeechobee five months later, he wanted things to be different. He swore he would never steal another car, not after she had died in one, not after this.

His mother had been too sad to go into the room he'd shared with Dominique. Her clothes were still on her bed, and her blue bookbag was on the nightstand. There were pink sheets on Isaiah's bed, from a sleepover she'd had with friends. Isaiah lay down on them, but he didn't sleep at all.

The next day would have been Dominique's 17th birthday. He bought flowers at Family Dollar, and his mom drove him to the cemetery on First Avenue S. There was no headstone where Dominique was buried; just a little pink nylon flag. Isaiah put the flowers there, with four "Happy birthday!" balloons.

From his sister's grave, he could see the Shell station where he had stolen that Porsche. He sat down in the dirt and weeds. He prayed that Dominique would watch over him.

Isaiah decided he would get a job. He'd go to school. Finish school. He was going to stay out of cars.

All of his friends were still stealing them. They were having fun and going places. He hung pictures of Dominique on his bedroom walls. He tried to hang out at home more.

It was hard, with her stuff still everywhere. Their room smelled like perfume.

He applied for a job at Dunkin Donuts. He applied for a job at Publix. He applied for jobs at Winn Dixie, Domino's and Burger King.

He went back to school, now at Gibbs High, and made B's and C's.

He smoked weed. He watched television.

He called to check on his job applications. They told him they'd get back to him.

Before, he'd find cash going through cars. Now he asked his mom for $20, $40. Isaiah hated taking her money.

She was involved with the International People's Democratic Uhuru Movement, a community group that believes police killed Dominique because she was black. Yashica spoke at rallies, saying her daughter was chased into the pond.

He started getting in fights again, at Gibbs, with kids from rival gangs.

None of the jobs got back to him. "Nobody wanted to hire me."

Months passed. He was kicked out of Gibbs. Went to an alternative school in Pinellas Park.

He would come home and sit in that room full of his sister.

***

There was so much time to kill and so few ways to do it. His world was only as east and west as his bike could take him.

But when he was in a car, he could drive around the city: "See what's around." He could drive around all night. He could listen to music, or he could listen to the quiet. He could cram the car full of friends, or he could be alone. He liked to be alone: "I really like to do everything by myself."

He didn't have to think about anything: "You just got to be focused on what you're doing." He didn't have to be home, or at a motel, or at a shelter. It made him feel free, Isaiah says: He could go anywhere.

But all those times Isaiah was in cars, all those times he could go wherever he pleased, all those times he was at the wheel and finally in control, he didn't. He wasn't.

Isaiah Battle has never taken a car as far as Tampa. He has never been to Busch Gardens to see if a real rollercoaster feels anything like when he threw his hands above his head in a speeding car.

***

It was a 60-degree morning in January. He was riding his bike from Childs Park to his cousin's, and he was getting tired. He still had 15 or 20 more blocks to go.

He knew what to look for, scanning the street now. His eyes searched until he saw it: heat coming from the tailpipe of an Acura. Someone had left it running in their driveway to warm up.

He slowed to a stop. He set his bicycle on the pavement. Did he think about her then?

Isaiah says he did. He always thought about Dominique. Every day, all the time.

But he was also thinking about himself. That he knew it was wrong, but he wanted to do it anyway. That what happened to her wouldn't happen to him.

He crossed the street. His fingers curled around the door handle.

He thought that people who try to do the right thing, even if they mess up once, or even a lot, over and over again, might still get to go to heaven.

He climbed into the car, and he drove away.

The aftermath

Isaiah was caught the same day he stole the Acura and charged with grand theft auto, fleeing and eluding, and driving without a license. Prosecutors charged Isaiah as an adult, deciding the juvenile system and the death of his sister hadn't been enough of a deterrent. He is expected to be sentenced to up to six years in prison at an Aug. 28 hearing.

About a Boy

The Oregonian

July 30- August 6, 2017

By Casey Parks

At 13, Jay told his family he wasn't the girl they thought he was. Then he began his journey to becoming himself

Jay woke in darkness, the summer and a girlhood behind him. A sharp pain stabbed through his stomach. In an hour, he would be a high school freshman.

Please, he thought, don't let anyone recognize me.

He dragged himself out of bed and lumbered through the double-wide trailer he shared with his mom and two sisters. His mother was at work, his siblings asleep. Only his dog, a 9-pound Chihuahua named Chico, marked Jay's passing from one life to the next.

Jay faced the bathroom mirror. He was 14. His dark brown hair spiked just the right way. His jaw was square, his eyebrows full and wild. But his body betrayed him. He was 5-foot-2 and curvy in all the wrong places.

He tugged one sports bra over his chest and then another. He pulled on a black T-shirt, hoping it would hide his curves. He eyed the silhouette, and his stomach rumbled with anxiety.

Not flat enough.

He had finished eighth grade with long hair and a different name. At his new school in southwest Washington, most of the 2,000 kids had never known the girl Jay supposed he used to be. As long as his contours didn't give his secret away, "Jay" was a clean slate, a boy who could be anyone.

He took one final look in the mirror. Puberty was pulling him in a direction he didn't want to go, and reversing it would take more than a haircut and an outfit. But how much more? He was a boyish work in progress, only beginning to figure out how to become himself. His mom and his doctors had little precedent for how to help.

He had taken great pains to start school as this boy with no past. His mom had met with the principal, and a counselor had created a plan. Jay could use the staff bathroom. Teachers would avoid his birth name, a long and Latina moniker that stung Jay every time he heard it.

Jay stepped outside and knew he should feel lucky. Whole generations had lived and died without any of the opportunities he would have. He was a teenager coming of age in an era *Time* magazine had declared the Transgender Tipping Point.

By his senior year, Jay's quiet life would ride a surge in civil rights.

Barack Obama would become the first president to say the word "transgender" in a State of the Union speech. Target would strip gender labels off its toy aisles. In Oregon, student-athletes would gain the right to decide whether to play on the girls' team or the boys'. Girls would wear tuxedos to prom.

That didn't make the path forward easy or safe.

North Carolina would forfeit $3.7 billion to keep people like Jay out of the bathroom. An Oregon city councilman an hour from Jay's house would threaten an "ass-whooping" to transgender students who used "the opposite sex's facilities." Even Washington, the liberal state Jay called home, would consider a bill rolling back his right to choose the locker room that felt right. Nationwide, President Donald Trump would take over for Obama and ban transgender people from serving in the military.

But that morning, Jay was just a teenager, just a boy walking to school. He didn't want to be a trailblazer. He wanted to be normal.

"That's Not Me"

He was 12 when "girl" started to feel like the wrong word for him. He didn't know what he was, yet.

I'm a ghost without a body.

He avoided mirrors, but his reflection found him anyway. There were mirrors in the hallway and next to the kitchen table. Turned off, the flat-screen TV was a black projection of the body he tried to hide. Even the coffee table, a glass-top smeared with after-school snacks, caught his form.

His face was round and so was his body. He turned away in disgust.

That's not me.

His family called him YaYa then. He dressed to disappear. He pulled his thick hair into a ponytail, the imperfect gathering too far left or right to be stylish. He wore an oversized gray sweatshirt every day and kept the hood up to hide his hair.

He tried to do what other girls did. He shaved his eyebrows and curled his hair. Both felt wrong. His stomach knotted every time someone called him "she."

In other parts of the country, people might have talked. Girls in guys' sweatshirts were tomboys or worse. In Vancouver, just north of Portland, most people looked the other way. He had friends who wore makeup, but no one ever pressured him to try it.

Still, some days, he couldn't bring himself to walk the hallways. He skipped class at least once a week in seventh grade. He passed whole days in bed, the sheets pulled up to his neck. In the shadows of his bedroom, Jay could be almost nothing at all.

His mother took him to doctors, but there was no word for the way Jay felt. He struggled to explain that he felt sick because he didn't feel like himself.

I feel like I am walking on glass, he wanted to say. But the words came out, "My stomach hurts."

The doctor gave him omeprazole for heartburn and Zofran for nausea. Jay trawled the internet for a better diagnosis. Surfing on a years-old iPod, he landed on YouTube, where every video was a current that pulled him toward another. Eventually the river carried him to a four-minute video called "BOYS CAN HAVE A VAG." A 20-something woman with long hair and perfect eyebrows laid out her argument.

Gender, she said, is like a suitcase. When you're born, doctors look between your legs and assign you one. Boy luggage contains sports, trucks and action figures. It comes with short hair and abs, toughness and courage. The girl suitcase has soft curves and graceful movements, dresses and jewelry, patience and nurturing.

But what if all those things felt wrong? she asked. "You might start to feel broken, like there was no room for who you were in that stifling suitcase."

That's it.

People who don't identify with their suitcase, the YouTube host explained, are transgender.

Jay typed "transgender" in the search box. He watched documentaries and first-person testimonials and began to imagine the possibilities. Puberty blockers could stop his period. Shots could deepen his alto voice. With surgeries, he could even rid himself of ovaries and breasts.

It might take years, he realized, but maybe the world would see him as a guy.

That recognition was a window opening and a door slamming shut. He'd never have a kid, he thought. He would always have this history —a girlhood that screeched to a halt. He was afraid of shots. He dreaded surgeries and secrets.

He didn't want to be that word, "transgender." He searched for other explanations, but nothing fit.

After a month, he resigned himself.

This is my label.

One afternoon while his mom worked, Jay called his younger sisters to the living room. They were 8 and 10 —old enough, he hoped, to understand.

"I need to show you a video," he told them. He streamed one of the YouTube videos on the TV. A trans guy appeared on the screen and explained how he came out to his family.

Jay stood while his sisters watched from the couch.

"This is how I feel," Jay said when it ended.

"So you're becoming a boy?" asked his youngest sister, Angie.

Jay paused. He couldn't bring himself to say it out loud.

"Kind of."

"Do you want me to tell mom?" Maria asked.

"No," he said. Jay hadn't talked to his mother much the past year, but he knew he had to tell her.

The next day, he crept to the other side of their trailer, his heart knocking. He pushed open his mom's bedroom door, stood in the doorway and watched her play Candy Crush. She was zoned out after a 12-hour workday. Maybe she'd be too tired to talk about it. She already had on her favorite pajamas, gray sweatpants and a tan tank top.

"I think I figured it out," he said.

He took a deep breath.

"I'm a boy."

His mom looked up from the phone.

"So you want to be a butch lesbian?"

"No," he said. He walked toward her.

"A boy."

"What Went Wrong?"

Nancy Munoz spent half her life dreaming of who her oldest daughter would become. Nancy was 16 when she gave birth, 29 when her 13-year-old told her everything she'd imagined was wrong.

That night, Nancy fell into bed and reminisced. Her oldest had been a perfect baby, fluffy and cute in tiny dresses. What went wrong? She racked her brain for answers. Nancy didn't wear makeup or skirts. Maybe she hadn't taught her kids how to be women. They saw their dad only once every few months. Maybe Jay wanted to be the man his childhood lacked.

Nancy couldn't help but think of the ways she had failed. She had wanted to be a secretary working in an office. Instead, she earned minimum wage working double shifts at a home for disabled adults.

She longed for her three girls to have all the things she never had, wedding dresses and quinceañera parties.

Had all her dreams been the wrong ones?

A thought came. Her perfect oldest baby had cried every time Nancy suggested dresses. Jay had wanted to wear only one outfit when he was young. It was green camouflage with a Scooby-Doo print. A boy's outfit.

When that outfit wore out, Nancy combed four stores for a replacement. She prided herself on being the kind of mother who would do anything to make her children happy. She bought them pizza even if she couldn't afford lunch for herself. She let them have cats and birds and hamsters.

But this? What would it take to make her daughter a boy?

The next morning, Nancy searched online. Doctors had spent two decades looking for biological proof of what makes someone transgender, she learned. So far, they had only theories.

Some blamed hormone imbalances or psychosocial factors. Others found proof in patients' brains. Some people, researchers believed, were just born transgender.

Nancy couldn't see inside Jay's head. As she read, though, the pieces started to fall into place. He had loved Hot Wheels. He'd never harbored crushes on boys. And that walk, she thought. Girls sway and glide through life. Her child traversed the world with stiff hips and steel legs.

Nancy kept reading. Nearly 80 percent of kids who came out as transgender had been harassed at school.

A third said they had been physically assaulted. Ninety percent of transgender adults had been harassed at work. Nearly half had attempted suicide.

That was not the life Nancy wanted for her child. And yet, she thought, what was the life Jay had now?

He had been depressed since he was 4. She had taken him to counseling, but still he spent so many hours in a dark bedroom. When he said he had figured himself out, his eyes had flickered.

There was a spark, she thought. I have to run toward that light.

"I Know She's a Boy"

They started slow. One afternoon at Walmart, Jay ventured to the boys section. His new life began with button-downs and boxer shorts.

He wore a men's T-shirt for his eighth-grade yearbook photo, a subtle victory his classmates didn't notice.

Jay's sisters tried to use "he" when talking about their oldest sibling. It didn't feel right. They still called him YaYa, a girlish name carved from the one his mother had chosen before he was born. He still had long hair. Everyone else thought of him as a girl.

In the winter of 2013, Jay spent an hour each week untangling his thoughts with a counselor. Jay had depression and anxiety, the counselor said. He also had what's listed in the Diagnostic and Statistical Manual of Mental Disorders as "gender dysphoria."

That feeling might go away, the counselor said. Some kids grow up and find there were other reasons their brains and bodies felt mismatched. The therapist suggested Jay practice living as a boy one day a week. If it felt right, he said, Jay could try longer.

Nancy told the girls to think of the process as a kind of ultrasound.

"Your sister thinks she is a boy," Nancy said. "We're going to find out. It's kind of like being pregnant all over again. What are we going to have? A girl or a boy?"

"She's a boy," Angie said. "I know she's a boy."

Jay tried, but the experiment felt too much like dressing up, as if Halloween came once a week. He wanted to be a boy all the time.

"Why don't we wait until you finish eighth grade?" his mother asked. That way, he could transition without 750 preteens watching.

On the first day of summer vacation, Nancy drove Jay to Supercuts. He pulled the hoodie off, climbed into the barber's chair and asked for a guy's style.

"Are you sure?" the stylist asked.

"Yeah," he said. "Not a pixie cut. A boy's cut."

The job was cheap and fast. When he left, his hair was a palm tree, a porcupine's splayed spikes.

It's ugly, Jay thought. But he didn't care. He was one step closer, he thought, to looking right.

Going Stealth

By the time Jay started high school in August 2014, his hair looked just how he wanted, shaved on the sides and high on top. He tramped through hallways in Timberland boots and black T-shirts. The cosmetic changes had worked, he thought. Everyone at school thought of him as a guy.

Other transgender kids wrote online that they longed to live undetected. But "going stealth," as Jay called it, had its limitations. Jay used the nurse's office to change clothes for P.E. His blood pressure rose anytime someone saw him emerging in gym shorts.

He was afraid to use the bathroom. People asked questions when he used the teachers' bathroom, and he didn't feel safe in the men's room. What if a guy came in and noticed Jay sitting in a stall? He just held it.

Jay lived in one of the most liberal regions of the country. His school had a day of silence for transgender rights. Still, he worried his classmates would treat him differently if they knew. They might ask what his name used to be. They might want to see pictures of the years he spent miserable and mistaken for something else.

Passing was a gift he tried to preserve. Jay played dumb when LGBT issues came up in class. He avoided the diversity club, a lunchtime gathering of ethnic minorities and gay students.

"I don't want everybody wondering, 'Why is this straight dude in here,'" Jay told his mom. "What would I say?"

Few people in his neighborhood noticed. Theirs was the last mobile home on a dead-end road where no other kids lived. When their favorite taco truck owner asked, "Didn't you have three daughters?" Nancy said no, she'd always had a son.

Then, a month into school, people started asking questions.

Roughly a quarter of the students at Jay's high school had also attended his middle school. Occasionally, old classmates noticed him in the throng. One guy stopped Jay at the end of biology class.

"Didn't you used to be a girl?"

"What? No way," Jay said. "Do you want to see inside my pants?"

Sometimes teenagers whispered. A few times, they shouted down the hallway.

"Jay, are you a girl?"

He joked in class, but he didn't invite anyone home after school. How would he explain the long-haired school pictures that hung on the walls?

Instead, he lived his life in video games. He remade himself into a businessman with a family on The Sims. He crashed through Grand Theft Auto as basic killa, a hipster renegade with nothing to lose.

Then, one day in health class, a tall girl with wavy blonde hair struck up a conversation. Jay had drawn a poster showing the rap group Odd Future's doughnut logo. Maddie liked it. They started talking about music, and soon, Maddie and Jay were inseparable.

She was, he thought, an ideal friend. They found the same pedestrian things funny. They spent whole afternoons and nights hanging out or texting. Maddie and Jay both possessed a quiet maturity that made adults say they had old souls.

Maddie had heard the rumors, and at first, she told people they were wrong. Jay just had a "small voice." That didn't make him a girl.

The more she thought about it, the more Maddie wondered. That Thanksgiving, she decided to ask him.

Jay was at home, sick with another stomach ache, when the text message came in.

People keep saying you're a girl.

His heart dropped. He wasn't ready.

Yeah ...

Maddie was shocked. She had never knowingly met a transgender person. She asked her mom for advice. When she texted Jay back, though, she kept her cool.

I'm not going to treat you different. You can tell me anything you want, and I'll never be here to judge.

As winter neared, other boys grew taller and deeper-voiced. Jay remained the same. His face was smooth, his voice high and lilted.

"People think I'm a late-bloomer," Jay told his mom.

Something had to change, he told her. He couldn't stay frozen in time while his classmates became men. He needed testosterone to do what his own biology would not.

The T-Clinic

If Jay had lived anywhere else, his journey might have stalled right there.

In the fall of 2014, most doctors didn't know how to help him. His pediatrician offered him birth control to stop his period. But Jay didn't want girl hormones.

Fortunately, Jay lived half an hour from one of the few doctors in America who knew what to do. Dr. Karin Selva was a pediatric endocrinologist in Portland. When she read Jay's chart, she recognized all the signs.

Depression. Anxiety. Frequent trips to the emergency room with stomach complaints.

Then Selva opened the door to her exam room and saw a boy with a fresh haircut and big grin. She was his only hope.

Selva knew how to treat hormone imbalances, but in the three years since a transgender patient first approached her, she'd had to learn on the fly. She'd hunted for research and mentors. Only one study, conducted in the Netherlands, examined how hormone treatments affected children as they became adults. Only one U.S. clinic, Boston Children's Hospital, specialized in transgender adolescent care.

By the time Jay arrived, Selva had treated 48 transgender patients. They made up less than 5 percent of her work, but that was enough to make her a national expert.

She traveled the country training other endocrinologists, and she convinced Randall Children's Hospital officials to set aside one day every other month for the program she called the T-Clinic. The appointments were always full.

Families came from six hours away, bringing children as young as 8. Selva's research suggested there might be thousands of transgender adolescents just in the metropolitan area.

A Portland Public Schools survey found that 3 percent of middle and high school students identify as transgender. Leaders at a local advocacy group told Selva they were working with 450 transgender kids, nearly two-thirds of whom were under 12.

The work could be daunting. Adolescent brains aren't fully developed. Teenagers take risks and try out identities. The more transgender patients she had seen, though, the more Selva thought of the oath physicians take: Do no harm.

"Abstaining is actually doing harm," she said. "Puberty is happening, and it's making it worse for these kids."

Once a child went through puberty, physical changes became much harder to reverse. She could arrest a patient's development to buy time and even re-route it.

Selva's task was to figure out when and how to intervene.

Jay was a week shy of his 15th birthday. Two years had passed since he told his mother he was a boy. He hadn't wavered.

The puberty blocker Lupron was a good place to start, Selva told Jay and Nancy. The medicine would shut down his production of estrogen. His period would stop.

The medication was completely reversible. Doctors had been using Lupron for 40 years on kids who started puberty too early. But the shots cost nearly $20,000 a year, more than Nancy took home annually. She earned only $10.80 an hour.

Jay qualified for public health benefits, Selva noted. Just a few months before, Oregon had become the first state to provide Medicaid coverage for transgender adolescents using the blockers. Washington was close to approving a similar plan, and Selva thought she might be able to lobby the state to pay.

"What about testosterone?" Jay asked.

Testosterone was cheaper, Selva told them, and more powerful. The hormone would change Jay in ways that could not be reversed. Once his voice deepened, it would never go back. With testosterone, Jay would grow facial hair and an Adam's apple. Those changes, too, could not be undone.

Jay was making a rest-of-his-life decision. Go home and think about it, Selva said.

"It Still Hurts"

Nancy's relatives told her she was making a mistake. What kind of mother lets her daughter become a boy? Jay's dad accused her of enabling Jay. Other people said she was a bad mom.

"He's still alive," she countered. "Would I rather have a dead child because I didn't support him?"

Nancy had already given up so many of her own dreams. She had never gone to college, never found a job she loved. She wasn't pushing him to transition. She was sacrificing, again, so he could have the life she had missed.

Every step forward took Nancy further from the daughter she raised. She stopped calling him YaYa, but some nights, Nancy flipped through her files and stared at the name on his birth certificate. She had spent 13 years calling that name to dinner, writing it on presents and permission slips.

After Jay cut his hair, he grumbled about the family photos Nancy shared on Facebook. He looked miserable in most of them, grimacing while his younger sisters beamed.

Over time, Nancy deleted the snapshots that showed him in white dresses. She took down the gap-toothed toddler in floral print. She removed the 8-month ultrasound that revealed a girl with big cheeks.

She kept his basketball photo for a while. It was a sporty pose, she assured him. He looked more like a Native American guy than a Latina girl.

"It still hurts," Jay told her.

Nancy deleted the photos and felt like she was erasing her baby from her life. It was as if YaYa had died and Nancy had inherited this teenage boy with no backstory.

What if she got old and couldn't remember anything? What if pictures became her only link to the past?

I'm going to ask myself, "Is this kid really mine?" And if he is mine, how come I don't have any pictures of him when he was a baby?

She searched her leather-bound albums for photos she could keep.

Maybe there was one of him in a diaper, she hoped, one shot that appeared genderless. She flipped the pages, looking for the Scooby-Doo outfit. How had she never taken a picture of her 4-year-old's favorite clothes?

Nancy wished she could start over again. She would shove him back inside her and deliver him right. His photos would be Hot Wheels and Scooby-Doo prints.

She didn't need him to be a girl. She just wanted proof that he was hers.

The Gift

The Christmas tree glowed pink that year. Jay's mom pointed to the big red box below.

"There's an extra present for you," she said.

He tore away the wrapping paper. Inside, he found another box. He opened it and pulled out a glass bottle. The vial was red-topped, smaller than his thumb.

"What is it?" he asked.

"Read it," Nancy said.

Testosterone cypionate injection, USP

200 mg/mL

It wasn't fair, he thought, that he needed medicine to trigger what happened naturally to other boys. He wished he had been born "right," a guy with all the guy parts.

He carried the vial to the couch in disbelief. He laughed, then cried, then laughed again. "Mom," he said. "It's so little."

The hormone would change him, the doctor had said, in ways he could never undo. Jay held up the vial. The testosterone gleamed in the Christmas lights.

A Big Question

Jay feels more himself, but at age 15 he's considering an irreversible path

Seventeen million people tuned in the night Caitlyn Jenner came out on national TV as a transgender woman. Jay watched alone.

He hadn't told many friends that he was transgender, too. His mom refused to watch.

"I have more important things to do than watch someone who's rich and has their life figured out," Nancy Munoz said. "My focus is on finding resources for you."

It was 2015, and Jenner was 65. That meant six decades of secrets in a spectacular body that always felt wrong.

Jay was 15. He retreated to his bedroom, stepped over his PlayStation into bed. He leaned against a Bob Marley poster and watched the interview on his iPhone.

Diane Sawyer's voice filled the room. For the past year, the reporter said, Jenner had lived "in a white-hot vortex of cameras, questions, speculation, jokes and ridicule."

That was how most people thought of transgender people, Jay knew. Men in dresses. Ugly women.

"As we sit down," Sawyer said, "the person whose face has changed so much over recent years is quiet, knowing the moment that carries you forward can also mean no way back."

Jay bit his lip. After four months of testosterone, his voice cracked with the first hints of puberty. A few dark hairs shaded his chin.

"Are you ready?" Sawyer asked.

Holding His Breath

Some days, Jay forgot he was transgender. For the first time in years, he volunteered to accompany his mom to WinCo for groceries. He no longer avoided mirrors. He gazed at himself before school. Had he grown taller? Had his face thinned?

The world saw him as he saw himself. He picked clothes that made him feel macho — gold chains and Timberland boots. Everyone called him "he."

Then his depression crept back. He stood in front of his closet before school and worried his 2Pac T-shirt revealed too much. He walked to class, and his brain looped reminders.

My chest. My chest. My chest.

He bandaged his A-cup breasts so tight that he breathed in bursts. He slinked down hallways, terrified of contact. People rough-housed with guys, he had learned. They slapped his sternum to say hello.

"Girls will touch your chest, too," his mom said. They lean in to cuddle. They rest a hand there as they kiss.

"If I wanted to date somebody now, or even in the future, how would I tell them?" Jay asked.

"Who's going to date you?" Nancy asked. "Lesbians?"

"Straight girls," Jay said.

"It's kind of lying, though," Nancy said. "What they see is a boy."

"It's not lying," Jay said. "That's who I am."

It'd be easier to be open, Jay thought, if his body looked more like he wanted. He didn't feel ready to consider genital surgery. Many transgender guys never did, he had read. But he couldn't think about girls or school or anything else until the breasts were gone.

"I've been on testosterone awhile," Jay told his mom in April. "I'm thinking about top surgery."

Nancy had struggled at first to accept that her oldest daughter was a boy. She still kept a few photos hanging on the wall that showed the kid Jay used to be. They captured him in scoop-neck T-shirts in fifth grade, with long hair in eighth.

He had been Jay for nearly a year. Nancy didn't want to make him wait to live like a regular teenager.

"Let's ask," she said.

Something to Discuss

Google Maps said the trip would take 34 minutes. But they had traveled the horseshoe route from one suburb to the other for an hour already, and Jay was sure they were lost again.

"It says turn right," he told his mom.

Nancy cursed Portland, its city traffic and confusing interstates. Jay believed the winding path would end his depression, so Nancy kept driving, missing turns and backtracking until they found it, a nondescript Beaverton clinic for young transgender patients.

Inside the Legacy Medical Group waiting room, Jay grabbed a Teletubbies book and pretended to read. The walls were yellow, the art kid-friendly neon. He peered over the book as another patient floated by. She was tall and graceful, more at ease as a girl than Jay ever had been.

Some Oregon school districts estimate as many as 3 percent of students identify as transgender. At Jay's school in Vancouver, the principal knew at least half a dozen kids whose gender identities and anatomies didn't match. But Jay had never knowingly seen another transgender person in real life. His long lashes froze as the patient made her way to the parking lot.

"Jay?" a nurse called.

Inside, the nurse weighed and measured him. Not quite 5-foot-2, she wrote in his chart.

The doctor barreled in, a whirl of energy in coral pants and a floral shirt.

"What's new?" Dr. Karin Selva asked.

Jay sat up straighter. "I actually have facial hair now."

"Where is it? Where is it?" the doctor asked, inspecting his chin. He had three tiny hairs.

"Stinking?"

"Oh, yes," his mom said. "He stinks a lot."

Nancy cleared her throat.

"Jay has something he wants to discuss," she said.

Jay tapped his black knock-off Vans nervously against the exam table. "Top surgery," he said.

Selva sat down.

By then, the pediatric endocrinologist had prescribed hormones for nearly 100 transgender adolescents. She traveled the country to share her experience with other doctors. She believed affirming a child's gender identity could save their life.

But Selva had never recommended a 15-year-old for surgery. She wasn't sure a surgeon would agree to do it.

The Endocrine Society's guidelines suggested waiting until a patient was 18. Teenage brains are too malleable, some thought. But Selva and other doctors had started to think allowing teenagers to have chest surgery earlier was OK.

Jay had three more years of high school. Three years of homecoming dances and pool parties. With surgery, those might be bearable.

"Hmm," Selva said, tapping her fingers on his chart. "Let me think about it."

The Road Ahead

Jay spent the summer fine-tuning himself. He tried to make his handwriting sloppier like a guy's. He and his best friend Maddie spent afternoons working out in the school weight room. And in August, eight months after his first dose of testosterone, he started injecting the shot himself.

He picked up the supplies at the Fred Meyer pharmacy, then laid them on the kitchen table. One syringe, two needles and a small vial of testosterone. His mother was at work, so he called his younger sisters to the living room to watch.

"If I start bleeding out, you guys are going to witness that," he told 10-year-old Angie and 12-year-old Maria.

"Do you need a cotton ball?" Angie asked.

Jay shook his head no and studied the inch-long needle. He stuck it into the vial and drew out the hormone.

"OK," he whispered.

His sisters moved to the couch and peered over the back. Neither spoke. Maria clutched a gallon-size freezer bag of bandages.

Jay shut his eyes tight. The needle stung. The hormone felt thick going in.

Later that week, Selva called. She and his counselor both believed Jay should have the surgery. The surgeon was willing to meet him to decide if she did, too.

Oregon is one of only three states that gives 15-year-olds the power to make their own medical decisions. As long as a doctor consented, Jay could have any surgery, including an abortion or a heart bypass, without his mom's permission.

He was still a kid, though. State law prevented him from getting a tattoo or piercing his nipples. At doctors' offices, his mom filled out his intake papers. The plastic surgeon, Jay knew, could meet him and decide he was too young.

Dr. Hema Thakar had spent much of her career helping women after breast cancer. By the fall of 2015, when she met Jay, transgender patients made up a third of her practice. She performed top surgery an average of three times a week, but only on adults.

"You are by far the youngest guy I have seen for this," Thakar told Jay.

Thakar had some reservations. Jay's body would grow and change for another few years. If Thakar removed Jay's breasts at 15, she likely would have to perform a revision surgery later. Both procedures would be expensive, with long recovery times.

Because Jay's breasts were so small, she said, Jay could consider a minimally invasive procedure called the keyhole. In that operation, Thakar would make small incisions in the nipples, then draw out most of the breast tissue.

"The incision gets hidden," she explained. "The other thing is your nipple sensation has a better chance of being maintained. For a lot of people, that's important."

Jay laughed nervously.

"He's young right now," Nancy said. "He doesn't care."

"Jay," Thakar said, her voice lowering.

"The last thing I'm going to say is — and it's going to sound really serious because it is — removing the breast, that's irreversible."

She paused.

"I really want you to talk about it with your mom," Thakar said. "The major reason is you can't breast-feed if your breasts are not there."

"Yeah," Jay said.

Nancy and Jay had discussed it. He wanted a family. They had talked about "the pregnant man," a transgender guy in Bend, who'd become famous when he stopped taking testosterone long enough to give birth. Jay figured he would adopt.

"Why don't we meet in December one more time?" Thakar suggested. "I want all of your doctors to be involved and have a group of us agree. We all want the best for you."

Jay had hoped he would have the surgery before school started. It was only four months, he told himself. One semester of his sophomore year.

He mustered a smile.

"Yeah," Jay said. "I guess we could wait."

"That Was Never Me"

Jay had watched enough YouTube videos to know the transition wouldn't be instant. His voice had deepened over time. Surgery, too, would be a process.

He went back to see Thakar in December 2015, and she suggested they wait another six months.

By early 2016, Jay was tired of waiting. That February, he slumped at the kitchen table while his sisters watched "Mulan." When he was a kid, he had loved the Disney movie's main character, a young girl who becomes a soldier by dressing as a boy.

Every day, it's as if I play a part, Mulan sang. When will my reflection show who I am inside?

He looked down at the table, too bummed to watch. His school's winter formal was that night. A friend had nominated Jay for the court, and he had scored enough votes to make it. A teacher passed out repurposed Burger King crowns for the princes to wear.

Jay tried to imagine himself swaying with a girl. If his date leaned in, Jay worried, her head might land on the soft curve of the breasts he worked so hard to hide.

Would a slow dance give his secret away?

He had almost talked himself into taking the risk, he told his sisters.

"Then the situation happened."

That morning, a girl had brought Jay's middle school yearbook to school. She cornered Jay and pointed to a picture. The hair was longer, and the name different, but there was definitely a resemblance. Jay played dumb, but the girl showed the yearbook around school.

Jay, she told people, used to be a girl.

He ran a finger over the black spray-painted crown. No, he realized, he couldn't go to the dance.

Jay left the crown on the table and dragged himself to his bedroom. He fumbled through his closet until he found the yearbook. He flipped to the page the girl had shown around school and looked at the picture. Sixth grade. He had tried to curl his hair that day. Not good.

It felt like the girl at school was trying to trap him, like she wanted to prove the person in the photo was the real Jay. He'd told her to stop. What was her agenda?

He stared at the picture and didn't recognize himself.

That was never me.

In the living room, the Disney characters were discovering Mulan was really a girl. Her chest gave her away. They dragged Mulan out of the tent and threw her into the snow.

Boy With Breasts

When the letter came in May 2016, Jay's mother tore it open. Nancy read it twice, then slammed the pages on the glass coffee table.

"This is so messed up," she said.

The state of Washington required transgender patients to send three letters of recommendation for surgery. Public health officials accepted letters from Selva and Thakar, but the note from Jay's counselor hadn't been good enough. Medicaid wouldn't pay for Jay's surgery, the letter said, unless he saw a psychiatrist.

Nancy dialed the number at the bottom of the letter. When someone answered, Nancy unleashed years of frustration.

"If anybody can say no, it's going to be me because I gave birth to him," she told the woman who answered. "I carried him in my womb for nine months. I couldn't even sleep at night— he was kicking me. I'm the one who has hopes for him. Every woman dreams of seeing their daughter marry in a church with a white dress. And a nice husband to the side and everybody crying. I'm the one who didn't get the quinceañera. And I'm saying yeah, he should have surgery. And yet you're saying no?"

Jay is a boy, Nancy told the insurance worker, just like any other. He was learning to drive. He loved his sisters and scary movies.

"Can you imagine?" Nancy asked the insurance worker. "What if you were a boy walking around with breasts?"

Nancy hung up. Jay sat quiet on the couch.

"We'll fix this," Nancy told him. "They just want to make sure. Minors change their minds sometimes."

Everything seemed to go wrong that spring. A week later, Medicaid stopped paying for his puberty blockers — $8,000 a shot. No one could tell him why. He woke up every morning terrified that his period would return. At school, the yearbook staff posted a survey online for class favorites. Jay's name was inadvertently listed on the girl's side. He called the adviser and asked her to change it. She did, but Jay couldn't help wondering if anyone had seen.

When Jay started transitioning, most people didn't know a transgender person. State legislatures introduced more than 115 anti-LGBT bills the year Caitlyn Jenner came out. Parents packed school board meetings and begged officials across the country to keep boys like Jay out of locker rooms.

He slept away the afternoons and skipped dinner. He snapped at Nancy when she tried to help. He picked fights with his best friend, Maddie.

Eventually, Maddie confronted him. It seemed like Jay went out of his way to be rude to her, she said. If she accidentally stepped on his foot, he purposefully stepped on both of hers. When Maddie started dating a guy, they drifted further apart. They fought one afternoon over text, and that was it.

"It's fine," Jay told his mom. "She was being overdramatic. It wasn't a big loss."

But he felt deeply alone. Maddie was the one person who understood him. She was his only tie to a teenage life. Now she had a boyfriend and a life chugging forward. Jay worried he might stay stuck forever.

That spring, he rarely left his room. He gained weight, and his chest looked fuller, he thought. His mom suggested a trip to Klineline Pond, but he didn't want to go anywhere near water.

"There are guys who have man boobs," Nancy said.

Jay sighed and shook his head. He didn't want to swim until his body was right.

He enrolled in driver's ed but learned in the first class he needed a permit. His birth certificate still listed his old name and marked him as female. A permit would do the same.

Nancy hated watching him suffer. That spring, she wrote to the state of Washington. The old name and gender no longer fit, she wrote. Her child needed a new birth certificate.

In May, she signed Jay out of school for a doctor's appointment. As they left the pediatrician's office, Nancy told Jay he needed a haircut. It had been a few weeks. His hair sprang in unwieldy cowlicks.

A barber re-shaped Jay's spikes, then Nancy told him it was time for school. They got in the car and she started the engine.

"Oh, wait," Nancy said. "Can you hand me the paper in the glove box?"

Jay pulled out a folded piece of paper and handed it to his mom. Nancy told him to open it.

He unfolded the paper and read.

"Born at 9:21 a.m.," he said. "Mom!"

He laughed and stared at the tiny miracle his mother had pulled off. She had changed his birth certificate. As of May 19, Jay was legally male.

Nancy suggested they go get his permit. They stopped for coffee, then strode into the licensing office all smiles. Nancy approached the front desk with a whisper. She needed to talk to someone who could be discreet, she explained. The receptionist looked confused.

Nancy leaned in.

"We're dealing with transgender."

The receptionist lowered her voice to a nearly inaudible level, then disappeared. Another worker eventually waved them over. Jay had a state identification card from childhood that listed him as a girl, she explained. He needed to apply for a gender change through the department's headquarters.

"We've got the birth certificate," Nancy said. "I scanned in his old ID, the application from the health department, the mental health professional's letter."

The worker was friendly but hamstrung by bureaucracy.

"Get this filled out."

Jay's face dropped. The woman handed them another stack of documents.

A Better Normal

A counselor, a doctor and a surgeon had all agreed he was ready. Why did he have to persuade someone else?

"You have to go to 100 different doctors and explain to them 100 different times in 100 different ways," he complained. "'This is who I am. Can you just help me please?'"

They went back to the T-Clinic in June. The office had expanded since Jay first visited two years before. Two doctors, two nurses, a psychiatrist and a psychiatric nurse practitioner worked together to decide when teenagers were ready to take irreversible steps. Together, they had treated more than 150 young people.

Selva suggested Jay discuss surgery with Valerie Tobin, the clinic's psychiatric mental health nurse practitioner. Tobin had worked with transgender children for more than a decade.

Every case was different, Tobin knew. Some patients were ready at 16. Others had bigger issues that needed to be treated before surgery. Sometimes, a kid was so depressed that Tobin believed hormones or surgery were the only fix. Other times, she thought it was best to treat the depression first.

Jay was in many ways a great candidate. Nancy would be there to help him recover. His school had offered to send classwork home. But Tobin told them she couldn't write the letter.

Jay hadn't seen a counselor in a year. The therapist he had seen didn't specialize in transgender kids.

Surgery would be emotional and painful in ways Jay couldn't yet comprehend. Even anesthesia could induce a depressive episode, and Jay's mental health history suggested he was more at risk.

Tobin thought Jay needed an ongoing relationship with a therapist who knew what to expect.

"And you need friends," she said.

Making friends was a vital part of adolescent development. Teenagers needed to learn how to form relationships, mess up and apologize.

With Maddie out of the picture, Jay had no close friends. That could be a sign that he had trust issues or other problems he needed to explore.

Tobin recommended Jay follow up with a psychiatrist closer to his house. He went that August, but that psychiatrist agreed with Tobin — no surgery until Jay made friends.

"Does she know why we're here?" Nancy complained after the appointment. "It's because being trans is not easy. You can't just say, 'Hey, my name is Jay. I'm trans, can we be friends?' You have to be very selective of who you are opening yourself to."

"I told her I'm not very confident about my body," Jay said. "If I want to make good, sustainable friends, it'd be better for me if I had the surgery because I'd feel more confident, and I'd feel OK with telling them more about it."

He was quiet for a while. He pulled his Chihuahua into his lap.

"If that's what she really wants," he said finally. "I can try. I can have a million friends."

Jay's town had meetup groups for young gay and transgender people. He couldn't bring himself to go. He spent a week talking to one girl and imagined telling her. But he wasn't ready.

He needed to start with someone who understood. Just before his junior year started, a friend of a friend messaged Jay on Facebook. Like Jay, he was 16 and transgender and living in Vancouver.

They met one Saturday afternoon at the mall. The guy was bigger and taller than Jay, with a style that skewed more emo-punk. His hair was shaved on one side. He wore gym shorts and a cartoon T-shirt.

They stopped first at a shop that sold ancient knives.

"This is so cool," Jay said, browsing through glass.

His friend shrugged. He didn't really like sharp things.

At an incense store, Jay bought sticks of musk. His friend preferred anime to scented oils. Eventually, their conversation turned to the one thing they had in common.

"What's it like being on T?" Jay's friend asked. His parents hadn't let him start the hormones yet. He had tried beard oil to thicken his facial hair and took a daily dose of men's vitamins. Neither helped.

Jay scanned the crowd as they walked, hoping no one could hear their conversation.

"It's just going through another puberty," Jay told him. It felt normal. A better normal.

"Expect your emotions to run crazy, but it settles down."

They tried talking about music and dating, but those conversations fizzled, too. His friend liked bands, Jay liked rap. His friend was pansexual, with plenty of boyfriends and girlfriends. Jay had no experience at all.

"The only thing we have in common is the fact that we're trans," Jay said.

Later, at home, Jay told his mom the trip had gone well. It was the first time he'd ever hung out with another transgender person. But Jay wanted a friend who liked the same things he did. Someone who listened to 2Pac and Odd Future.

Someone like Maddie.

They hadn't talked in nine months, but he regretted how mean he had been to her. He missed life with his best friend. He had laughed more when she was around. When they went to the mall, they spent hours browsing. The conversation never lagged.

That Thanksgiving, he saw a picture Maddie's mom posted on Facebook. The photo showed all of Maddie's Christmas presents perfectly wrapped. He clicked like.

A few hours later, a text message came in.

Hey how was your summer, I hope you had a good Thanksgiving.

It was Maddie.

Did you ever have your surgery?

When the Medicaid letter arrived a week before Christmas, Jay texted Maddie first. His psychiatrist thought he was ready and had sent in the final recommendation Jay needed. Washington health officials had made a decision.

He held up the envelope. His fate was sealed inside.

Wait Over, Weight Lifted

Free from the body that held him back, Jay starts to share his story as a 17-year-old

On the last night Jay had breasts, the snow began to thaw. Weeks of white stuff had blanketed his Washington suburb. School had been canceled, the mail delayed.

Jay picked up his phone, and his thumbs skated across the screen. He checked the weather, then the post office's tracking system. He was expecting a pair of cheap headphones.

"It says local weather delay," he told his best friend, Maddie. "That always happens to me. I order something, and it comes way later than it says."

He dropped the phone and made circles around the dining room. He talked fast in a British accent. He and Maddie mimicked the "Wheel of Fortune" contestants on TV guessing letters for money.

In the kitchen, his mother cooked carne asada on an electric griddle. The steak sizzled.

"You need protein," Nancy Munoz told him.

"Maybe," Jay said. Then he collapsed onto the couch. Outside, the temperature had climbed to just above freezing, but he worried the weather might postpone his surgery, too.

He was 17 and impatient. No one at school knew why. From a distance, Jay's life looked perfect. He was sarcastic and smart-witted. He wore the same tapered pants and streetwear brands other guys did. His schoolmates didn't know how deliberate he'd had to be, how he gave himself a shot every week to look that masculine, how he strapped down his breasts so his shirts fell on a flat chest.

He had waited two years for the final step. In the morning, he hoped, a plastic surgeon would sculpt his feminine frame into a masculine one. Then, he thought, his transition would be complete. Then he'd feel normal.

On screen, the "Wheel of Fortune" letters fell into place. A contestant guessed the answer: MAKE YOUR DREAM A REALITY.

Jay smirked. He knew it wasn't that simple.

"Do You Feel Different?"

He slept easily, and in an instant it was 3 a.m., time to drive to Portland for the surgery.

Jay pulled on a pair of blue jeans and grabbed an elastic compression shirt out of his closet. It had been three years since he'd left the house without some kind of binder smashing his breasts. He stretched the tank top between his hands, then tossed it on the floor. He wouldn't need it again.

Time barely existed that January day. One moment he was in the backseat with his best friend, barreling south toward a new life. The next he was in a Legacy Good Samaritan hospital bed, the curtains pulled close around him. His aunt and uncle came to pray in Spanish. His mother kissed his forehead, then grew small as a nurse wheeled him away.

His hand burned cold as the anesthesia made its way through the IV. He shivered in a pale green gown. The anesthesiologist told him it was normal.

"Usually I ask people if they've had a mimosa in the morning," she said. "It's kind of like that. But you're a little young."

He giggled when he saw the surgeon. Her assistants said their names, then all their faces disappeared. He didn't hear the beep of the machines or the radio playing "Mr. Big Stuff" in the background. He didn't feel the knife or the surgeon's hand as she pulled a pound and a half of tissue away.

When Jay woke up three hours later, the breasts were gone.

"Do you feel different?" his mom asked.

His mouth was dry. His lips felt cracked. In the movies, people woke up and they were free.

"I feel like I did a really hard workout on my chest," he whispered. He had never done a really hard workout, but he imagined the dull, everywhere pain must be the same.

He looked down, but there was nothing to see. A stiff girdle covered his chest. Bandages dug into his armpits. Two plastic cups collected a fluid the color of cherry Kool-Aid as it drained from his chest.

"Was it freaky?" Maddie asked.

"I don't remember," he said.

"Do you feel less weight?" she asked.

"Just tired."

He watched Cartoon Network. His eyes grew heavy as Scooby-Doo's gang faced costumed monsters. When he was younger, he'd worn his Scooby-Doo outfit until it frayed. In cartoons, the mask always came off before the show was over.

He woke the next morning, and his mom smiled from across the room.

"When I got pregnant with you," she said, "the first ultrasound I got, they told me it was going to be a boy."

At the second ultrasound, the doctors told her she was having a girl. Nancy's mom believed in old wives' tales and a traditional form of witchcraft. She grabbed a needle and thread.

She dangled the needle by the thread so the tip was just touching the back of Nancy's hand.

"She said, 'If it goes like this, side to side, it's a girl. If it makes a circle, it's a boy.'"

Jay looked up from his hospital bed. He'd never heard this story before.

"The needle went like this," Nancy said and shook her hand side to side. Girl.

"Then," she said, as if possessed from something beyond, "the needle started making circles."

Jay laughed.

"My mom told me," Nancy continued. "She said, 'You're having a boy.'"

Get Well Soon

The next morning, Jay lay in the hospital bed and imagined returning to school. Only Maddie knew he was having surgery. Only Maddie planned to visit while he stayed home the next eight weeks.

What would it be like to tell people?

He had rid himself of the breasts. He needed to break free of the secret, too.

Jay picked up his phone and opened Snapchat. He surveyed the room, looking for a photo to take. A balloon floated in the air conditioner's breeze. GET WELL SOON. A dry-erase board charted his pain, just a mild ache at 9 a.m. His mom reclined in a chair, still wearing the black T-shirt and jeans she had worn the day before.

He settled the camera lens on the television screen. He tapped the shutter. He didn't write a caption, but soon, his friends would see the inside of his hospital room, and they'd wonder.

"I'll probably start to tell people," he told his mom.

At home, they binge-watched "Grey's Anatomy," and Nancy wondered aloud if the show's portrayal of surgeries was true. Had Jay's doctors listened to music? Did they take dance breaks?

After several episodes, Nancy checked the clock. It had been 48 hours since Jay's operation.

"You can shower now," she said.

In the bathroom, he leaned against the sink and faced the wall. Nancy pried apart the girdle that protected his chest. She removed the white bandages.

Jay looked down. He could still see the lines the surgeon had drawn to mark her cuts. His nipples were red and swollen. Two thin tubes jutted from his sides.

"My stomach does poke out more," he said.

His mom left to search for gauze, and Jay was alone with the mirror. He exhaled, then turned to face his reflection.

"That's nice," he said.

His grin was sheepish and silent, the muted excitement of a teenage boy.

"Figure It Out"

By February, he'd forgotten what his body looked like before. Daytime TV droned in the background as he sat stewing at the kitchen table.

His chest felt numb. The surgeon said his nerve endings wouldn't recover for months, maybe even a year. No one had been able to tell him when he might feel different emotionally.

He picked up an appointment card for his next doctor's visit. He bent it in half. His mom walked by and grabbed for it, but he held on.

"I have no love life," he said.

His friends had asked him why he never dated anyone. What could he tell them?

"Just say, 'I'm too focused on my career as a doctor,'" Nancy said.

"I'm not trying to lie to them," he said. "It's my fault. I don't make the effort to do anything because this whole thing I'm going through might make people feel weird."

Even if girls weren't bigots, even if they accepted transgender people, that didn't mean they wanted to date one, he thought.

Jay tore the appointment card into four even pieces. Doctors had helped him in every way he'd asked. He was happier. Now that he looked like a guy, he was ready to date.

Eventually, Jay realized, he would have to tell girls he liked that he was transgender.

"It would have been easier if I was born right," he said.

He tore the card into smaller pieces. Nancy sat down in a chair beside him.

"I get it," Nancy said. "You were born in the wrong body. But you also have to see the positive. People wouldn't even guess that you had boobs at one point."

"It's not being positive or negative," Jay said. "It's being realistic."

"If you want to speak realistically," Nancy said, "you have to think of all these people who are now going to be suffering under the Trump laws."

Donald Trump had become president a few weeks earlier, and Nancy spent hours reading the news. She worried Trump would make life tougher for LGBT people and families living in poverty. She, Jay and his two sisters lived off about $1,500 a month. Medicaid had paid for Jay's surgery. Other kids might not be so lucky. Trump had promised to cut back the Affordable Care Act expansion that guaranteed coverage to transgender patients.

Jay knew how grateful he should be. Nancy reminded him all the time of the opportunities he had that older transgender people had not. But he didn't compare himself to other transgender people. He measured himself against other teenagers.

Some of his classmates had already had sex. They'd gone on dates and lived through heartbreak. He hadn't even had his first real kiss.

"I feel like I am behind," Jay said.

"What's the next step?" Nancy said.

"I don't like questions like that," Jay said. "I don't know what to do."

"Hang out with Maddie. Break some windows. Be a teenager."

"I don't know," he said. "I feel like it won't be easy."

"Figure it out," she said. "Otherwise, 10 years from now, you're going to be sitting in the same chair. You're going to be saying the same things. 'I'm behind. I'm behind. I'm behind.'"

She stood and grabbed her car keys. It was time to pick up Jay's sisters from school.

"That's not very helpful," Jay said. "I ask you what to do and you say, 'Go figure it out.'"

Nancy opened the door then closed it again. She turned to face him.

"You think you're behind," she said. "Let me tell you, I'm way behind. I didn't have a youth. I didn't get to go out and socialize with my friends. I didn't have any time to go to the mall, to go to the movie theaters, to experience drinking or running crazy with my friends or dating all these boys. I became a mom."

She sat down again. She had spent more than half her life trying to make him happy. She had sacrificed so he would have the teenage years she had missed.

"I don't want you to be like me," she said.

Nancy looked at him. She couldn't spot a hint of anything girlish about him anymore. His voice was so deep that Nancy often forgot that he hadn't always been that way.

"I have to pick up your sisters," she said finally.

The door shut behind her. Jay looked at the mess he'd left on the table. He tried to reassemble the appointment card, but he had ripped it into in so many pieces he didn't know where to start.

"I Like You for You"

Things started to change the week Jay went back to school. He'd missed cell division, polynomials and "The Great Gatsby." Eight weeks of gossip.

"Where've you been?" his classmates asked.

"Home," Jay said.

"Just because you felt like it?" one girl asked.

"Sure," he said, then continued down the hall.

Maybe it was his air of mystery. Maybe he seemed more open to the world. His first day back, a girl told Jay's best friend she thought Jay was cute. Maddie gave the girl Jay's Instagram username.

"Hit him up," she told her.

They started chatting on Instagram at midnight. They talked about school and family. Within a few days, they had evolved to text messaging. She was exactly the kind of person he had hoped for: Mexican, shorter than him and girly-girl cute.

One day after school, Maddie told Jay his crush had heard the rumors. She'd asked Maddie if Jay had been a girl in middle school.

Jay slouched at the kitchen table as Maddie recounted the conversation.

"I asked her, 'Well, if this was the situation, are you comfortable with Jay being that way?'" Maddie told him. "'Like does it change your feelings at all about him?'"

A car pulled into the gravel driveway, and Jay motioned for Maddie to change the subject.

"My mom doesn't know," he said. "I just don't want to say anything because she's going to make everything weird."

Later that night, alone in his room, he clutched his phone and decided it was time.

It's better to hear it straight from the source, he thought. But what do I say? I'm a transvestite?

He typed a message.

It's true, he wrote. I've been living this way the last four years.

Her reply came immediately. It didn't matter, she wrote. Her mom was a lesbian who had taught her to be open-minded.

I like you for you.

They started texting each other good night and good morning. He liked her so much, he clammed up when he saw her at school. Over text, he could phrase things just the right way. He was funny and flirty. In person, he could barely speak.

He tried to brainstorm ideas for a date. He knew she liked the outdoors but wasn't sure if hiking sounded romantic. What if he got sweaty? His mom suggested he take the girl to see "Beauty and the Beast," but that was a movie his younger sisters wanted to see. He didn't even have his license. How could he take her out?

They had been text-flirting for a month, but Jay still hadn't made a move. A few weeks before prom, the girl told him she'd started seeing another guy, someone who knew how to woo a girl, someone who knew how to hold hands and kiss her in the dying light of a sunset.

"She friend-zoned me," Jay told Maddie.

"At least you got that experience," Maddie said. "There's plenty of people out there who will accept you."

In a funny way, he was grateful. He'd done one thing teenagers do. He'd put himself out there and lost the girl he wanted. It wasn't a happy ending, but it was progress.

In May, he skipped prom, the last dance of his junior year, but he got his driver's license. The next time he met a girl, he'd be ready. He started going places just to explore. He picked up Dairy Queen for his sisters and ran errands for his mom. One weekend, he drove all the way from Vancouver to Portland, rap blasting from the radio.

Jay never had a big movie script ending. Over time, he just felt lighter. He wore his backpack with both straps now and didn't worry that his breasts would stick out. He slept shirtless. He researched colleges and applied for a job at Panda Express. When a teacher asked students to include their baby photos in a school project, he even brought a few gender-ambiguous snapshots to share.

One cloudy morning in July, he and Maddie headed to Sauvie Island. They curved along a gravel road and stopped at a berry farm. They loaded a metal wagon with boxes and hiked through the fields. The cart squeaked behind Jay. His white Converse turned brown with dust.

He stopped and looked down a row red with possibility. He snaked his hand through the bushes and pulled raspberries out by the half dozen.

"You're getting all the big ones," Maddie said.

He shoved a few in his mouth, then grinned.

"I think I just ate a spider," he said.

They picked their way through the field, joking until they grew tired and quiet.

Jay had spent three years obsessing about his chest. Now, he thought about the future. He imagined going to Canada. The country was so beautiful and so close to Washington, maybe he could hike there. He dreamed of going to Switzerland to eat cheese, to Iceland to play in the snow.

He checked his phone for messages. He'd started talking to his crush again. Her relationship with the other guy hadn't worked out, and she still liked Jay. This time, he wouldn't blow his chance. He felt relaxed, more like himself.

The sun broke through the clouds. They had plenty of raspberries, so he wandered toward the blueberries.

Jay knelt in front of a bush. Most of the berries were green still, not ripe enough to eat. In another week, they'd be ready. He pulled off four berries and popped them into his mouth.

He didn't need to wait for perfect.

HOPE FOR THE REST OF US

THE DALLAS MORNING NEWS

MARCH 5, 2017

By Jennifer Emily

BETRAYAL

When an unthinkable crime shatters a family, a father is forced to confront the emotional wreckage. A three-part series

Gunshots startled Buz Caldwell from sleep. They filled the room with hot light and blew him from bed. He came to on the floor, his feet toward the headboard. Blood soaked the carpet.

Buz shouted to his wife, Rosalyn, who had been asleep next to him in her pink nightgown. "Roz? Roz?"

Silence.

He tugged open the nightstand drawer and reached for his pistol. It was gone. So was the intruder. Buz never saw the shooter.

He checked his digital alarm clock: 11:47 p.m. He struggled to his knees, then crumpled. Somehow, he inched toward the phone across the room.

Every breath hurt. When he tried to raise his head, he blacked out again. A light flicked on in the hallway just as he reached for the phone.

"Krissi, is that you?" he called out. The shadow of his 16-year-old daughter filled the doorway. "I need your help," he said. "I've been shot."

Krissi called 911. Her words were so matter of fact, so calm, that the Frisco police dispatcher at first believed the call was a hoax.

The plot

What the dispatcher heard in Krissi Caldwell's voice was not deceit but disappointment. The teenager entered the bedroom expecting— hoping —to find both of her parents dead.

Krissi's relationship with them had been fraying for years. She skipped school, stayed out late, called her mother a bitch. She had illusions of taking her parents' money and playing house with her 15-year-old boyfriend, Bobby Gonzales. All she had to do was get rid of Buz and Roz.

So she plotted two murders. To get Bobby to go along, she lied to him, saying her father sexually abused her and her mother allowed it. She swiped her father's gun and gave it to Bobby.

On March 6, 1992, she and Bobby ditched school after second period and rode around in Krissi's black Blazer with Buz's gun under the passenger seat. Bobby played a little basketball that afternoon. After dinner, Krissi told her parents she was going out to see friends. She met up with Bobby instead.

Late that night, wearing a polo shirt, jeans and Air Jordans, Bobby stepped into the Caldwells' bedroom.

When the police got to the house, Roz Caldwell, just 41 years old, was already gone, killed by a bullet to her chin that traveled into her brain. Buz, shot twice, was still alive, stubbornly drawing breaths in his bloody T-shirt and underwear.

Krissi had committed the worst kind of betrayal. Once, she had been Buz's baby girl, but now, he grew determined to seek vengeance. He testified against Krissi and demanded the harshest possible sentence. He got what he wanted, but for years after, his heart remained cold.

Then something happened to Buz Caldwell.

Think of the worst thing a loved one ever did to you. Think of the shock and pain you felt when you saw this person's other face. How long did you carry that rage, that scar on your heart? Do you carry it still? What would it take you to forgive?

Here's what it took for Buz Caldwell. If there's hope for him, there's hope for the rest of us.

School sweethearts

For Buz, it all began with Roz.

They met on the school bus when she was in fourth grade and he was in fifth, back when Frisco was a patch of dirt in the country. On their first date, in high school, he took her to church, then out for ice cream.

He was chocolate and way too serious. She was strawberry and giggles.

They were country kids. He was an only child who grew up doing chores on his family's farm. She baled hay, drove a tractor and put peanuts in her Coke.

They got married in 1969, before she finished secretarial school and he got his degree from what is now Texas A&M—Commerce. He would go on to work with military contracts at Texas Instruments. She did bookkeeping and secretarial work.

Their daughter Brandi was born in 1972; Krissi, three years later. Buz worked long hours and Roz stayed home, sewing, cooking and singing Charley Pride songs in the kitchen with her girls.

Roz was "the love of my life," Buz said one morning on the patio of a Frisco Starbucks. He looked away, a catch in his voice. "There are days you look ahead and still expect to see her."

At 67, Buz's hair has thinned and turned a grayish white, as has his mustache. He often wears a baseball cap and a long-sleeved T-shirt under a short-sleeved one. He's retired but finds himself busy every day, helping his mother, working in the yard, meeting up with old friends. He likes to have things his way and considers himself "a crusty old bird." A fight with throat cancer has left his voice gravelly and weak; he calls it his "Godfather voice." He always has a bottle of water so he can keep talking just a little bit longer.

When Krissi was a child, she and Buz "were pretty much inseparable," Buz said. "If I would sit down, and she spotted me, I was going to have company. She was very close, very warm, very affectionate."

He read her Snow White and the Seven Dwarfs, Alice in Wonderland and Winnie the Pooh. She pointed out if Buz accidentally skipped a word.

Years later, Buz sounded both weary and wistful as he talked about those simple times. "I got sick of reading Pooh Bear," he said.

A sudden change

Krissi's big sister, Brandi, remembers Krissi as "an angel child" who followed the rules and excelled at school.

Then, in seventh grade, Krissi's grades dropped. She failed classes. She lied— about big things, little things. It didn't matter.

Mood swings aren't unusual for adolescents, but Krissi changed so suddenly and intensely that her own parents barely recognized her. Every disagreement turned into a fight. She would scream and yell for 10 minutes, then retreat to her bedroom and slam the door. She'd return a short time later just as loud and angry as before.

Buz had little patience for Krissi's tirades. "My dad's temper was way beyond my mom's," Brandi said. Buz spanked Krissi when she acted out. Once, he even grabbed her by the hair to pull her away from her mother.

"It was absolutely a miserable existence for all of us," Buz said.

The family went to counseling, but any improvement was fleeting.

When Krissi was 15, the school nurse called Roz and said Krissi was "out of it." She had overdosed on Roz's Valium pills.

Buz and Roz had her hospitalized, and doctors diagnosed her with major depressive disorder. When she was discharged, she seemed better. Medical records show Krissi was "in stable condition ... she was nonhomicidal and nonsuicidal."

Krissi and Bobby

Bobby Gonzales was nearly a year younger than Krissi, but they were in the same class at Frisco High. He was the second of five sons born to a truck driver dad and a mom who worked a variety of jobs. Bobby was small, 5 feet 8 and 130 pounds. He played junior varsity football and did just OK in school. He had never been in real trouble.

Krissi and Bobby had dated on and off since eighth grade, but Krissi always tried to hide the relationship. Her parents didn't want her dating. They were especially concerned about Bobby because they didn't think she could handle the complications of dating someone from another culture. Bobby is Hispanic, and the Caldwells are white.

Once she was on her own, Buz told her, she could decide for herself.

She ignored him. Once, she took a sonogram photo to school and told her classmates she was pregnant with Bobby's baby. The photo actually belonged to Brandi, who'd had a daughter just after she finished high school.

Despite Buz's strong feelings about Bobby, he'd never actually met him. Somebody had once pointed him out from a distance, but that was it.

Intense strain

Buz worked 10 to 12 hours a day, leaving Roz to deal with Krissi on her own much of the time. "This really devastated Rozie that one of her kids, one of her children that she loved dearly, could be that difficult," Buz said. "And the longer it went, the more difficult it became. Difficult almost to the point of becoming debilitating."

Sometimes the couple would escape the chaos by flying their small plane to Longview or Texarkana or some other place. They'd eat lunch and fly home.

"It was just kind of a day out. We wasn't gone but three or four hours total," Buz said. "But it was always kind of a joke at the house that we went and had our $100 hamburger."

One night, heading home from Greenville, they flew mostly in silence, just listening to the rumble of the engine. Then Roz spoke up.

"You know, that really worries me," Roz said, looking out into the night. "What worries you?" Buz asked.

"I feel like I'm being pulled into the blackness," she said.

In all the years they'd been married, she'd never said anything that caught Buz so off guard.

Fateful night

On the night of the shooting, Roz and Buz got ready for bed early, as usual. Some people check all the locks before they turn in. Some check on sleeping children. Buz usually opened his nightstand, just to see if his 9 mm Browning pistol was inside. It always was.

But on this night, Buz didn't open the drawer. Even today, he doesn't know why.

He and Roz were asleep before 10. A short time later, Buz was awakened by the snap-snap-snap of gunfire in the bedroom. Roz was killed immediately. A bullet struck Buz above the right pelvic bone and traveled to his left shoulder, piercing a lung. Another hit his left arm, just below the shoulder.

Bobby ran outside. Krissi, who had been waiting in the living room, joined him, and they sped off. They listened to Metallica, continuously rewinding the cassette tape to hear Bobby's favorite song, "Nothing Else Matters." It was the tune Bobby used to build his confidence before football games.

Krissi returned more than an hour later and "discovered" her parents shot.

At the hospital, doctors put Buz on a ventilator. Friends and family rushed to be with him. Uncles, aunts, grandparents, work friends, church friends.

Brandi planned her mother's funeral, not knowing if she'd need to do the same for her father.

Buz missed the funeral. Krissi showed up in a white dress and boots. Bobby came with his mother but left early.

Nearly every day for two weeks, nurses summoned Brandi, Krissi and Buz's mother to his ICU room. "There's just no way he's going make it," they'd caution, preparing them for the worst. Somehow, he did.

Once the nurses removed the ventilator, Buz asked about Roz. Brandi told him she had died, but he kept forgetting, so Brandi had to say it again and again.

"Dad, Mom passed away."

Buz vomited each time she told him. She learned to have a bucket ready.

Cracking the case

Solving the case wasn't particularly challenging. Investigators learned about the secret relationship between Krissi and Bobby and showed up on Bobby's doorstep the next morning. From Krissi's friends, they discovered she had long talked about wanting her parents dead.

One day, Collin County sheriff's investigator Dave Waldschmidt stopped by Buz's hospital room. Buz quickly realized that his questions weren't routine.

"Are you sure that Krissi was involved in this?" Buz asked.

Waldschmidt's reply has stayed with him: "At this point in time, I would say they are both the top two suspects."

Buz had to live with that sickening idea— and sometimes with Krissi — for weeks. After the shootings, Krissi stayed with relatives and rarely visited him in the hospital. But after he moved in with his mother to continue healing, Krissi joined them. The tension was thick with the things they didn't say.

Finally, Buz simply asked Krissi if she and Bobby shot him or knew who did. Krissi blew off the question. Buz never detected a hint of remorse or sadness.

Nearly a month after Roz's murder, the principal summoned Bobby from Spanish class. Bobby walked into the hallway, where two deputies in cowboy hats were waiting. They frisked him and cuffed his hands behind his back. Bobby's classmates poured into the hallway to watch as he was taken to the Collin County Juvenile Detention Center.

Detectives were closing in on Krissi. She had confided to a friend at school: "I can't believe he lived. He was supposed to die." Some of the most damning evidence was in Krissi's own handwriting. The cops found letters she wrote to Bobby on school notebook paper about what would happen if her parents died.

"Mom & Dad went and updated their will today. So now if they die Brandi & I will live here together on our own for as long as we want. God that would be nice, just think I'd be able to do what ever I pleased w/out anybody bothering me," Krissi wrote in August 1991. "I think I am wrong to wish something would happen to them, but I can't seem to help it."

Years later, Buz would change in ways he never imagined possible, and this selfish, calculating teenager would again be his baby girl. Recovering from her betrayal would prove far harder than healing from bullet wounds.

THE PIT

Anger and despair consume an aggrieved father—until a more powerful force removes the darkness
Four months after his daughter's boyfriend shot and killed his wife, Roz, and seriously wounded him, Buz Caldwell returned home for the first time.

He felt Roz's presence with every step. The house was decorated just as she wanted it. The marble countertops. The tan carpet. The dark brown bathtub and matching toilet Buz abhorred and Roz loved.

Nearly 25 years later, the memory of that day was almost more than Buz could bear. He faltered, then said, "It's going to take a minute." Tears trickled down his cheeks. He pulled off his glasses and swiped at his face with the sleeve of his gray sweatshirt.

"You walked in the house and her stuff was everywhere. And, honestly, you absolutely didn't want anyone else there," Buz recalled. "Every time you walked in the house, you had to go through that. It never got what you'd call easier."

He was drawn toward, yet repulsed by, the bedroom where Roz had died.

The police had sliced away large portions of the bloodstained carpet. Interior doors no longer hung from their hinges. Fingerprint dust covered the furniture.

Buz lugged away scraps of long, shaggy carpet left behind.

"I actually found bullets that had hit me or Roz and gone through us that had been missed," he said. "Don't ask me how."

On Monday, July 6, 1992, deputies arrested Buz's daughter Krissi as she stood outside her car at summer school. She was booked into the same detention center where her boyfriend, Bobby Gonzales, had been taken.

Though expected, the news still crushed Buz. He pushed away everyone but family and barely tolerated them. In his grief and rage, he became unrecognizable, even to himself. He descended into what he calls "the pit," a lonely hole where he existed but didn't really live.

He put in 90 to 100 hours a week for Texas Instruments, traveling as much as possible so he didn't have to be at home with his memories. He read voraciously, not caring about the subject as long as the books took his mind somewhere else.

He had never played golf, but now he watched the game incessantly on TV, the sound muted, his eyes fixed on a world more serene than his.

He didn't seek help. Shrinks, he thought, were for people who were spiritually and intellectually weak.

"I don't guess I have ever really believed in emotional shock," he said. "I learned shock is real." Buz would get peace of mind by getting even. That was the plan. He would testify against Krissi and Bobby, and they would be convicted and sent away for a long time. That would be justice, and justice would bring closure.

"I was out for blood," Buz said. "I'll make no bones about that."

Tried as adults

In his fury, Buz supported prosecutors' plan to try the teenagers as adults. Today, judges and juries consider factors such as brain development in cases involving kids, but nobody thought about that when Krissi and Bobby were tried. The public and lawmakers believed dangerous kids should do adult time.

Buz visited Krissi in jail before her trial, but when she found out he was seeking the maximum punishment, she told him to stop.

"I love you, but to me it seems that you have become my enemy. I know that you're going through some rough times, and I'm praying for you," she wrote from the Collin County Jail. "This next month is going to be hell on both of us, and there's no point in either of us making it more difficult on the other. You may be right, they may lock me and Bobby up for 35 years. At least your wish will be granted, huh?"

Still, she signed off: "I love you Daddy."

Buz didn't stay away. Father and daughter didn't have much to say to each other, but Buz had to see her. Once, he pressed his hand against the window as a sign of affection. Krissi returned the gesture.

When the trials came, Buz wasn't allowed in the courtroom unless he was on the witness stand, so he didn't have to see the flower-patterned bedsheets stained with his and Roz's blood.

When Buz testified, prosecutor Bill Schultz homed in on Krissi's lies and how Buz and Roz struggled to help her.

"Does she have the capability to manipulate those around her that care about her?" Schultz asked.

"She's one of the best you'll ever meet," Buz responded as his daughter sat at the defense table, dressed in white.

"How dangerous do you think Krissi is, by the way?" Schultz asked.

"Very dangerous," Buz responded. But he also told jurors: "She's my daughter, she always will be, and I'll always love her."

Krissi and Bobby were convicted in the killings, and both are serving life sentences. They are eligible for parole in 2027.

"She was the brains of the outfit, to the extent the outfit had any brains," recalled Bobby's lawyer, David Haynes. "She wanted them both dead. Kill both parents, collect the insurance and live happily ever after. That's the kind of crazy plan a teenager comes up with."

Buz told himself the verdicts were victories. But he felt hollow.

"I walked out of that courtroom just as angry as I walked in," he said.

Krissi's lawyer, Donald McDermitt, was struck by how much Buz still cared for Krissi.

"He had a certain grace about him," McDermitt said. "I sensed a tremendous amount of sadness. He had lost his wife, and he was going to lose his daughter. He loved her very much. He didn't hate her. He hated what she did."

Awkward conversations

Krissi left the Collin County Jail for the Gatesville Unit of the state prison system on June 29, 1993, 15 months after the shootings.

Buz kept visiting. Still angry, still empty. The two spoke, at first, on opposite sides of the glass, and then, as years passed, across a table. The physical barrier was removed, but the pain, loss and anger erected their own wall.

"It was a conversation based on obligation as a parent," Buz said. "Not that there wasn't love there, but there was not that emotional connection."

Climbing out

One day, Buz got a call from a woman he worked with. Would he like to go with her to a company party?

He said no.

"Not because of you," he told her. "I just don't want to be social."

They talked more over the next few months, beyond the usual "hello" and "how are you?" Eventually, Buz asked her out and she accepted.

The time seemed right. Roz was gone and Buz believed she wouldn't want him to be lonely. Linda Wallace already knew his story. She'd known Roz. They had all played cards and eaten potluck dinners together a few times a year.

With Linda's help, Buz began the climb out of the pit.

"I fell in love with her, and the rest is history," Buz said. "I was very surprised, not because of her. But because of me. She had a good sense of who I was, and she knew what I'd been through.

"She understood how much baggage I drug."

Buz married Linda in 1995. "I hope that you and Linda well have a happy feeling in your hearts this year during the holidays," Krissi wrote that December from prison. "I feel like mommas heart would somehow be lighter because of your new marriage."

A different feeling

It's hard to identify the precise moment when someone lets go of anger. It happens slowly, gradually, like a campfire burning down until the last tiny orange ember fades away.

Buz doesn't know when things changed for him, but if you press him, he'll point to a night on the porch at his house— the house where Roz died and where he and Linda now lived.

It was in 1998, Buz remembers. He sat in an aluminum lawn chair, smoking a cigarette and drinking iced tea. All around him, plants grew in pots his grandparents once used for hog boiling. He and Roz had often sat here together, talking or not, it didn't matter.

The night wasn't too hot. The bugs hadn't begun to bite. Stars brightened the dark sky. Summer hadn't fully arrived and neither had the urban sprawl that would make the constellations harder to see.

His thoughts turned, as they always did in this spot, to Roz. To Krissi and Bobby. How did he end up here? How did everything go wrong?

On this night, Buz realized, something was different. He had a startling realization: "I feel good."

He couldn't remember when he'd last felt this way— physically, spiritually and emotionally. Anger didn't consume him, and he no longer wanted retribution. He was happy.

Buz knew then he would forgive Krissi one day. Bobby, too.

"I had two simple choices. They weren't hard. They weren't complex, but they weren't easy," Buz said.

"I could continue to hold on to that hate and let it dictate my life going forward. Or I could forgive those two guys. I wish I could forget, but I can't. But I can forgive."

It occurred to him that Roz would have forgiven them long ago. She would have chided him for not doing the same.

Putting faith into action
Prophets and poets have written about mercy and forgiveness for centuries.

The Rev. Martin Luther King Jr., the Dalai Lama and the prophet Muhammad have spoken of the need to forgive and be forgiven. No less a sage than Willie Nelson sings that forgiveness is "the only way that I'll find peace of mind."

In religion, forgiveness is often associated with purification: Sin is a stain on the sinner, and forgiveness is the cleanser. Buddha overcame anger before he found enlightenment. Jews ask God for forgiveness on Yom Kippur, but only after requesting the same from those they've wronged.

When God says "vengeance is mine," he is not just issuing threats; he's taking on the burden of anger to lighten our load. The rage is too much for us to carry. The lesson in all of this: Forgiveness is something you do for yourself. Those who forgive are no longer defined by how they were betrayed.

We have all borne witness to astounding acts of forgiveness by seemingly average people. The families who forgave the man who slaughtered their loved ones inside Charleston AME Emanuel Church. The wrongly imprisoned North Carolina man who hugged the woman who misidentified him as her rapist and said, "I've never been mad at you."

Then there is Buz Caldwell, who no longer goes to church but still holds to the Southern Baptist faith he grew up with.

"I believe God sent his only son to die on the cross for our sins," Buz said. "If he could send his son to the cross to die, how was it that I could not forgive these kids? I either had to practice what I believed in or had to stop believing— and I wasn't going to stop believing."

'I forgive you'

Not long after that night on the porch under the stars, Buz made the nearly three-hour drive to the Mountain View Unit in Gatesville, near Waco. Until then, his visits with Krissi had been just another item on his to-do list. Check it off. Head home.

This was the first day he truly looked forward to their time together. Krissi met him in the visitation room in her white jumpsuit. She was 22, a veteran of the dull routines and indignities of prison. She was prepared for another awkward visit with her dad.

His words were simple and unrehearsed: "I forgive you."

Years later, Buz remembered the scene: Relief flooded Krissi's face. She gripped his hand and began to cry, then immediately tried to stop. Guards disapprove of tears.

Buz kept talking. The decision to forgive her didn't come quickly or easily, he told her. He was doing it for her, yes, but mostly for himself.

Buz and Krissi didn't say everything they wanted that day. She was too emotional. Buz told her they'd talk on his next visit, a few weeks away.

His heart felt lighter on the drive home.

"Forgiveness has enabled me to live," Buz said. "Had I stayed where I was at after this happened, I would have not survived."

His lasting regret is not what Krissi did, but what his rage cost him.

AN UNUSUAL FAMILY

Visits to prison, lingering regrets and a love that knows no end

Krissi Caldwell is an inmate at the William P. Hobby Unit near Waco, where she is Prisoner No. 00644824. She works as a seamstress and has learned Spanish by talking with other inmates.

Her father sends her books and keeps money in an account she can use to buy toothpaste, a fan, shoes, and food she can eat in her cell.

She's in her early 40s now, no longer the teenage girl in the defendant's chair. She's kept her brown hair long, even longer than it was when she posed for a family picture before her mother's murder.

In an interview at the prison, she seemed uncomfortable. She'd never spoken publicly about her crime or her family. But over time, she opened up, smiling and sometimes growing teary as she talked about her dad, Buz Caldwell, and their relationship.

Krissi waved off questions about the night of the shooting and parts of what led up to it. The only question that interests her now is an essential one. Sometimes, when Buz visits, she will cry and ask him, "Why did we do this?"

"I wish it could be as easy as saying that I think it was a mental health issue," she said. "I don't think Bobby and I had that excuse."

The truth, she said, is that she was angry because her parents wouldn't let her date Bobby Gonzales. She said the plot started as a joke that got out of control.

During all the fights and yelling and anger, before shots were fired, Krissi forgot a simple truth: Her parents loved her.

Krissi remembered sitting on Buz's lap when she was a little girl and twisting his wedding ring on his finger.

"Find the beginning of the ring," he told her.

She searched and wanted to please her father, but she couldn't find it. "Find the end of the ring," he said.

Again, she examined it without success.

"Me and your mom's love for you and your sister is just like this ring," Krissi recalled her father saying. "It doesn't have a beginning and an end."

Telling the story years later, she seemed wistful, saying she's sorry she didn't understand years ago.

"I was like, 'Oh, OK. I know, Daddy.'"

Sometimes, she asks her father about her mother's life. "Dad, I'm 37, what were you and mom doing when you were 37? Dad, I'm 40 ..."

With age has come the realization that Roz Caldwell died very young. Krissi turned 41 in October. Next fall, she'll have lived longer than her mother, who died weeks before her 42nd birthday.

"My sister is now older than she was when she died," Krissi said. "It's not fair that she didn't get to live out her life."

That sister, Brandi, remained bitter toward Krissi much longer than Buz did. But eventually, she started going to church again, and the right amount of time passed. Also, she learned that kids' brains don't fully develop until their 20s. Until then, young people, especially teens, overreact and don't make reasonable decisions.

Brandi has seen her sister change. She notices that she can do something nice for Krissi without her sister asking for more. She encourages her two children, now adults, to get to know Krissi. That's new.

Not long ago, Buz and Brandi visited Krissi together. Buz watched as his daughters acted more like two sisters in elementary school than two middle-aged women.

"They sat down there and held hands like two kids," Buz said. "The guards would come by and they had them where the guards couldn't see."

Krissi believes Buz's love for her— and his Christian values— allowed him to see her as more than a murderer.

"He knew me whole as a person," Krissi said. "'This is still my daughter, and I remember and I know her. She's really not a monster.' I think that kind of helped him forgive."

She hasn't given herself the same grace. When she thinks back to quiet moments with her mom, sipping Diet Pepsi on the porch, her betrayal of her family hits her like a gut punch.

"How do you know when you've forgiven yourself?" she asked, choking back a sob. "If the answer is when it stops hurting, then the answer is never."

Visiting Bobby

From the beginning, Buz wanted to hate the kid who shot him and killed his wife.

During the trials, he had looked for confirmation that Bobby Gonzales was evil. Surely Bobby hurt animals and beat up his little brothers.

But Buz asked around, and that's not what people said. They said Bobby had always been a good kid who was close to his parents and four brothers.

Quiet. Friendly. An athlete.

"Had you known Bobby," a school administrator told Buz, "you would have liked Bobby. Everybody in this school respected him."

A couple of years after the shootings, Bobby showed that character by writing to Buz to apologize.

"I've prayed a lot about what happened, and have asked GOD for forgiveness many times, but I've realized that part of the forgiveness I need has to come from you," Bobby wrote.

Buz hadn't wanted to hear it then. But in time, he came to see his forgiveness of Bobby as a "package deal" with Krissi. Not because of who they were, but because of who Buz had become.

"It was easier for me to forgive Bobby," Buz said. "Bobby was an unknown to me. I felt like Bobby was led into this crime. Had it not been for Krissi, he never would have been involved."

Finally, years after the shootings, he drove to the Jim Ferguson Unit in Midway, just north of Huntsville. While the guards sent for Bobby, Buz waited in an uncomfortable chair pulled up to a window. Soon, a young kid walked toward him and took a seat on the other side of the glass. Certainly, the prison had sent the wrong person.

"He looked so young, so baby-faced," Buz said. Bobby was in his mid-20s.

This was the first time they had ever formally met. They began by talking about this and that. The outside world. How good it was for Buz to visit. After 10 or 15 minutes, Buz saw the person others had told him about.

"I saw a kid sitting there in an adult prison surrounded by guys who were 10, 15, 20 years older than he was," Buz said. "All of a sudden, you realized what a tough world he had."

Buz said what he had come to say: He had long since forgiven Bobby. Yes, he still felt angry sometimes. But he held no animosity.

Tears spilled onto Bobby's cheeks.

"Well, I've not learned to forgive myself," Bobby said. Buz told him it was time he did.

Then, Buz remembers, Bobby said something that shocked him: Bobby had always assumed Buz would use his military connections and high-level security clearances to have him killed.

Buz found himself apologizing to the guy who shot him.

"I'll ask your forgiveness," he recalled telling him. "I should have been down here a long time ago or had your family tell you I wasn't out to get you."

"I just felt so bad"

Bobby remembers tearing up when Buz came to see him.

"Here's this guy that I took so much from. All this regret and all this sorrow. It just hit me," Bobby said, sitting at a picnic-style table in the Alfred D. Hughes Unit where he has been since 2013. "What did I do to this man's life, and he's right here in front of me now. I couldn't even describe how I felt. I just felt so bad."

Buz doesn't visit often, but he and Bobby talk on the phone every few weeks.

"We've got where we chitchat like a couple of teenage, high school girls. I mean, it's pretty nauseating," Buz said with a laugh. "Things on the outside, things he'd like to do, what he does on the inside. From a reality standpoint, what it was like to grow up inside prison."

Buz shares tidbits about Krissi's life with Bobby and tells his daughter about him. The two briefly married early in their prison terms but divorced a short time later. They said they realized their marriage wasn't good for either of them. Today, prison rules forbid them from communicating because they were convicted of the same crime.

Buz has also gotten to know Bobby's family, especially Bobby's mother, Eloisa Salomon. A while back, Buz, his mother and Brandi spent an afternoon at Eloisa's house with Bobby's brothers watching Dallas Cowboys football and eating brisket. For Bobby, this is another way Buz shows he has forgiven.

"If I were in his shoes, I don't think I'd be so easy to forgive a person," Bobby said.

Looking back

Twenty-five years after the shootings, Buz finds it easier to live with what Krissi and Bobby did than what he himself did: He supported the decision to try the two teenagers as adults. He hates that he did this, hates that he so badly wanted life sentences.

Now, he believes Krissi and Bobby couldn't truly understand the consequences of their decisions. "I know the crime is horrible. I know the loss of life is horrible," said Buz. "But I still go back to looking at that young person and being able to understand that, physically, they may look like an adult. But they're still just a kid."

Buz wonders if the courts and juries would have looked at Krissi and Bobby differently if they'd known about teenagers and brain development back then. That science is one of the reasons the U.S. Supreme Court banned the death penalty for those who commit capital murder before age 18.

The justice system is beginning to think differently about cases involving kids.

In 2015, a 14-year-old girl in Dallas plotted and carried out the drowning of an infant. A judge gave the girl a 40-year sentence that will begin in a juvenile facility instead of a state prison. She'll undergo therapy and go to school. It's possible she could go free and never spend a day in adult prison. A judge will decide before she turns 19.

For now, the soonest Krissi and Bobby can hope to get out of prison is 2027, when they're eligible for parole. But Buz hopes the criminal justice system will make an exception for them because they were locked up so young. He talks about meeting with state legislators interested in changing the laws for child criminals.

Buz wants the state to conduct early evaluations of these inmates. The ones who have changed should be released early, he believes, and those who haven't should stay.

These thoughts consume him in retirement, as he mows the grass and walks his dog, Rose. Krissi worries about how her father will cope with disappointment if he's unsuccessful.

"He is twice the victim," she said. "One, for having been the victim of this crime and, two, for having to be the father. It never quite ends for him."

A distant vision

Buz wants to be there when Krissi and Bobby get out. In his mind, he knows just how it would go. In this idyllic reunion, he'd drive his truck down Interstate 35 to Waco and head west to Gatesville, where he would pick up Bobby. Together, they'd drive east for an hour to get Krissi.

"It would be absolutely joyful. I can't begin to tell you how happy it would make me to go do that," Buz said. "It's kind of like a dream come true. I've been thinking about this for years and years."

He'd buy them lunch— their choice after years of prison food— and then they'd all head home to Frisco. He'd invite Bobby to move in with them, too. Buz imagines everyone living together peacefully under one roof, the past in the past. An unusual but loving family.

This new life wouldn't happen in the house where Roz died. That place is gone.

Years ago, Buz watched as a bulldozer plowed into the porch and mashed the house into rubble. In the end, the splintered wood and concrete were swept into a deep pit and covered with dirt.

Buz still drives by sometimes and sees the field where the house used to be. He glances that way and moves on.

THERE'S NOWHERE TO RUN

THE WASHINGTON POST

DECEMBER 13, 2017

By Kent Babb

CONVINCED HE IS LIVING WITH CTE, FORMER NFL STAR
LARRY JOHNSON BATTLES SELF-DESTRUCTIVE IMPULSES

He inches forward, with jets overhead and the ground 50 stories below. Larry Johnson can feel it happening: the arrival, he calls it, of the demons.

They push him toward the barrier of a rooftop deck of an apartment building where he sometimes comes to visit a friend, and, in moments like these, there's a strengthening urge — an almost overwhelming curiosity, he describes it — to jump.

"One is telling you to do it; one is telling you don't," says Johnson, a former NFL running back. "One is telling you it'd be fun."

It is early November, less than two weeks before his 38th birthday. He played his last game in 2011, and he now believes he suffers from chronic traumatic encephalopathy, the degenerative brain disorder linked to more than 100 former football players. For now, CTE can be confirmed only after death, but Johnson says his symptoms — anxiety, paranoia, the occasional self-destructive impulse — are consistent with those of past victims.

On this afternoon, he shuffles closer to the ledge, past the drainage fixture a foot or so from the glass barrier. His body is tingling, he says; his thoughts are filled with static.

"They say when you die," Johnson says, looking down toward Southeast 1st Avenue, "you feel that euphoric feeling."

Closer now. He's frightened, less of the fall than the direction of his own mind.

"What would it be like," he says, "for this to be the day for people to find out you're not here?"

Fading memories

At a red light back on terra firma, Johnson glances into the back seat. "Let me see the homework," he tells Jaylen, his 7-year-old daughter. He flips through the stapled pages: math problems and reading comprehension about bicycles and roller coasters. The light changes, and Johnson hands the papers back and hits the gas on his Porsche SUV. For the next half-hour, Johnson — prone to fits of volatility, jarring mood swings, extreme periods of silence — will say almost nothing.

Johnson says father and daughter have many things in common, including a quiet personality and a running stride that made Johnson a 2002 Heisman Trophy finalist at Penn State and a two-time Pro Bowl honoree. He was a rusher so durable and fierce that, while playing for the Kansas City Chiefs in 2006, he set an NFL record with 416 carries. That same year, groundbreaking neurologist Bennet Omalu published additional concussion research that linked football-related head injuries with degenerative brain trauma, the beginning of an NFL crisis that still rages and one of the reasons Johnson's carries record probably will never be broken.

Jaylen doesn't know much about that part of her Papi's life, in part because Johnson thinks his daughter is too young to understand how football brought him both glory and ruin. But it's also because there are widening chunks of his career that he can't remember: Two full NFL seasons have disappeared from his memory, he says, and even some of his most memorable plays have grown hazy.

Which is why, in the past few years, Johnson has begun making video compilations of his football highlights, in part as reminders to himself that he was involved in them — but also, when she's ready, as a time capsule for Jaylen.

Johnson fears that, by the time he's 50, he won't remember his own name. If that proves to be the case, Johnson is taking steps for Jaylen to watch her Papi run, to learn who he was, to maybe understand why he was so unpredictable — even, on occasion, with her.

"If I can't remember who I was, I've got YouTube; I've got music videos that I'm making for myself, so when I watch these things I can remember," he says. "I'm trying to get these things in order so she knows who I am and what I came from."

The project became urgent a few months ago, after a particularly severe case of CTE was discovered in the brain of Aaron Hernandez. The former New England Patriots tight end, with a history of erratic and explosive behavior, was convicted of first-degree murder in 2015 before hanging himself in his prison cell in April.

"I could be Aaron Hernandez," Johnson says, and indeed he sees the former Patriots star as a kindred spirit as much as a cautionary tale.

Like Hernandez, Johnson has a history of erratic behavior and violence: He has been arrested six times, and several of the incidents involved Johnson physically assaulting women. The ex-running back says his decision to publicly describe his darkest thoughts is meant not as a way to excuse his past but rather a way to begin a conversation with other former players who Johnson suspects are experiencing many of the same symptoms.

Johnson says he frequently gets brief but intense headaches, often triggered by bright lights or noise, and is increasingly jittery and forgetful. He has no idea how the Porsche's passenger-side mirror got smashed, nor can he remember the full sequence that led to the cluster of dents in the vehicle's rear hatch.

"Blank spots" are what Johnson calls the empty spaces in his memory, and there are seemingly more of them every year. But there's another similarity with Hernandez that scares him most.

Johnson says he has considered violence toward others and himself, and perhaps the only reason he hasn't acted on these impulses is sitting quietly in the back seat, looking out the window at the South Florida flatlands.

"Chicken, steak or spaghetti?" Johnson asks, and Jaylen chooses spaghetti. Her voice is soft as a whisper. Her father believes it's also the only one, when the demons push him to the edge, strong enough to pull him back.

"Sometimes he was the reason"

Almost three decades ago, on a youth field in Oxon Hill, a 9-year-old kick returner caught the ball and sped toward the sideline.

Hoping he'd be tackled quickly and painlessly, young Larry kept running and tried to get out of bounds — but then an opponent crashed into him from the side, spinning his helmet sideways.

The boy got up, dizzy and with no idea where he was, and spent the rest of the game on the sideline with a headache. Though it was never diagnosed as a concussion — Johnson says, in 23 years of football, he was never diagnosed with one — he now suspects this was his first of many.

But more than the impact, he now says, he felt then that he had let his father down. Larry Johnson Sr., at the time a well-known high school coach in Maryland, was in the bleachers, and the boy felt he had shown everyone that the coach's son was soft.

"I didn't know how to redeem myself," Johnson says, though soon he was going into the family's basement for extra blocking drills, studying footage of prodigious NFL hitters Ronnie Lott and Mike Singletary, looking for any chance to prove his toughness.

He grew, and by middle school he was researching which opponents came from broken homes; those were the kids he'd taunt before plays and, for an extra psychological advantage, the ones he'd tackle from behind. If Johnson was benched, he'd blow up at coaches; if an opponent or teammate challenged him, Johnson wasn't above the cheap shot.

Then he'd look to the bleachers.

"I'd be like: 'Dad, you saw that?' It was a point of pride," he says now, and he came to believe, in an era that glamorized masculinity and intimidation, that "this is what tough means."

Larry Johnson Sr., now an assistant head coach at Ohio State, says that wasn't exactly the intention.

"He ran with rage, and it was just his way of saying, 'I'm not going to let this opportunity get away,'" the coach says. "It might have taken him to places he didn't think he would go."

Some of those places, as Johnson became a college player and eventually a pro, included the backs of police cars or disciplinary meetings with coaches. He says he began experiencing symptoms of depression in college, and he sought to prove his toughness in nightclubs and fights with women. He tried to numb himself with alcohol, which took him deeper into the shadows.

Months after Kansas City selected him in the first round of the 2003 draft, Johnson was arrested for aggravated assault and domestic battery for an incident involving a woman. A misunderstanding, Johnson would say. Less than two years later, he was arrested again for shoving a different woman to the floor of a bar. An overly aggressive local law, he'd say.

"There's always a reason" for Johnson's mistakes, says Tony Johnson, the ex-player's brother and his day-to-day manager during his NFL career. "And sometimes he was the reason."

Johnson could be cheerful and social at times, sullen and isolated at others. He collected slights and bad habits, to say nothing of the guns he kept strapped to his shoulders at high-end restaurants or under the seat of his white Bentley. Some nights he'd fire rounds into strangers' lawns or palm a pistol at a gas station, he says, hoping someone would challenge him for a late-night lesson in toughness.

"Me against everybody," he says, and on and off the field that became his code, driving him to rush for a combined 3,539 yards in 2005 and '06. His dominance and persona made him an A-list celebrity and opened doors to a friendship with Jay-Z and dates with R&B singer Mýa.

Whether it was brain injuries, immaturity, celebrity or some combination, Johnson says, aggression became "a switch I couldn't shut off." After a while Jay-Z cut him off via email for being arrested so often, Johnson says, and Mýa once stopped him from jumping from a window.

After two more arrests and a suspension, the Chiefs released Johnson in 2009 after he insulted his head coach on Twitter and for using gay slurs toward a fan and reporters. Years after trying to adapt his personality to an unforgiving game, Johnson found himself too volatile for the NFL. Over his final two seasons, with Washington and Miami, he carried the ball six times.

"Those two combinations, of being angry and not being able to shut that switch off, started to disrupt who I really was," he says. "And it was just waiting to eat me up."

Sound and fury

They're in the living room now, Papi and Jaylen, surrounded by walls undecorated but for the blotchy spackling compound behind them. That's where, a few years ago, Johnson punched through the drywall.

Jaylen was there, and Johnson says he sent her upstairs before making the hole. The way he describes it, the best he can do sometimes is to shield her view.

"Did you think it was something that you did?" Johnson recalls asking Jaylen afterward, and the girl nodded. "I had to explain it: It's never your fault."

But her little mind is expanding quickly, and he worries that these will be some of her earliest memories. And so he tries. It might not seem like it, he admits, but he tries.

On this afternoon, father and daughter play a racing game on Xbox — bright colors, loud sound effects, rapid movement — and after a few minutes, Johnson pauses the game and walks onto his balcony. He stands alone for a minute or two, hands clasped behind his head; he'll say later he felt the onset of a headache and needed to step away.

He returns, and now it's homework time. Johnson has high expectations for Jaylen, and he believes the universe was making a point when it gave him a daughter. How better to punish him for shoving or choking women than to assign him a girl to shepherd through a world filled with Larry Johnsons?

"My greatest fear is my daughter falling in love with somebody who's me," he'll say, and he believes if he's honest and tough with Jaylen, she'll never accept anyone treating her the way her father treated women.

With the sun filtering between the blinds, Johnson plays with her curly hair as she slides a finger across her sentences.

"All people," Jaylen reads aloud, and her father interrupts.

"No," he says. "Why would it say 'all people?' It ..."

He stops, sighs and presses two fingers into his eyelids. She looks back at him, and he tells her to keep reading. He rubs his hands, massages his forehead, checks his watch. He'll say he sometimes forgets she's only in second grade.

They move on to her page of math problems: 27 plus seven.

"How many tens?" he asks her.

"Two."

"And how many ones?"

"Seven."

"No," he says, visibly frustrated until Jaylen reaches the answer. Next: 57 plus seven. She stares at the page.

"So count," he says. "Count!"

Thirteen plus eight. Again staring at the numbers. Johnson's worst subject was math, another trait Jaylen inherited. But his empathy is sometimes drowned out by more dominant emotions.

"You start at thirteen and count eight ones," he tells her, and in the kitchen, a watch alarm begins to beep. Jaylen counts her fingers.

"No," her dad tells her, again rubbing his face. The beeping continues in the next room. "No!"

Abruptly, he stands and stomps out of the room without saying anything. Jaylen's eyes follow him, eyebrows raised, and she listens as her father swipes the beeping watch from a table, swings open the back door and throws it into the courtyard.

In the minds of both father and daughter, it is impossible to know what's happening. Will she remember this, or has Johnson shielded her from something worse? Is he managing his impulses as well as he can, and even if he is, will Jaylen someday come to view moments such as these as emotional milestones?

For now, when her Papi returns, Jaylen's eyes dart back to the page.

"So what's the answer?" he says.

"A bittersweet thing"

Nighttime now, and Johnson takes a pull off his Stella longneck and hits play on the remote.

There he is, or more precisely there he was: a wrecking ball in Penn State blue, highlights of Johnson overpowering defenders interspersed with pictures of Jaylen. The background music, which he selected, is the Imagine Dragons song "I'm So Sorry."

"This is who I really am," he says is the intended message of his self-produced video. "I can't change who I am, regardless of who you are."

He points the remote again, and next is a video of some of his best moments in the NFL: cheers and chants and line-of-scrimmage assaults that, in this era of increased awareness, are both exciting and devastating. The background song is "War Pigs" by Black Sabbath.

In the fields the bodies burning

As the war machine keeps turning.

Death and hatred to mankind

Poisoning their brainwashed minds.

Johnson lifts the remote again. "This may ..." he says, choking up. "I get emotional."

He hits play.

"I did this for her," he says, and a moment later the piano begins.

A few years ago, Johnson woke into a hangover and felt drawn to his computer, spending hours navigating a video-editing program. What emerged was more than a gift for Jaylen's second birthday, Johnson says; these next 5 minutes 17 seconds were meant to say goodbye.

Back then, the demons could be overpowering. Johnson, drifting in the months and years after his NFL career ended, went searching for a new identity. He was arrested again for an incident with an ex-girlfriend, and he cycled among peddling bootleg makeup kits on South Beach, being turned down for a job stocking shelves, researching how to join the military. Usually it was just easier to go to a nightclub and chase salvation down the neck of a tequila bottle.

Trying to spend his way into new friends or purpose, Johnson says he sometimes dropped $50,000 in a night, torching his savings. In 2007, he signed a contract with the Chiefs that included $19 million in guaranteed money, but now, he says, he has enough for Jaylen's college and for himself to get by, and not much more.

Then, he says, he sometimes began evenings with the intention of starting trouble. Other times, he could feel himself losing control — an approaching cloud, he says, impossible to stop. Alcohol and noise were kerosene on his smoldering patience, and friends became used to Johnson turning into, as one friend put it, the Incredible Hulk.

"You could see the mood swings, and they were drastic," says Chantel Cohen, who has known Johnson for most of the past decade. "He could be super happy one moment, and an hour later, he's just ready to blow up. You're like: What just went wrong?"

Once, Johnson says, he sat with a group at a crowded table, and a man he'd just met was being loud. Johnson says he asked, profanely, for the man to shut up; a second later they both stood, and Johnson says he experienced one of his blank spots.

"When I came to, he was already on the ground, like, leaned over, and I'm kind of like: 'Damn, I must have did that,'" he says. As Johnson tried to get away, the man went after him with a chair, and that's where the dents in the back of his Porsche came from.

He would call his parents at all hours, cursing and making strange accusations. Tony Johnson woke to so many worried texts from his brother's friends that he stopped checking his phone in the morning and made peace with how his brother's story might end.

And so did Johnson himself. Working on that video for Jaylen years ago, he was aware he was about to go destroy himself. Like the time he punched through the wall, he explains, he could delay the explosion, but he couldn't avoid it.

Now re-watching the video in his living room, he says he wasn't exactly considering suicide but that he was preparing to go away to stay. Prison was a possibility, and so were a few others, considering he'd decided that if he did something to get himself arrested, he wasn't planning on going quietly.

There was, he recalls, something calming about it.

"A bittersweet thing: I'm going to be free of everything that's holding me down," Johnson says now, and he wonders whether Hernandez experienced similarly intense feelings in his final days. "The same way Aaron thought: I'm going to be gone from this world, but I'm still going to be able to take care of my child, because that's all I care about."

A moment later, he continues. His voice cracks.

"When you're that down deep in it," he says, "you don't want to be talked out of it."

And so that day a few years ago, he worked on the video until it was perfect, the music and images and sequence just right. A text banner — "I will always Love you," it reads — flutters past near the beginning, and with the Christina Perri song "A Thousand Years" in the background, it closes with a photograph of Johnson kissing Jaylen. It pans out before fading.

Then he posted the video on Instagram before loading his pockets with painkillers and ecstasy, he says, and set off into the space beneath a dropping curtain.

"He definitely has something"

A few weekends ago, friends invited Johnson to join them at a bar, have a few drinks, meet a woman he might like.

He agreed, and indeed he was drawn to her. They talked, and so did the friends — a little too much, maybe — and after a while Johnson could feel the shadow falling. The Hulk was coming, so at one point he excused himself and, without explanation, just left.

Distrustful of his own mind, Johnson says now that he wasn't just annoyed by his chatty friends. He noticed himself staring at one of them, feeling a growing urge to punch him. Almost in a heartbeat, Johnson went from sociable and joyful to deeply angry and potentially violent — frightening, at least this time, only himself.

"Something so easily dismissed," he says. "But it's just — once I get in that mood, I can't stop it. And it comes out of nowhere."

Even so, is this truly a look at CTE's corrosive effects in real time? Or has Johnson, with his history of blame deflection and self-validating reasons, simply found an unimpeachable — and unprovable — excuse?

"Do I think he's a special breed? Yes," says Tony Johnson, who suggests the family will consider donating Larry's brain for study after his death. "Do I think he might have CTE? I just can't say."

Others, who point out the brain's frontal lobe is the portion that regulates judgment and behavior — and the region most under attack during on-field collisions — see it more Johnson's way.

"I'm pretty sure that he definitely has something going on," says longtime friend Cohen, who claims she knew Junior Seau, the Hall of Fame linebacker who in 2012 shot himself in the chest so that his brain could be studied; indeed, CTE was discovered in Seau's brain. Cohen sees some similarities in the behavior of Johnson and Seau.

Johnson says years ago he was diagnosed with type-1 bipolar disorder, a condition he blames on head injuries. Though this cannot be confirmed in Johnson's case, brain injury experts have found possible links between bipolar symptoms and mid-life behavior issues and CTE.

"Certain things happen in your life," he says, "that you just can't come back from."

After making the video for Jaylen a few years back, Johnson says, he spent the next 72 hours cycling from one party to the next, daring bar patrons or police or even death to bring him down. When nothing did, he kept going.

At one point he sat on a sidewalk, exhausted and struggling to breathe, and thought of his daughter. She was living with her mother at the time; Jaylen's parents now share custody.

Johnson went home, slept it off, and not long afterward, he says, he sold his ownership stake in a club on South Beach and reduced his intake of hard liquor. He still found trouble sometimes, including a 2014 arrest for aggravated battery involving another man, and Johnson says he has since made more changes.

He moved out of a trendy high-rise in Miami and into a quiet townhouse in Fort Lauderdale, got rid of his guns, took a job with a nonprofit that uses the arts to mentor disadvantaged children. Johnson also quit therapy and refused to take his prescribed medication; he says it's because he's better equipped to manage his impulses himself. All these years later, it's still Johnson against everybody — even himself.

He has, more recently, filled his bookshelf not with reminders of his playing career but with photographs of Jaylen and her paintings. If friends invite him out, more and more he turns them down.

"You kind of create your own prison," Johnson says. "I've kind of barricaded myself in my surroundings [with] certain things that I can handle. That's kind of how I beat it."

That's easy when his daughter is here — Jaylen spends most weekends with her father and weekdays with her mother in a nearby town — and a challenge when she's not. On the nights he's alone, Johnson is more likely to sulk or drink or venture into the depths of his restless mind. If she's here, bedtime is at 8:30, and they play games or watch television or draw.

"She's, like, a good distraction I have," he says. "She sees something in me that most people will never see."

Occasionally they watch football together, Jaylen in her Penn State or Kansas City jersey, and she asks why the announcers sometimes say his name. He explains some of it, and very carefully he has begun to explain some of the rest.

"Papi," he says he tells her, "used to be really bad."

He doesn't offer much more, and though he's uncertain what the future will bring, Johnson says he wants to tell her his whole story eventually.

Johnson figures that in seven more years, or when she's 14 or so, Jaylen will be old enough to absorb the paradoxical nature of her father: the life of the party and the introvert, a man capable of violence and tenderness, the person he actually is and the one he wants to be.

He wants his mind to hang out at least that long. Jaylen might not like what she learns, but he wants to be present for those conversations.

His biggest fear, if he were to disappear now, is that Jaylen wouldn't remember him; his second biggest is that she would.

"That scares me more than anything," he says. "Sometimes it scares me to tears."

Back to the unknown

He's driving again, steering the Porsche south on a highway not long after sunrise. Jaylen, who like her Papi is not a morning person, is dozing off in the back seat.

Earlier, the vehicle's back latch wouldn't close, and in the 20 or so minutes since, Johnson hasn't said a word. He weaves through traffic, occasionally touching 90 mph, and a radio commercial plays a doorbell sound. The tone repeats again. And again. Johnson jabs his finger into the preset button to change the station.

He cracks his knuckles, sighs loudly, checks his phone.

He looks behind him occasionally, Jaylen napping or drawing imaginary circles on the glass. She's spending the next few days with her mother, and Johnson is already nervous about the upcoming time by himself. What if friends call and ask him to go drinking? Or if someone crosses him at the wrong moment?

How will he react this time if the demons come?

For now, she's with him a few more minutes, so Johnson parks the Porsche and lifts her from the back seat. He carries her toward the elementary school and kisses her cheek as they cross the driveway and fall into a line of students.

The line starts moving, and he tucks in her shirt and kisses her again. "I'll see you this weekend, okay?" he says, and then he turns toward the crosswalk.

He's alone again, left to face the next few days — and whichever emotions and impulses are waiting — with his mind as his only company. He looks behind him to see Jaylen toddling toward the entrance, and with little more than uncertainty ahead, Johnson stands on the curb and waits for her to drift out of sight before stepping, finally, off the edge.

The House on the Corner

Tampa Bay Times

November 22, 2017

By Lane DeGregory

Anthony Roy felt threatened in his own back yard. So he got a gun.

When the couple retired to Clearwater four years ago, they moved into a little house on a big corner lot. Across from a Stop-N-Shop. Next to a police substation.

The two-bedroom home was supposed to be their slice of the Florida dream.

But soon, Anthony James Roy, and his wife, Irene Quarles, started seeing people hanging out in their yard, drinking and smoking weed. Strangers plugged their phones into outlets on the couple's patio. They sat on their outdoor furniture, selling drugs.

The couple tried to make them leave. They complained to the police. When that didn't work, they tried to build friendships, hoping they could charm the squatters into respecting their property. Sometimes, they hid in their house.

For three years, the tension built. Until one sweltering summer night in 2016.

The events are captured in police reports, videos, depositions, evidence files and interviews. The story is recounted here in their own words.

Roy doesn't deny shooting another man 17 times. He just wants to explain why.

***

At the police substation, on the night of the shooting, Roy, 50, and Quarles, 60, spoke to officers in separate rooms. They explained what had gone on in recent years, how they'd felt trapped and powerless.

ROY: The man just scared me to the point where I had to do something. I thought he was bonafide.

QUARLES: It didn't happen in the yard. But it started there. I been having a problem with these people since I moved down here about getting in my yard. They slept in my yard. All their crackheads come by ... I just wish somebody would listen to his story. Sit down and really listen.

ROY: I'll tell you everything you need to know. I'm a humanist. I'm not here trying to hurt nobody. I even buy his dope, smoke his s---, just for argument sake. ... I mean, what would you do if you was in my situation?

***

Anthony Roy was born in Washington, D.C. His parents joined the Air Force when he was young, and he grew up all over the country. He attended high school in Alaska, where he and his mother say classmates hurled racial slurs at him, and he started getting into fights. In the 1980s, he moved to Los Angeles — in the middle of the Crips and Bloods feud. He was back in D.C. by the '90s, where he installed air-conditioning systems, had a daughter and got arrested for cocaine and marijuana possession. His wife, Irene, worked for a caterer. When they moved to Clearwater, Irene's 32-year-old daughter and 9-year-old grandson moved with them.

ROY: My uncle is from here, down here in Clearwater. I've been coming down here since 2004. I would come here to get away from the pressures of D.C. And then, when I got tired of D.C., I said, "I'm moving to Florida."

QUARLES: We came down here to chill and relax and retire from the drama that's going on in D.C. Too much killing. We wanted to come where it's peaceful. We looked at brochures and said, "We can do this!"

***

Patricia Roy, Anthony's mother, is a retired master sergeant in the Air Force. She lives in D.C., winters in Florida and bought the house on the corner as an investment about seven years ago. With the police substation so close, she thought it would be a nice place to rent.

PATRICIA ROY: Well, I was wrong. My first tenant, she stayed there for the whole year, and I was really surprised. And the second tenant had their hubcaps robbed, and they just moved out. I started to go over there and noticed how the guys were all out on the street. It'd be like 15 guys hanging around the house, well, on that corner. I had a third tenant move in and, Lord, she complained. She would call the police on them. And what happened was, at the end, somebody threw a rock into her bedroom window. That upset her so bad she moved out.

ANTHONY ROY: Mom couldn't keep a tenant in the house, because of all the traffic on that corner. So I told her: "You need somebody like me to move down in there. I could live in the house. I'm not gonna be scared."

PATRICIA ROY: My son, he's one of those kinda guys that, you know, he can adjust to his situation. He's very charismatic, very intelligent, likes being around people. So I figured that he would be able to handle it over there. And you know, they set up house real nice, and they were comfortable.

In their shady back yard, Anthony Roy and his wife set up a canvas gazebo with twinkling white lights, a wicker couch and cushioned chairs. A makeshift bar squatted in the sandy grass.

ROY: Me and my wife's first house. We painted, transformed that house. Redid everything: walls, floors, bath. I wasn't planning on ever leaving that spot. I used to love my mornings waking up right there. I mean, couldn't nothing have been more right. And I met a lot a people. That was the one thing I liked about Florida is how people just wave at you, don't even know you, they come up and speak to you. Thought that was all nice and fine. But the house where I lived at had a lot a drug dealers out there.

QUARLES: When I got the furniture, that's when it really got bad. We had a tent, a bar, a smoker. I guess it was just too comfortable.

ROY: People walked up and sat in my yard like it was a park. I had homeless people, dope fiends, all that.

QUARLES: People hiding drugs in our trash can. We found a needle out there, out by the tree. We got rid of that 'cause, you know, I got grandkids. And you might find some weed. I had to put a lock on my shed to keep people from walking in. They'd unplug my freezer, my food go bad because they wanna charge a phone. They ordering meals, delivery knocking on my door. "I didn't order that." Then some fool come running up, "I did." And eat it in my yard!

ROY: I would ask 'em, "Hey, can't you go down the street with that? I'm not here to tell you what to do, or how you gotta make your living. I'm just asking you not to do it at my expense." But half the people that ended up being my friends, weren't my friends. They were all just trying to have somewhere to go and sit there all day and do what they do.

QUARLES: People out there in my yard cutting hair for money, using my electricity. If I wanna go out there and enjoy my own furniture, I couldn't. You gotta step over people. You gotta tell 'em, "Look, don't come in my yard the day I'm having company." Everybody sitting in the yard was drug dealers, selling pills, crack. I tell 'em: "Y'all got to go. You can't sell drugs out my yard." When you tell them this, they get angry. We started looking for another house but couldn't find nothing in our price range. The police seen all that going on and just didn't do anything about it. We went to them a lot. Never nothing done.

***

Over three years, Roy, Quarles and his mother say they called or talked to police in person more than a dozen times, asking for help. His mother had an officer's number on speed dial. Police spokesman Rob Shaw said the substation is not staffed full-time. Officers stop by there, he said, to work on paperwork or hold meetings. In six visits to that corner, a Times reporter and photographer never saw anyone there.

PATRICIA ROY: I complained to the police department next door, and they told me to get a no-trespassing sign put on the property. I went downtown to see about getting the sign put up, and they told me because it wasn't a commercial business, they couldn't do it. The only thing that I could do was go to the Home Depot and buy a sign that says, "No Trespassing." But that wasn't gonna do any good.

ANTHONY ROY: If the police came around in my yard, people would come over there just to make sure I don't say nothing. You know what I'm saying? I'm the only outsider there. I'm not from there. The police just always tell me, "I know it's not you. It's the people that be over there at your house." I used to tell 'em all the time, If you see somebody doing something and they run in my yard to duck you, come up in my yard and approach 'em. You got my permission." Maybe one police did that.

PATRICIA ROY: My son would say, "Mom, you need to put up a fence to keep 'em out, from coming in the yard." Well, I was gonna do that, but they said it couldn't be a 6-foot fence, because it was a corner lot, they say only a 3-foot fence. I said, "What good is that going to do?"

***

Police logs show numerous traffic stops and drug calls around Roy's house. Officers acknowledge that it was a "known problem area." Chief Daniel Slaughter said people question whether officers respond to complaints in poorer neighborhoods as quickly as in more affluent areas. He said some also assume that African Americans are unwilling to cooperate with police. Officers were making arrests in Roy's neighborhood. But those people seldom stayed in jail long.

SLAUGHTER: It's the revolving door of justice. That breeds a culture of people not wanting to rat out other people. It's frustrating. We spend a lot of time focusing on those chronic offenders that are well known to us. Five percent of the criminal population creates 80 percent of the crimes.

QUARLES: I started noticing somebody hanging out back there, like every day. I used to look out my kitchen window sometimes at night and see him sitting out there with some girls, on my furniture. Three o'clock in the morning.

ROY: That dude got locked up four times. Every time, he came right back to the same spot. My spot! He was constantly getting kicked out of his baby mama's house. So he's in my yard, sleeping under my gazebo. Slinging dope. I ask him, "You got anywhere you wanna go?" I would take this dude anywhere to get him out of my yard.

***

Bernard Antonio Richards, a.k.a Big Tony, 31, grew up in Florida and played high school football. When he wasn't in Roy and Quarles' back yard, he stayed in an abandoned apartment nearby. He weighed close to 300 pounds and stood 5 foot 10. Roy was just as tall, but weighed half as much. Richards' criminal record spans 16 years and includes arrests for selling cocaine and hallucinogens, battery and sexual assault.

QUARLES: My daughter, she used to hate to go out of the house because of that guy. He used to grab her and try to hug on her and pull her. She used to hide to keep him from putting his hands on her.

ROY: He pulled a gun on me twice, come up in my face showing me, "This gun right here I just bought." He always used to make comments about my house not having nowhere to hide. He'd knock on my window 2 o'clock in the morning 'cause he see me sitting on my bed watching TV, just to let me know like, "I see you sitting right there in front of the window."

QUARLES: We never had a gun in D.C. Never needed one. But now it's time to do something. The police aren't going to protect you. You gotta protect yourself. That's why I bought the gun.

***

Richards' mom, Margie Mills, lives nearby. She used to manage a Popeye's and a Burger King. Her son moved out at 16, and she didn't see him often.

MILLS: I'm not gonna sit up and say that Tony was that type of child that's staying outta trouble. He was a decent boy and he mind. But he also could have an attitude and get mad. He was a big boy so he could hit hard. He didn't hit me, but he would charge at me like he wanted to. So I figured to bring him down from his high horses, I told the police on him. Sent him to jail.

BIG TONY'S FORMER GIRLFRIEND, NIKI MASON: He was actually a good person. He'd do anything for anybody if you asked him to. He was great helping me with my kids. He was working at a moving company. He'd just started a job there. He had a wonderful smile.

MILLS: He intimidated people, you know? 'Cause he's big. I heard that they said on TV that he was arrested over 30-some times. Caught walking down the road with weed. Battery charges. Went and just jumped on somebody, you know, just to fight somebody.

MASON: He was friends with that guy whose yard they all hung out in. As far as I knew, they'd always been talking, chilling. I don't understand what could've went so wrong.

***

On July 9, 2016, a Saturday, a dozen men sat in Roy's back yard all day. Drinking Budweisers. Smoking blunts. Roy stayed inside for a while, playing Battlefield on his Xbox. Until one of the guys coaxed him to join them for a beer. It was hot. Going on dusk when an old van pulled up. A woman got out and walked toward the men.

WOMAN: Hey! I need $30 worth.

ROY: What you want? (He stood up) Ain't no one slinging out of my yard. I don't care who you looking for. Don't disrespect my yard. Take your f----- ass down the street. This is my house. I live here. These f----- n----- don't live here. Who you here to see?

WOMAN: F--- you.

Quarles stepped out the back door.

QUARLES: We don't sell drugs here. You get away from my yard.

WOMAN: Listen, you b---- ...

ROY: I'm fed up with this s---. Who you think you are? (Roy lunged toward the woman. Other men pulled him back.) You don't know who you f----- with.

NEIGHBOR ERIC CASON, AKA EBAY: Chill out. Chill out. It's not worth it.

ROY: I can't do this no more. I feel like they took over my s---. Anything I try to do, it's not working. I'm fed up. I ain't s--- to them. I ain't nobody.

CASON: Calm down.

Roy went inside, grabbed his wife's loaded 9mm Glock from under her pillow. He came back out, pointed the gun at the woman, who ran down the street. He chased her and fired two shots into the dirt. When he returned home, he stashed the gun, then grabbed two baseball bats. He stepped back outside, where a dozen men were still smoking and drinking. And now laughing.

ROY: I'm tired of you disrespecting me and trying to run over my s---. I'm 50 years old. I ain't come down here for this. No man run over me. I'm gonna stand my ground ... Now, unless you want to be a witness, leave. Or one of you all is gonna get your ass whooped.

RICHARDS: Who you talking to?

ROY: I'm talking to you, fat ass mother f-----. I'm tired of you.

Richards reached his right arm behind his back, into the waist of his gym shorts.

RICHARDS: Who you talking to?

ROY: I'm talking to you.

RICHARDS: Well, I got mine. You better go get yours.

Roy stomped inside, grabbed the Glock, shoved in an extended magazine. He came back out, pointed it at Richards.

ROY: I'm gonna shoot his fat ass.

CASON: No! Calm down. You ain't gonna whip nobody's ass. Please. Don't do it, bro. Come on. She was asking for crack. She wasn't asking for no nuclear weapons or no crazy s---.

Richards walked away, pulling a phone from his shorts' pocket.

RICHARDS: You ain't gonna do nothing to me. You ain't got shit. I'm gonna call some people ...

As he crossed the sidewalk, heading toward the Stop-N-Shop, Richards turned and shouted.

RICHARDS: Yo! Miss Irene! You better get on outta the house. I'm fixing to shoot it up!

Roy followed Richards across the street, into the convenience store parking lot.

ROY: What the f--- do you mean by that? What the f--- did you say? Ain't no one gonna threaten my wife!

RICHARDS: I'm right here, n----. I'm right here. I ain't scared. You say you got a gun? Use it!

ROY: Come on, n----. Come on. (Raising gun.) You still threatening me?

Richards stopped, spun to face Roy.

RICHARDS: Oh, you gonna pull it out? You better use it. Man, you gonna shoot me? You better shoot me.

He turned and took a step toward the convenience mart. Rapid gunfire pierced the night. Richards fell on his stomach in front of the store, by the trash can, blood pooling around his head. Roy fired 17 times. The bullets hit Richards' chin, neck, chest, stomach, both shoulders, arms and legs, left hip, and back. When Roy ran out of bullets, he kicked Richards in the head. A video camera outside the convenience mart recorded his rage.

ROY: You touch my g--d--- woman, I'll kill your ass!

Roy walked back to his house where his wife stood behind a tree, trembling. Without saying a word, he gave her the gun. They went inside, sat on the couch. While they waited for police, he held her hand.

***

The 911 call center lit up.

OPERATOR: Clearwater police. What is your emergency?

CALLER 1: Um, there's a shooting on Woodlawn and MLK ... It was probably the whole entire clip. People started screaming.

OPERATOR: How many shots did you hear?

CALLER 1: Like 10, maybe a little more.

OPERATOR: Clearwater police. What is your emergency?

CALLER 2: I was in my car, and I was backing out. But the guy, whoever he was arguing with, went across the store. So I ran back in the store for my own safety, okay. Pop, pop, pop. And he is not moving.

OPERATOR: Clearwater police ...

AMBULANCE DRIVER: Rescue is responding ... for gunshot trauma.

OPERATOR: Thank you.

AMBULANCE DRIVER: This was outside the front of the store. He said they heard a gunshot and now there's a guy ... he thinks he's dead.

Later that night, just after 10 o'clock, red and blue police lights striped the corner. Officers wrapped the parking lot in yellow crime scene tape and started interviewing witnesses. Richards' body lay on the ground. Police found a green lighter in his pocket, a baggie with what looked like marijuana and one nickel. But no gun.

STOP-N-SHOP MANAGER REDOUNE BOUSNTRA: So we're working in the store and this girl, she went to drive her car. She came back, "Red, Red, they're fighting outside." I grab my phone and call you guys, the police. I lock the door. I heard: Pop, pop, pop, pop, pop!

OFFICER: This gentleman, the victim there that's dead, do you know him?

BOUSNTRA: Yeah, he come by the store. He's always shopping. He buys the chips, he buys soda. He's always there. He just lives across the street.

OFFICER: Was he in the store tonight?

BOUSNTRA: Yeah, he was at the store right before that happened, like an hour maybe, I'm not sure. He comes in the store 10 times a day, you know? He was always quiet.

OFFICER: Did he seem agitated?

BOUSNTRA: No. I seen him happy. He was just talking on the phone, buying, paying me. "Alright, Red! Have a good one." That's it.

ICE CREAM MAN STEVEN MONROE: So I heard those two arguing ... going back and forth. So then the next thing you know, he come walking cross the street with the gun in his hand.

OFFICER: You could see the gun in his hand?

MONROE: Yeah. He pointed it straight at him, and then Tony, like, threw his hands up and got mad. He's like, "Man, you gonna shoot me? Go on and shoot me then." Turn around, and then he did, like, boom, boom, boom ... And then he just fell to the ground.

OFFICER: And you never saw if Big Tony had a firearm?

MONROE: I didn't see nothing in his hand.

CASON: And bro came out with the baseball bats. He said nobody was gonna do anything to him. Then he came out with the gun. But he wasn't gonna shoot Tony. Not until he said Miss Irene's name.

OFFICER: Who said that?

CASON: Tony tell Miss Irene, "When I come back, you better be outside the house."

OFFICER: So he did threaten Miss Irene?

CASON: He did, yeah.

OFFICER: Tell me how you would take that threat. What do you think he meant?

CASON: Ain't nobody gonna let a man say that.

***

Inside the police substation, on the night of the shooting, Roy was amped and angry. Quarles looked exhausted.

ROY: He held us hostage too long. I've been telling him for years about serving people in my house.

OFFICER: Was he out there trying to sling today?

ROY: Every day. That's what he do. I gotta fight these n----- every day. In my yard. Ain't nobody helping me. I'm out here by myself. You hear me? I was always the one that backed down. Let him get his way. I got tired of it. ... I swear to God if I could bring that stupid son of a bitch back, fat bastard. But when he said that s--- about my old lady, I snapped. I'm not gonna let these n----- run me, man. I'm gonna stand my ground. You understand?

OFFICER: I understand. Makes sense.

ROY: What I'm supposed to do? Sit there and wait for this fool to shoot me? I ain't gonna play that. I'm a bonafide street motherf-----. You understand? I'm old school. I went through a lot of s---. I made it here. ... And now I threw away my life for this f---ass n----. I'm sorry. I can't take it back.

OFFICER: Did he have a gun on him tonight?

ROY: I didn't see it. But he act like he did. I thought he was serious about his s---. He came at me.

OFFICER: You did what you thought you had to do. I understand.

ROY: I had to protect my old lady. I'm worried about my family. ... Tell Irene I'm sorry.

***

In Margie Mills' apartment, a bible lay on the table, a portrait of MLK hung on the wall. On the floor by the TV, she had created a shrine to her son: a photo of Richards and the program from his funeral.

MILLS: I dropped the phone. I fell backwards. I didn't know what to do. I'll never see my son ever again. Never have an argument with him again. I'm gonna miss that.

She sobbed as she recounted her son's funeral.

MILLS: They just had all these blankets around his body, torn apart. I would say 50, maybe 60 people there. Tony's grandmother, she were there, and the aunts were there, my brother. And of course I broke down. My last chance to see him.

Irene Quarles still had to deal with people squatting in her back yard, plugging their cell phones into her outlets. She was terrified to confront them. Devastated to have lost her husband to jail.

QUARLES: He was just ... got pushed too far. People just trying to disrespect him. My husband did what he did to protect his family.

Patricia Roy was in D.C. when she got the call but quickly flew to Florida to see her son.

PATRICIA ROY: Irene, she told me that (Anthony) had shot a man. First thing I thought, "Is he dead? Or is he just shot?" I didn't raise him for this type of thing to happen to him, you know?

I didn't know of an attorney. The only person I thought of was a person who worked for the Justice Department. So I called and asked did she know anyone I could get to defend him? The lawyer said, "What do you want?" I said: "I don't want my son to be, what do you call it? I can't ... electrocuted."

***

Roy hired Lee Pearlman to defend her son. He told her that it isn't a stand your ground case, because Anthony Roy left his property.

PEARLMAN: This case is about a man defending his family in a circumstance that nobody ever wants to be in, which is a person who has made it clear to you they are going to come back and shoot your house up. What was the right way to react? Does a jury believe that this was an imminent threat? The defense would be focused entirely around that: an argument of self-defense.

The greatest hope is we have a case where we can put this to a jury, potentially, and reach a not-guilty verdict. That's our best-case scenario. The worse-case scenario is, potentially, the death penalty.

One potential version is that these two were friends, and this was just a bad day for Mr. Roy. Is that validated by somebody who allegedly shoots somebody 17 times? Or is this something that has been building for a long period of time and results in this outcome, because my client couldn't get help from the police?

Slaughter, the police chief, said officers were frustrated, too.

SLAUGHTER: It's not like someone is saying this neighborhood, this problem, isn't important. We engage with the neighborhood, increase our visibility. There's just a whole resource constraint. Anyone who has a drug house in their neighborhood says the police aren't working fast enough. ... Dealing drugs, however, is not a legitimate explanation to assassinate another human being.

PEARLMAN: It's a brutal video. You see the outcome of what that was, but you don't see the lead-up. The context is so important. This person continues to be arrested, continues to come back on his property. This is a man who, over and over, comes to his window, knocks. "Man, you ain't got no cover in here. Somebody opens fire, where you gonna go?"

If you had that kind of emotional stress over you and you're looking at your wife, the person that you love, your kids, the people you're responsible for caring for, what does that do to you?

PEARLMAN'S INVESTIGATOR, JEFF BARKER: I took this case because I could see myself in this man's position, as a parent and, you know, protector, so to speak, of my family. I think for anyone, if you've been threatened enough, there comes a breaking point.

PEARLMAN: For me to be able to articulate that to a jury ...

BARKER: If he would have done this five minutes earlier, when the guy was on his property, it would have been more of a justified-type thing.

PEARLMAN: There's differences between stand your ground and self-defense. Stand your ground is a basic legal defense that the judge makes. Self-defense is a jury question. So we try for self-defense and hope to get manslaughter. With manslaughter, you reduce the minimum mandatory sentencing to 12 or 13 years.

Prosecutor Scott Rosenwasser said Roy was charged with first-degree murder because the shooting seemed premeditated. After Richards' threat, Roy went back inside. Loaded the extra clip. Followed Richards across the street. The prosecutor said Pearlman offered 15 years for a guilty plea.

ROSENWASSER: That's not even close to the ballpark. If they want to make another offer, we'd consider it. But he's facing life.

***

Nearly a year after the shooting, Mills drove her Jazzy scooter a mile to the funeral home to pick up her son's urn. She added his ashes to the memorial beside her TV.

MILLS: I just want (Roy) to be in there for life. He need to sit back and think about everything he take away from me. Not just even my family, even if he could step back and see he done took it away from his own family.

For a time, Patricia Roy visited her son twice a week. She gained 20 pounds from the stress. In May, she headed back to D.C. — and sold the house on the corner to pay for her son's defense.

PATRICIA ROY: I wake up and say, this is not really happening. And then I have to go see him behind that screen. Oh, it just tears me up to see him like that. Couldn't you have done something else?

Quarles left the corner behind and moved with her daughter and grandson to a trailer. She looks emaciated, having lost 50 pounds. Her walls are covered with drawings her husband sends: The Obamas, Muhammad Ali, an angel saying, "Do all the good that you can as long as you can."

QUARLES: I visit him three times a week or more. My new mobile home is, like, three blocks from the jail.

It took us almost a year to sell that house 'cause a lotta people that came, they just didn't like the area. Too much hanging out in the front of the store, across the street.

I never said he shouldn't go to jail. I just don't think it's fair for the time they're trying to give him for protecting his family. Because I think if the shoe's on the other foot, they woulda done the same thing.

***

In the Pinellas County jail, Roy met with his lawyer over the summer.

PEARLMAN: The prosecution is at 25 years. There was a discussion about potentially coming down to 20, but ... If you feel like you're going to die in jail anyway ... We've got nothing to lose by going to trial.

ROY: A jury? No way. They can't put their self in my place or what I've been through. Three years I put up with that crap. No human being should have to tiptoe around another person, be scared to even come around that person. The worst thing you wanna do is scare somebody to the point where you got 'em so scared, they'll mess around and kill you. ... Nobody wants to die ... A jury don't even care about what his record is ... With what they got on video, I wouldn't risk that ... Even though, if I had the right jury ...

In August, Roy stood before the judge in a Pinellas County courtroom. During the last year in jail, he shaved his head. His goatee went gray. And beneath his left eye he had another inmate etch a tattoo: A tear drop.

PEARLMAN: My last offer was 18 years, and that was rejected. I'm going to make another offer ... but I'd also like to set a trial date.

JUDGE NANCY MOATE LEY: Are there a lot of witnesses?

PEARLMAN: Probably 10 to 15.

The judge scheduled a trial for April. Rosenwasser has agreed to meet again, to talk about a plea bargain. Pearlman has offered to take Roy's case to trial, pro bono.

PEARLMAN: There are assumptions that get made about people. Issues of race and class always play a factor. There was a growing tension in that neighborhood, but nothing was done about it. I can't think of too many situations in other areas that wouldn't warrant a response.

Roy is not optimistic about his chances. He's in poor health, and at his age, a long prison term feels like a death sentence.

He already lost his freedom, his wife, his little house on the corner.

CPSIA information can be obtained
at www.ICGtesting.com
Printed in the USA
FFHW020912140519
52457343-57863FF

9 781574 417524